THE RELIGION OF THE PEOPLE

Methodism was the most important religious movement in the English-speaking world in the eighteenth and nineteenth centuries. It helped reshape the old denominational order in the British Isles and North America and deeply affected the lives of many millions of people.

Although taking account of broader patterns of growth, the focus of this book is Methodism in the British Isles in the period 1750–1900. David Hempton begins with a discussion of why Methodism grew when and where it did and what was the nature of the Methodist experience for those who embraced it. The distinctive religious beliefs and practices of Methodism appealed mostly to women and men of the lower middle and working classes, and its harsh disciplines and tender pieties have been closely related to many other important questions such as class formation, increased political consciousness, the rise of industrial capitalism and market economies and the growth of religious pluralism.

Hempton considers four of the important figures in the early history of Methodism: John Wesley, the founder; Jabez Bunting, the most powerful man in the connexion in the nineteenth century; Thomas Allan, the connexional lawyer and political adviser; and Gideon Ouseley, a representative of the much neglected order of itinerant preachers who spread the Methodist message. *The Religion of the People* concludes with an exploration of the themes of law, politics and gender which lie at the heart of Methodist influence on individuals, communities and social structures.

David Hempton is Professor of Modern History in the Queen's University of Belfast. He is the author *Methodism and Politics in British Society 1750–1850* (1984) and co-author of *Evangelical Protestantism in Ulster Society 1740–1890* (1992).

'This lively and highly readable cluster of essays takes the reader to the heart of recent debates over popular religion (especially popular Protestantism). It offers not only the ripe fruits of the author's work but along the way provides a critical synthesis of much recent research by others. The tone is refreshingly fairminded: Hempton avoids both the clichés of the old denominational history and the reductionism of some modern writing on the social role of religion. An important book.'

John Walsh,
Jesus College, Oxford

'*The Religion of the People* is an extraordinarily good book – distinguished for the lucid complexity of its arguments as well as for its compelling use of wide-ranging sources. . . . This is historical writing at its best.'

Mark A. Noll,
Wheaton College, Illinois

'Those who want the latest word on Methodism's first century can do no better than turn to this collection of essays by David Hempton. . . . A pleasure to read.'

Hugh McLeod,
University of Birmingham

THE RELIGION OF
THE PEOPLE

Methodism and popular religion *c.* 1750–1900

David Hempton

London and New York

First published 1996
by Routledge
11 New Fetter Lane, London EC4P 4EE

Simultaneously published in the USA and Canada
by Routledge
29 West 35th Street, New York, NY 10001

© 1996 David Hempton

Typeset in Palatino by
Ponting–Green Publishing Services, Chesham, Bucks
Printed and bound in Great Britain by
TJ Press (Padstow) Ltd, Padstow, Cornwall

British Library Cataloguing in Publication Data
A catalogue record for this book is available from the
British Library

Library of Congress Cataloguing in Publication Data
Hempton, David
The religion of the people: Methodism and popular religion
c. 1750–1900 / David Hempton.
p.   cm.
Includes bibliographical references and index.
1. Methodist Church–Great Britain–History–18th century.
2. Methodist Church–Great Britain–History–19th century.
3. Great Britain–Religious life and customs.
4. Great Britain–Church history–18th century.
5. Great Britain–Church history–19th century.
I.   Title.
BX8276.H47   1996
287'.0941'09033–dc20   95-32861
CIP

ISBN 0–415–07714–1

For Reg Ward and John Walsh

CONTENTS

ILLUSTRATIONS

FIGURES

TABLES

PREFACE

This book has been a decade in the making and had its origins in the immediate post-completion depression of *Methodism and Politics in British Society 1750–1850* (London, 1984) in 1983. As is the way with historians, I was struck more by the questions I had failed to address than the ones I had tried to answer. Each of the ten chapters in this book, therefore, represents an attempt to answer a specific question, grouped around three overarching categories of growth, people and themes.

With so much of the historiography of English Methodism encaged within the 'little Englander' tradition of scholarship, the question at the heart of Chapter 1 is how was it that a religious movement with broadly similar theological content and organizational structures had such different patterns of growth, not only *within* England, but right across the North Atlantic world in the Age of Revolution? Moreover, an appreciation that Methodist growth was yet more spectacular in the USA than in England further erodes the attempts that were made to explain such growth purely within the peculiarities of English economic and social history. Methodism, in short, was an international religious movement (with roots in European pietism and with branches all over the world), not an English epiphenomenon.

Methodist growth needs also to be earthed in the specificities of time and place. Chapter 2 serves the dual purpose of seeking to explain the dynamics of Methodist growth in a particular geographical location and of supplying a proper social context for Irish Methodism, the political influence of which formed an important part of the argument in *Methodism and Politics*. Chapter 3 represents a progress report on a lifetime mission to penetrate to the heart of popular religion in the modern period. The immediate stimulus on this occasion was the conviction that the picture of popular religion that emerged from Victorian novels and oral evidence was not the same as the one presented in the great statistical surveys so beloved by middle-class Victorians. I have also made an effort in this chapter to bring the situation up to date by referring to some fresh work in the field.

Part 2 has to do with people, and the questions addressed have to do with the quality of the surviving evidence which is unusually lavish for all four biographical portraits. My chapter on Wesley is an attempt to get to the heart of his political theology by looking at his attitudes towards those four cornerstones of the eighteenth-century state: monarchy and constitution, Established Church, property and law. The purpose of the chapter on Bunting is not to heap more abuse on this most abused of ecclesiastical bureaucrats (though that was very tempting), but, through a close reading of all his surviving correspondence, to understand the processes by which this son of a radical Manchester tailor forsook his early career as a Methodist revivalist for the trappings of connexional power. Moreover, Bunting should not be seen in isolation from the forces unleashed on the religious world by the French and Industrial Revolutions. The peculiar relationship between power and piety worked out in the 'solid, mathematical' mind of Jabez Bunting was worked out in thousands of different ways in the Methodist circuits of early industrial England. Jabez Bunting's 'deformity of the sensibility', to use Edward Thompson's characteristic phrase, may have been particularly odious, but the processes that produced it were not unique to him.

The chapter on Thomas Allan partly reflects my sense of historical guilt that someone should do something with the largest collection of papers of any layman in the connexion in the fifty years after the death of Wesley. Occasionally guilt results in more positive emotions, however, and this chapter brought its own rewards in the shape of a first-hand glimpse of the murky political waters Methodism had to chart in the era of the French Revolution, the Napoleonic Wars and the rise of popular radicalism. Allan, as the connexional solicitor and as the chief political negotiator with government ministers, was at the centre of most of the political controversies associated with Methodism in the first quarter of the nineteenth century. With the future of itinerant preaching constantly under threat, his papers show how Methodism was pushed in a conservative direction in order to protect both religious toleration and the early gains of religious pluralism upon which the whole future of the connexion depended.

Chapter 7 on Gideon Ouseley is an attempt at an engaging squib on a larger than life character, but there is a more serious purpose behind it. Too many studies of Methodism have bypassed the religious motivation and Herculean labours of the itinerant and local preachers who spearheaded the Methodist movement. Denominational historians have been too embarrassed by the vulgarity of the early Methodist itinerants, and social historians have been too fond of attributing early Methodist success to anomie, to spend much time on the lives of those who suffered many humiliations and not a few privations in their quite remarkable itinerant mission. What made them do it? And why are historians so uninterested in what made them do it? The unusually rich collection of private papers and diaries recording the life of the most famous Irish itinerant preacher at least supply the basis for the beginnings of an answer to these questions. Happily, more work is now in progress on the American itinerant and female preachers, and the time may not be too distant when we shall have accounts of the lives of local preachers and class leaders.

The themes in Part 3 are the ones that interest me most and seem to raise, if not entirely to answer, the most important questions relating to the early history of Methodism and popular evangelicalism. In particular, what kind of a movement was it? What did it offer people? And what was its impact on other structural changes in British society? Chapter 8 on law was stimulated, as is so often the case, by the work of early modern historians of popular religion. Professor Collinson's presidential address to the Ecclesiastical History Society, entitled 'The English conventicle', alerted me to the fact that I did not know the precise status of Methodism before the law in the eighteenth century, and the creative work of Martin Ingram and others on law and morality persuaded me that legal history offered a particularly creative avenue into the heart and centre of Methodism as a popular religious movement. An investigation of the way in which Methodism disturbed communities, exploited legal loopholes and challenged conventional assumptions about the social function of religion opened up vistas which had previously been closed to me. It also brought home to me the part played by Methodism in eroding a centuries-old pattern of ecclesiastical discipline based on parishes, and in constructing new religious disciplines based on voluntary commitment. The social and mental adjustments that had to be made to accommodate such changes require fresh treatment. Law, in a special way, helps to crystallize the precise issues at stake in the rise of Methodism in the eighteenth century.

The ninth chapter on popular evangelicalism and political stability represents a new roasting of an old chestnut. My twofold purpose is to introduce readers to the major landmarks of Methodist historiography since the Second World War, and to move on from the narratives which have dominated the historical discourse on the relationship between Methodism and political stability, but which have proved so singularly sterile in bringing to life the chapel communities they are meant to represent. That my interpretation offers little more than yet another provisional staging post on the way to answering this question I have not the slightest doubt, but my aim has been to shift the debate away from the implausible oscillation theories of Edward Thompson (and their recent refinements) to processes of cultural brokerage which seem to me to offer a more realistic way forward.

The final chapter on gender, as with many another male historian I imagine, started out from motives of political correctness and evolved into something rather more important. The work pioneered by women historians on the domestic piety, language structure, moral prescriptions and organizational pragmatism (extending even to gender) of Methodism has not only filled in the experience of more than half of Methodism's adherents, but has opened up fresh lines of enquiry for the movement as a whole. The many ambiguities and paradoxes at the centre of Methodism and its social influence are revealed in a particularly acute form in the experiences of women. It is appropriate that they should have the last word.

Some of the chapters in this book have appeared in earlier versions in different places but none has been left unaltered and all have been brought up to date with the recent literature. I am grateful to the holders of the copyright for permission to reprint substantial parts of these publications. These include: the council of the Royal Historical Society (for Chapter 2); the editors of *History* (for Chapter 6); the committee of the Ecclesiastical History Society (for Chapter 7); the editors of the *Bulletin of the John Rylands University Library of Manchester* (for Chapter 8); to Epworth Press (for Chapter 4); and to Routledge (for parts of Chapters 3 and 10).

Perhaps the chief pleasure in writing a book is the rare opportunity it affords to acknowledge one's debts. My accumulation is far from inconsiderable. Nathan Hatch, Mark Noll and George Rawlyk helped introduce me to Methodism on the other side of the Atlantic and taught me to think better about it. Hugh McLeod, Martin Ingram and Myrtle Hill helped launch me into the seas of popular religion, law and gender, and baled me out periodically with better ideas than my own. My colleagues at Queen's have put up with the unpleasant side-effects of my interest in 'religious enthusiasm' with great tolerance and forbearance. Peter Jupp, Ian Green, Martin Lynn, Alvin Jackson, Lucy Wooding and Chris Marsh, in their distinctive ways, have all encouraged me to press on. John Bowmer and Marion Kelly have kept Methodist archives alive in unfavourable circumstances and have taken appropriate steps to preserve rich materials for posterity. I am grateful to Edward Thompson, whom I never met, for stirring up my religious complacency. My chief academic debts, however, are to Reg Ward and John Walsh, the best of scholars, and, in their different ways, the very best of Methodists. Their generosity of spirit to an Irish interloper has been quite astonishing. The same goes for Claire L'Enfant of Routledge who has too often found herself at the receiving end of my prose, but who copes with it, and more often with the lack of it, with patience and humour.

A Wolfson Scholarship and a Nuffield Foundation Research Fellowship supplied the much needed quantities of time and money without which this book would not have been brought to a successful conclusion. I hope that what follows, in however small a way, helps repay the faith that both organizations have shown in my work. I am immensely grateful to them.

My children, Stephen and Jonathan, are old enough to love to see their names in print, but, fortunately for me, are too young to know what it is with which they have been associated. For Louanne, the pain inflicted on her with each successive book is sadly not diminished, but her selection of painkillers is nearing perfection. She has a special reason for delight at seeing her name in prefaces. It is the delight of knowing that it is over.

David Hempton
Belfast, 1995

PART I

GROWTH:
COMPARISONS AND EXPERIENCES

The two most important questions to be asked of Methodism are why did
it grow when and where it did, and what was the nature of the Methodist
experience for those who embraced it? As with the great hub airports of
the modern airline industry all other questions stretch back to those two
and cannot be answered without reference to them. The quest for answers
is essential; the prospect of supplying them is intimidating.

The first two chapters represent two very different approaches to the
first question. The first seeks to understand Methodist expansion within
the widest possible geographical area (with the notable exception of
Canada) in the North Atlantic world in the Age of Revolution. The second
is an intensive local study of Methodism in the border counties of southern
Ulster in the same period. Each approach has its strengths and weaknesses.
The former inexorably leads the historian into other big questions about
the relationship of Methodist expansion to other simultaneous social
processes, including the rise of industrial capitalism, the growth of market
economies, the rise of religious pluralism and the democratization of
religion and politics. The answers are inevitably speculative, though the
process of comparison from place to place imposes its own intellectual
disciplines and throws up new frameworks of interpretation. Less ink
would have been wasted by nationally bound historians of Methodism if
they had paused to think how it was that Wesleyan Arminianism, itinerant
preaching, lay leadership, class systems, love-feasts and hymn-singing
came successfully to be exported to many different social contexts in
different parts of the world in the period from 1750 to 1850.

Bigger canvasses naturally facilitate the treatment of bigger themes, but
there is room also for the fine etchings of the miniaturist in the reconstruction of Methodist communities. Methodism did not simply blow
across the North Atlantic world like some giant cloud propelled by other
more powerful forces, it was rooted in the particularities of time and place.
Its tender pieties and harsh disciplines were embraced by individuals and
expressed in communities. Methodism needs to be earthed and the second
chapter is an attempt to do just that. The advantages of a local study are

1

that it is possible to reconstruct the economic and social setting of Methodism and relate it quite precisely to the growth and decline in membership. Southern Ulster was chosen because most Irish Methodists lived there and because Irish Methodism has not as yet been overlain with the same kind of cultural baggage as exists in England. It represented a rare opportunity to paint a picture almost from scratch.

In their different ways what these chapters show is that Methodism profited from the erosion of old structures and the weaknesses of the established denominations. Methodism thrived in expanding and plural-istic societies and found the going much tougher in places where old authorities or old conflicts retained their power throughout the revolu-tionary period. Methodism's own expansionist mechanisms either oper-ated in symbiosis (though not necessarily always in harmony) with wider economic and cultural patterns or clashed with them. The former, as in the USA, England and Wales, produced remarkable growth, while the latter, as in Ireland and France, could throw up periods of intense religious excitement, but could not convert them into durable religious cultures. On one level Methodist growth obeyed a tautology: growth and expansion created the minimum conditions of religious pluralism which in turn opened the way for further growth and expansion. Soil already steeped in Roman Catholicism or Presbyterianism was rarely as fertile for Methodism as that already cultivated by the Anglicans or that which had never properly been cultivated before.

Whatever the patterns that emerge it is good to be constantly reminded that Methodism was carried by people to people. It is sadly instructive to compare the many thousands of books devoted to Methodist theology, ministry and organization with the mere handful devoted to religious motivation, meaning and experience. Both in this section and in the others at least some effort has been made to restore this horrid imbalance.

The third chapter, therefore, represents an attempt to penetrate to the heart of popular religious (not only Methodist) cultures in the British Isles in the modern period. Oral evidence (and, later, participant observation), literary evidence and the decoding of religious rituals and rites of passage all show how unsatisfactory are the crude divisions into which statistically based studies have consigned their subjects. The religious census of 1851 still casts a great shadow over the writing of nineteenth-century religious history. Only slowly have we begun to shake off the statistical and utilitarian inquisitions of the Victorian bourgeoisie to move on to the questions which could neither be addressed nor answered by such methods. Numbers and the way in which they line up are far from unimportant, but they can no more get to the essence of religious belief and practice than Samuel Butler's bees were able to extract pollen from flowered wallpaper.

2

1

'MOTIVES, METHODS AND MARGINS': A COMPARATIVE STUDY OF METHODIST EXPANSION IN THE NORTH ATLANTIC WORLD, c. 1770–1850

Whether one was stimulated or angered by his work, there is no denying the fact that the regrettable death last year of Edward Thompson has robbed us of one of the most widely read and admired interpreters of popular religion in its cultural setting during the Industrial Revolution. A man of razor-sharp intellect and passionate convictions, Thompson was not only one of Britain's greatest ever social historians, but also has had a remarkable influence over Methodist historiography, especially in the United States, since the publication of his great work *The Making of the English Working Class* in 1963.[1] In a sense, however, his is a name that will not be regarded with particular fondness by those interested in the history of Methodism as a popular religious movement. The ringing phrase 'psychic masturbation' along with his other attempts to get at the heart of Methodist experience through a psycho-sexual treatment of hymns and images created an immense stir at the time and has never been forgotten or indeed forgiven by those who felt that a great religious tradition had been immolated on the altar of the sexual faddism of the 1960s.[2]

But Thompson was no mere dedicated follower of fashion. In the midst of the controversy surrounding his interpretation of Methodism it is easy to forget that Thompson wrote as he did as a result of asking penetrating questions which seem genuinely to have perplexed him and which still need to be addressed. With a sharp eye for the way the historiography was shifting, he stated that

> too much writing on Methodism commences with the assumption that we all know what Methodism was, and gets on with discussing its growth rates or its organisational structures. But we cannot deduce the quality of the Methodist experience from this kind of evidence.[3]

It was his attempt to penetrate to the heart of Methodist *experience* – as opposed to its structures, organization and theology – that stimulated

3

Thompson to address a number of subsidiary but linked questions. Why did working people, for example, accept 'this passionate Lutheranism' and not the more politically literate and rational faith of the English dissenting tradition which Thompson considered a more appropriate vehicle for working-class interests in the age of the French Revolution? How should one begin to interpret recorded Methodist experiences when they were so often couched in the most high-flown supernaturalistic language about Satan and his demons and described in the most surreal of images?[4] How can one explain a religion allegedly founded on the principles of a loving sacrifice which nevertheless 'feared love's effective expression, either as sexual love or in any social form which might irritate relations with Authority'? How can the remorseless mechanics of societary discipline be squared with the remarkable outbursts of folk revivalism which seemed to operate on the rawest edge of emotional extremism? How could Methodism simultaneously act as the religion of the industrial bourgeoisie *and* wide sections of the proletariat given that both Weber and Tawney had confined themselves to explaining why puritanical forms of religion had appealed almost exclusively to the middling sort with economic aspirations?

In answering these questions and in facing up to the many apparent paradoxes of Methodist experience, Thompson imposed several analytical frameworks; I say imposed, because, as is the way with many of the most influential histories of Methodism on both sides of the Atlantic, his conceptual apparatus and sheer power of historical imagination were generally more impressive than his detailed evidence. For convenience he split Methodist history into three epochs: the era of the Wesleyan pastorate, the war years and 'the sober years of ascending respectability and social status'.[5] It was the middle period, Methodism's great age of rapid expansion, that interested him most. In this period he sought to explain Methodist experience in terms of the psychic disturbances occasioned by war, food shortages and revolutionary political and social changes, which he synthesized in the memorable phrase 'the chiliasm of despair'. He meant by that not so much that Methodism was a kind of millenarian sect – like those which came to the fore during the English Civil Wars and Interregnum – but that social and political anomie produced the kind of psychological climate within which a religion like Methodism could flourish.

His second broad conceptual framework had to do with Methodism as an inculcator of work discipline and structured leisure at a time when industrial capitalism was eroding the traditional patterns of labour and popular amusement. 'The argument is thus complete', he wrote, 'the factory system demands a transformation of human nature, the "working paroxysms" of the artisan or the outworker must be methodized until the man is adapted to the discipline of the machine.'[6] It is here that he quotes

4

with approval D. H. Lawrence's words in *The Rainbow* that the miners 'believe they must alter themselves to fit the pits and the place, rather than alter the pits and the place to fit themselves. It is easier.'[7] This then, as far as Thompson was concerned, was the essence of Methodism's impact on the workers in the early Industrial Revolution.

His third main conceptual framework was based on his view of Methodist theology, and, in particular, its doctrine of grace. Grace, according to Thompson, was maintained primarily through service to the church, cultivation of the soul by means of conversion, penitence and study, and the creation of methodical discipline in every aspect of life. Passion and the workings of the heart were thus to be confined to the religious spheres of dramatic conversions and service to the church and not to the secular world. In this way 'the box-like, blackening chapels stood in the industrial districts like great traps for the human psyche'.[8] It was in this psychological disorder that Thompson located the sexual repression and womb imagery of the Methodist hymns. Why then did working people in such large numbers put up with it? The explanation he offered was a combination of indoctrination through Sunday schools and a desperate search for community in a fragmenting social order. Indeed, anything worthy of admiration in Methodism, and in Thompson's scheme there is very little, was owing to the ability of the English working classes to import some of their traditional compassion and common sense into the 'religious terrorism' of the Methodist experience.[9]

This is not the time or the place to engage in a point-by-point rebuttal of some of Thompson's arguments. The purpose of describing them at some length is to highlight one of the most imaginative and conceptually fertile attempts to get to the heart of the Methodist *experience* by answering the basic questions: what is it and why did it grow where and when it did? In answering these questions Thompson put more stress on the *motives* of the faithful, the *methods* of transmission and the various *margins* which Methodism exploited than any of his predecessors. What restricted him was not so much the inappropriateness of the questions he asked as his own ideological convictions that since religious belief is essentially ir-rational then religion must always be explained in terms of displacement and repression. In short, his Methodism could not be allowed to display agreeable characteristics because no religion of any kind can by definition produce good fruit. Another weakness in Thompson's approach to Methodism, which surfaced also in his influential study of crowd behaviour in eighteenth-century England, was his assumption that the essence of the Methodist experience was more or less the same from person to person and from place to place. As with English crowd behaviour, he assumes a 'unanimity of conceptualization' among Methodists which fails to do justice to the important variables of age, gender, location and level of commitment.[10] In particular, his attempt to link Methodist experience to the dynamics of industrial capitalism fails to explain why both the Wesleyan and Primitive connexions often made their most spectacular gains in primarily rural or village communities.[11] It would nevertheless be a misjudgement to ignore Thompson's shrewd questions simply because the answers he supplied were unsatisfactory.

What I wish to do, therefore, is to look more closely at motives, methods and margins in attempting to explain the quite remarkable expansion of Methodism in different parts of the world in the period 1770–1850. I shall begin with some of the implications of Professor Ward's work on the European origins of the great awakening, before saying something about Methodist growth in Britain and the United States. I then want to compare those stories with a different and less successful pattern of Methodist growth in Ireland and France in the same period. What accounts for the difference and how can a comparative treatment help to answer some of the questions posed by Thompson in a purely English context? I shall then offer some concluding reflections on the three words that frame my rather contrived alliterative title.

The roots of the great religious revivals of the eighteenth century – from eastern and central Europe to the middle colonies of America – are to be found, according to Professor Ward, in the resistance of confessional minorities to the real or perceived threat of assimilation by powerful states and established churches.[12] He locates the seeds of future revival in the eighteenth-century Protestant frame of mind which was a compound of low morale, fear of confessional conflict, eschatological neuroses and pious devotion – all serviced by an astonishing array of devotional publications and popular preachers. The spiritual life of Europe was quite simply breaking free from confessional control at precisely the time when such control was pursued with renewed vigour. As a result the pietism of Halle and Herrnhut was fanned into revivals in various Protestant corners of the Habsburg Empire and was then carried to the British Isles and North America by sweeping population movements and by a remarkable collection of revivalists who knew of each other's labours and who believed themselves part of a worldwide movement of grace. One of the most attractive and important features of Ward's fine study of the Protestant evangelical awakening is the way in which he is able to bring to life the many sturdy individualists who preached revival, without either etherizing their religious motivation or piously glossing over their most disagreeable qualities. In terms of religious motivation, therefore, we are presented with personalities with mixed qualities of egocentricity and heroism who experienced grace and preached it in ways that Thompson's models of sexual repression and work discipline cannot begin to encapsulate.

Above all, Ward's interpretation is based upon the idea that popular evangelicalism had the capacity to act as a radical and unsettling force in a world order in which the Christianization of the poor was regarded as the exclusive function of politically manipulated and spiritually pragmatic state churches. There are still further radical dimensions to this story which would not surface in an interpretation based on social class alone. The re-emergence in theory and in practice of the doctrine of the priesthood of all believers, for example, challenged the notion of a traditional priesthood based on clerical hierarchies and established mechanisms of social control.[13] In addition, the idea that spiritual enlightenment and instruction were not confined to adult males alone opened up surprisingly influential roles for women and children in early revivalism. Thus, popular Protestantism, for all its carping narrowness and bitter controversies, had the capacity to expand the religious potential of the laity and to have a civilizing and humanizing effect on its humble adherents.[14]

How does all this relate to Methodist expansion in England in the late eighteenth and early nineteenth centuries? The most conceptually integrated alternative to Thompson's interpretation, and the one based on the best command of the evidence, is once again supplied by Ward.[15] With all due attention to Methodist theology, organization and personal motivation, he nevertheless views Methodism's great age of expansion in English society as part of much wider structural changes in the generation overshadowed by the French Revolution. In this period a complex of social tensions caused by population growth, subsistence crises and the commercialization of agriculture, and further exacerbated by prolonged warfare, sharpened class conflict and undermined the old denominational order. The rising social status of the Anglican clergy and their unprecedented representation on the bench of magistrates cemented the squire and parson alliance at the very time that establishment ideals were most under attack. In such circumstances the Church of England was in no position to resist a dramatic upsurge in undenominational itinerant preaching and cottage-based religion which even the various Methodist connexions struggled hard to keep under control.[16]

Methodism thus made its fastest gains in areas least amenable to paternalistic influence, including freehold parishes, industrial villages, mining communities, market towns, canal- and sea-ports and other centres of migratory populations. James Obelkevich's classic local study of South Lindsey is a vivid illustration of how the Church of England's attempt to reinforce an older paternalistic, hierarchic and integrated society was vigorously challenged by more emotionally vibrant and populist forms of religion such as that offered by the Primitive Methodists.[17] The result was a mixture of class and cultural conflict which reflected the economic and social structure of the area and led to the growth of an agricultural trade unionism almost entirely under Methodist leadership.[18]

From this perspective, Methodism was a form of popular religion peculiarly well adapted to the kind of economic, social and political transformations that were changing the face of English society and which were inexorably loosening the control of the Established Church at the end of the eighteenth century. Religious associations eroded the Church of England, therefore, not primarily by political means, which for long had been the fear of the Church's most ardent defenders, but through the cottage prayer meetings and itinerant preaching of a vigorously mobilized laity. In that respect, at least, Methodism, in its fundamentally religious challenge to the religious structures of England's confessional state, may be seen more as an expression of social radicalism than as a reinforcement of *ancien régime* control.[19] Its alternative structure of voluntary religious societies, organized into a connexional system, posed the same kind of threat to the Church of England as the Corresponding Societies posed to the British state.[20] As Alan Gilbert has stated in his most recent contribution to this old debate,

> The labourers, artisans and tradespeople, the school teachers and other minor professionals, and even (albeit to a much lesser extent) the merchant and manufacturing groups who became Methodists in early industrial England, were the kinds of people who, in matters of politics, industrial relations or social status, often found themselves at odds, in one way or another, with the norms, values and institutions of the ruling classes. . . . Not only were the social groups from which the movement drew the bulk of its members already predisposed towards radical or independent politics, but the very act of becoming a Methodist was often interpreted by non-Methodist neighbours and local civil authorities as one of social defiance.[21]

As long as the state and the Established Church were prepared to acquiesce in a limited toleration for religious enthusiasts – which for all practical purposes hinged on the right to engage in itinerant preaching[22] – and as long as the Methodist leadership was prepared to propagandize its own membership on behalf of the established order, the 'social defiance' alluded to by Gilbert was generally kept within acceptable boundaries.[23]

Equally important in terms of social order was the capacity of Wesleyan Methodism, and subsequently its offshoots, to separate from the Established Church and then from the main connexion in a relatively ordered and disciplined fashion. But the key here is not so much the libertarian sentiments of the sects (that much at least can be conceded to Thompson), as the profound impact of legal and institutional frameworks in helping both to articulate grievances and to manage their consequences. Popular evangelicalism did not create the free-born Englishman, nor did it single-handedly create the English capacity for disciplined protest, but through Methodism and the connexional system it offered a vibrant religious vehicle for both to operate outside the confines of the Established Church without seriously destabilizing the British state in the era of the French

Revolution. Moreover, it was in this period, from 1780 to 1830, that the growth rates of the Methodist membership reached their most spectacular, and from year to year their most volatile, levels in the history of Methodism in England.[24] The most convincing explanation for that pattern is not that Methodism offered a convenient religious vehicle for counter-revolutionary forces, but that it supplied the means by which England's confessional state was eroded from within at the same time as it was challenged from without by pressure from Roman Catholics in Ireland.[25] Ironically, it was when the Methodist leadership self-consciously acted as agents of social control in the Peterloo years from 1817–20 that Methodist expansion sustained its most serious check before the crippling internal disputes of the late 1840s and early 1850s.[26] Nevertheless, the extent to which Methodism had refashioned the religious landscape in England in the period of the Industrial Revolution was made clear by the religious census of 1851. The number of Anglican attendants was just over half the total number, and the number of Methodist attendants outstripped all the other Nonconformist denominations put together.[27] By 1851 the Church of England was still the only religious denomination in England with a truly national coverage, but it had taken a fearful pounding in those parts of the country where the population was growing most rapidly.

An even more dramatic transformation of the old denominational landscape took place in the United States in the period 1776–1850. In 1776 Methodists accounted for only 2.5 per cent of religious adherents, comfortably behind the established colonial denominations, whereas by 1850 the Methodist share was 34.2 per cent which was almost double the proportion of Presbyterians, Congregationalists and Episcopalians put together.[28] In a period of remarkable demographic expansion, Methodist growth rates considerably outstripped those of the population as a whole.[29] By the 1840s a veritable army of over 10,000 itinerant and lay preachers was servicing the fastest growing religious movement between the American Revolution and the Civil War.[30]

In the most recent history of Christianity in the United States, Mark Noll states that 'the Protestant churches that flourished most decisively in the first half of the nineteenth century were the Baptists and the Methodists, the two bodies that succeeded in joining most efficiently a democratic appeal with effective leadership'.[31] Similarly, Nathan Hatch, in an important book, calls this period of Methodist expansion the democratization of American Christianity which 'has less to do with the specifics of polity and governance and more to do with the incarnation of the church into popular culture'.[32] The popular religious movements of the early republic, in their refusal to defer to the clergy and learned theologians and in their willingness to take the religious experiences of ordinary people at face value, articulated a profoundly democratic spirit. The rise of a popular religious culture of print, the place of origin of which shifted from eastern

9

seaboard cities to west of the Alleghenies, together with the widespread dissemination of personal stories of transforming religious experiences, further contributed to the notion that the religion of the people no longer depended on clerical mediation.

The style of religious communication and worship also changed. There was a move away from refined sermons of doctrinal exposition to populist addresses employing humour, sarcasm and popular wisdom. Similarly, the content and expression of religious hymns, ballads and verse became more accessible to popular taste. 'Better than any other source, popular poems and songs capture the force of the early republic's populism', states Hatch, 'they translate theological concepts into the language of the marketplace, personalise theological abstractions, deflate the pretension of privileged church leaders, and instil hope and confidence in popular collective action.'[33] The most common themes are anticlericalism, anti-Calvinism, anti-formalism, anti-confessionalism and anti-elitism. Empowerment was from God, knowledge was from the Scriptures, salvation was available to all and the spirit was manifested, not in structures and ecclesiastical order, but in freedom and heart religion. There were, of course, raw edges to populist religious enthusiasm. Frenetic revivalism, apocalypticism and sectarian fragmentation were all in evidence as an energetic lay leadership of both men and women struggled free from the control of traditional religious structures. Methodism, with a relatively coherent Wesleyan theology and with its distinctive combination of ecclesiastical authoritarianism and connexional discipline, was in a good position to accommodate popular enthusiasm without capitulating to its most bizarre manifestations. The paradox at the heart of Methodism in the United States in this period is of the creation of an authoritarian religious structure empowered by the authority of the people – an egalitarian spiritual message which did not result in democratic ecclesiastical structures. Methodism in the United States after the Revolution was therefore a form of popular religion that successfully attacked social, ecclesiastical and professional elites rather than a genuine movement of political or ecclesiastical democracy. How then is this remarkable growth of Methodism to be explained?

As with explanations for the growth of English Methodism in the same period, historians of American Methodism have approached the problem of causality from a bewildering, but by no means mutually exclusive, variety of perspectives. An older generation of scholars, whose work is in danger of being ignored entirely by their more conceptually fertile successors, drew attention (partly from motives of denominational self-interest and partly from inherited pride in a great religious tradition) to Methodism as a civilizing and ordering movement in a disorderly and potentially savage environment. Hence William Warren Sweet, writing mostly in the 1950s, painted a picture of Methodism as a tiered structure of moral courts supervised by a self-educated and disciplined cadre of local and itinerant preachers. Even the apparent wildness of frontier camp-meetings had, according to Sweet, an internal discipline imposed by ritual, architecture, hymn-singing and even spring shoots of literacy in a pre-dominantly noisy setting. 'Frontier Methodism was far more solidly based than is usually pictured', he wrote,

> it was by no means all froth. The long lists of books, Bibles, hymn books, Disciplines and church periodicals sold to the people by the circuit-riders, all of whom were agents for the Methodist Book Concern, is evidence that the amount of religious instruction af-forded the people of the frontier was not inconsiderable.[34]

There are clear echoes here of the work of Robert Wearmouth, the distinguished historian of English Methodism and working-class political movements in the nineteenth century. Writing in the period from the 1930s to the 1950s, Wearmouth, in the words of Harold Laski, showed 'that the psychological influence of Methodism was to teach its votaries self-confidence, the ability to organise and the ability to formulate their ideas'.[35] Methodism was thus the midwife of social and political progress by bringing self-discipline, order and organizational skills to the working classes of early industrial England. For Wearmouth and Sweet, therefore, Methodism was explicitly a movement of moral and social discipline, which appealed to those in search of an ordered community against the confusion of early industrialization in England and the chaos of the frontier in North America.

That Methodism could serve such functions is not seriously in doubt. There are important local studies of Methodism on both sides of the Atlantic which have shown in a more sophisticated way how popular Protestantism could impose a degree of cultural order on its adherents,[36] but there is another side to early Methodist expansion that does not show up in such tidy categories. The white heat, passion, physical prostrations and sheer 'noise' of the early Methodist revivals were not, on a superficial level at least, characteristics associated with order and civility. Compare, for example, the following contemporaneous and hostile descriptions of Methodist revivals in Yorkshire and South Carolina at the turn of the century:

> Their meetings are frequently noisy and long continued, often till midnight, frequently till morning. It is not unusual for persons to be crying out in distress in various parts of the chapel, and others praying for them. Now a number of stout fellows, kneeling around a sinner in distress, cry aloud, 'Come Lord Jesus, come quickly'. Anon, the captive being set free, they seem to shake the very house with crying, 'Glory be to God'. The noise and confusion sometimes

11

are very great, and one could wish it otherwise. . . . They had gone beyond all bounds of decency, such screaming and bawling I never heard. Divided into small companies in different parts of the chapel, some singing, others praying, others praising, clapping of hands, etc., all was confusion and uproar. I was struck with amazement and consternation.[37]

About a week past there was a methodist conference in this place which lasted 7 or 8 days & nights with very little intermission, during which there was a large concourse of people of various colors, classes & such, assembled for various purposes. Confusion, shouting, praying, singing, laughing, talking, amorous engagements, falling down, kicking, squealing and a thousand other ludicrous things prevailed most of the time and frequently of nights, all at once – In short, it was the most detestible farcical scene that ever I beheld.[38]

American scholars, on the whole, have been more sensitive interpreters of what is going on in such gatherings than their British counterparts for whom such 'events' have been a more marginal expression within the English religious tradition than has been the case in North America. Donald Mathews, for example, in his creative exploration of the 'psycho-dynamics of orality' in Methodist revivals concludes that it was preaching and its manifold congregational responses 'that actually brought the interior life of each person out into a communal sharing of the drama of salvation and commitment'.[39] The 'liberty' of the New Birth and the shared enthusiasm of the community of the faithful were, literally, 'sensible experiences' which translated the intensity of private faith into the most sensuously prolific of public encounters – the revival meeting. E. P. Thompson, in his work on English revivalism, thought that human sexuality was at the heart of such experiences, as did many contemporary observers; but why should sexuality be the only available category for the expression and interpretation of profoundly sensuous experiences? Some fresh light has been shed on this problem by the new historical writing of women who were, after all, allegedly the chief 'victims' of the psycho-sexual peculiarities of Methodist revivalism. Diane Lobody has suggested that it was 'the very subversive spirituality of Methodism' that 'coaxed women into speech' and that the strikingly eclectic use of the word 'liberty' in early Methodist discourse is not merely incidental, but is suggestive of much deeper resonances for both men and women. Women were therefore 'the hearers, the receivers, and the bearers of liberty, just as the preachers were'.[40] Popular religious enthusiasm, for women and men, was as much a vehicle for personal freedom as it was for social discipline or social control.

What this brief discussion of the carnival of the revival meeting has tried to show is that, notwithstanding the proper emphasis on discipline and

12

order in Methodist spirituality brought out by Sweet, Wearmouth and others, there was also a sensuous and subversive dimension to it which lay at the heart of the raw emotions described in the accounts of revival in South Carolina and Yorkshire. What is particularly striking about such accounts is the sheer vitality and variety of oral and bodily expression that onlookers at the time, and religious historians ever since, have struggled unsuccessfully to interpret. The repeated use of the word 'confusion' by contemporary observers shows the extent to which the traditional boundary lines of time, gender, decency, noise and emotional restraint were blown away by the libertarian implications of the 'New Birth'. There is also a powerful element of mutuality in this experience which was sustained by the corporate expressions of praise and prayer as they were transmitted through hymn-singing and communal 'noise' of all kinds.

The attempt to come to terms with the interior dialectic of Methodist experience – its combination of spiritual freedom and order – goes some way towards explaining what kind of a movement it was in its pioneering phase, but it does not in itself explain the geographical and chronological patterns of Methodist expansion. In each country in which it took root, Methodism never attracted more than a minority of the host population and was clearly stronger in some areas than in others. The English pattern has been alluded to already, but Methodist expansion in the United States was also quite distinctive. On the eve of the American War of Independence, Maryland and New Jersey accounted for more than half of the entire Methodist membership in the colonies, a fact which caused Edwin Gaustad to conclude that 'if Methodism had not been able to adapt itself readily to the conditions of the settled East, it would never have survived to share so boldly in the conquest of the beckoning West'.[41] By 1790 Methodist societies were most thick on the ground around the Chesapeake, in northern New Jersey, eastern Connecticut and the Albany Valley, and there were significant beginnings in southern Virginia, northern North Carolina and eastern and western South Carolina. There were also considerable numbers of African-American Methodists in Maryland, Virginia and North Carolina. Some of the reasons for the remarkable Methodist success in the Chesapeake area have been clearly presented by William H. Williams in his classic regional study of the Delmarva Peninsula.[42] Methodism developed a formidable ascendancy in this area due to the compelling power of its message, its attraction to primarily English settlers (especially in the wake of the American Revolution when the appeal of Episcopalianism diminished for obvious reasons), its disciplined espousal of an alternative values system and its ability to attract African-Americans and women in large numbers. In short, Methodism, by substituting 'seriousness for frivolity, co-operation for competition, compassion for brutality, and egalitarianism for deference', was a religion ideally suited to the social, political and economic conditions of rural

Delmarva towards the end of the eighteenth century. Moreover, the Methodist ascendancy around the Chesapeake gave the movement a solid base from which to move westwards, and, according to Russell Richey, enabled it to establish a religious and cultural pattern which was subsequently exported inland to the demographically growing states of middle America.[43] Part of that pattern was a characteristically Methodist ambivalence about race and gender. Although Methodism's early repudiation of slavery was not sustained, and although women preachers were thin on the ground, there were nevertheless sufficient opportunities for both African-Americans and women to find an emotionally satisfying niche within a movement led and directed for the most part by white men.

Methodism may have established a religious ascendancy in and around Baltimore and the Chesapeake, but its powerful itinerant-led expansionism ensured that it was well placed to take advantage of the opportunities presented by the western march of the frontier. By 1800 the Methodist system had been established in western Pennsylvania, Kentucky and Tennessee and had begun to push its way north into New England. Fifty years later there were more Methodist than any other churches in twenty states of the union, a proportion unmatched by any other religious denomination.[44] A remarkable revolution in religious practice had taken place, but the gnawing question *why* still remains to be addressed. As with the historiography of British Methodism in the same period, there has been an almost unseemly rush for a single narrative, the 'big idea', within which Methodist growth in all kinds of different social and cultural contexts can be interpreted as part of a much more profound and more unitary pattern. The most intellectually influential idea is that of the market revolution, and its most striking presentation is from the pen of Charles Sellers in his book on Jacksonian America. The essence of the argument is that religious enthusiasm of the evangelical and Methodist kind was a way of managing the shock of the market. Methodism, in particular, became the main bearer of 'antinomian universalism' (as against the grim, sovereign selectivity of Calvinism), and established a system at odds with the competitive, consumerist, flesh-ridden, usurious and egotistical values of the marketplace. Methodists were thus spiritual 'come-outers' – millennial visionaries – in a world increasingly at odds with their spiritual values. Only later, and partly as a result of the 'ethical athleticism' of Methodism's theology of entire sanctification (echoes here of Thompson), did Methodists capitulate to the capitalist imperatives of the market. 'Eventually capitalist transformation', wrote Sellers, 'would obliterate from the memory of both great popular denominations [the Methodists and the Baptists] their origins in a massive cultural mobilisation against the market and its ways.'[45]

Religious historians will blink and rub their eyes with puzzlement at Sellers' cavalier and often inappropriate use of theological terminology, but a far more serious problem is that his concept of the market as applied to religion explains at once too much and too little. Too much in the sense that his sequential approach to Methodism and the market (from early repudiation to later accommodation) simply does not do justice to the evidence in both Britain and America that early Methodists were by no means consistently pious opponents of enterprise and competition. The failure of Wesley's early experiments with the primitive church's ideal of sharing resources, along with his almost hysterical warnings against the perils of accumulation, show how inured many of his followers were to the vision of material renunciation.[46] The truth of the matter is that in both Britain and the United States, Methodists exhibit a spectrum of opinion from radical suspicion of the grinding ethics of the market – as represented by men like Stilwell and Hersey in the USA and Rayner Stephens and Skevington in Britain – to a welcome embrace of the opportunities afforded by an expanding economy.[47] That there were more of the latter breed of Methodists as a proportion of the whole by the middle of the nineteenth century than there had been at the start of it is not seriously in doubt on either side of the Atlantic, but it would be a mistake to conclude from such a proposition that Methodism as a religious movement was either a puller or a pusher in some kind of metaphorical tug of war with the values of the market. Indeed, if secession is the ultimate litmus test of strength of feeling within the Methodist polity, embourgeoisement stirred up a great deal more trouble in Britain than in the USA, and the reason for that is not that the two Methodisms were essentially different species, but that social class and establishment religion operated far more powerfully in the British environment than they did across the Atlantic.[48]

If Sellers' application of the market to popular evangelicalism attempts to explain too much, it also succeeds, because of its essentially *economic* imperatives, in explaining too little. Where the metaphor of the market really does apply to American Methodism (to a much greater degree than its British counterpart) is in the realm of denominational competition on the one hand and the marketing of religion itself on the other. The Methodists not only engaged in cutthroat competition with the Baptists and other popular enthusiasts for the souls of the masses, but the very fact of doing so, in the words of Lawrence Moore, 'committed revivalism to a market logic and ultimately to market strategies'.[49] Moreover, while the emotional heat of American Methodism remained hotter for longer than its British sister movement, Americans were also better (and still remain so) at presenting popular religion as a form of mass entertainment, without the same neurotic fear of vulgarity and disorder that obsessed British Christians of all denominations in the nineteenth century. Methodism, as a religious movement rooted in itinerancy and conversionism, and with a structure designed for growth and flexibility, had therefore more to gain than to lose from the market revolution, but, as the preceding discussion

15

has tried to elucidate, the cultural exchanges that took place in both British and American Methodism in the early nineteenth century do not easily yield their secrets to the crude application of economic metaphors.

Another approach to the problem of accounting for the remarkable growth of Methodism, particularly in the USA, is to borrow explanations of processes of social change from the sociologists. In a rapidly expanding society like the United States with its relatively fluid and inadequate structures of institutional control there was virtually unlimited social space – without hardened distinctions, whether of social class or religious denomination – within which dynamic new religious movements could take root.[50] Methodism, by appealing both to the authenticity of religious experience and to the disciplines of class and church membership, offered an attractive combination of individual assurance and corporate responsibility for those experiencing the fearful exhilaration of rapid social change. In the words of Richard Carwardine, Methodism, within a generation, became the largest religious denomination within the United States due to the 'appeal of an Arminian theology whose individualistic, democratic, and optimistic emphases found a positive response in an expanding society where traditional patterns of authority and deference were succumbing to egalitarian challenge'.[51] The parallels with England, and indeed Wales where evangelical Nonconformity flourished in the expanding crevices of an industrial frontier society, are striking.[52]

Nathan Hatch's recent attempt to assess the significance of American Methodism in four propositions could therefore, with minor modifications, be applied with equal validity to England.[53] In both countries Methodist reconstruction of the church along voluntary lines contributed to a more pluralistic and competitive religious environment; equally, in both countries, Methodism was able to construct a vernacular religiosity which could appeal, at least in the short term, both to those who were at the raw edges of social change and to those who stood to profit from it. Finally, Methodism, as the sheer complexity and variety of its political expressions in England and the United States clearly demonstrate, was an infinitely flexible and adaptable religious species. Not only were Methodists to be found supporting each of the main political parties in both countries in the 1830s and 1840s (though the majority was democrat in the United States and liberal in England), but the various pressures thrown up by anti-Catholicism, legal disabilities, moral reformism and social, ethnic and denominational competition produced a rich mosaic of political allegiances.[54] Environment, context and locale shaped, and were shaped by, Methodism. It was in recognition of that reality that I stated back in 1984 that, notwithstanding the well-known homogeneous features of the Methodist revival in England, there were in fact 'many Methodisms in many places at many times'.[55] Those who prefer their religious history encased in tidy theories will no doubt find this dispiriting, but sooner or

16

later it will have to be admitted that the capacity for variety and adaptability within the Methodist tradition in Britain and the United States was one of its most marketable features. It swept over rural areas, established footholds in towns and cities and appealed to sections of populations whose other interests were sometimes antithetical to one another. Above all it changed over time, not monochromatically as is often assumed, but in relation to its date of arrival in a particular locale, and the speed with which it acquired social and cultural power.

In both England and the United States Methodism not only grew faster than the total population in the first half of the nineteenth century, but its growth resulted in a dramatic reconfiguration of the old denominational order. It nevertheless remains to be explained why both the numerical growth and cultural penetration of Methodism in the United States was so much more dramatic than in England.[56] It must be stated at the outset that there is a deep-seated disagreement among scholars of English Methodism about the reasons for the limits and the deceleration of Methodist growth. Some emphasize the part played by the preachers and wealthy chapel trustees of Bunting's generation who pushed inexorably for connexional control at the expense of ranters, radicals and revivalists.[57] As Methodism became more centralized, more bureaucratic, more clerical and more respectable, it became less attractive to the increasingly class-conscious proletariat of early Victorian cities. Others, with a more jaundiced view of the potential religiosity of the English poor, combined with a much less jaundiced view of those who had to run the Wesleyan connexion in the early nineteenth century, take the view that the Methodists could not have achieved very much more than they did.[58] The most insightful studies of urban Methodism incline more to the former view than to the latter,[59] but perhaps the main reason for the relative weakness of Methodism in England by comparison with the United States was a combination of the remarkable resilience of the frail old Established Church and the inability of early Victorian Methodism to articulate the class and cultural aspirations of most English urban workers. The former effectively denied Methodism a truly national coverage and access to the emerging mechanisms of welfare policy, while the latter set boundaries to its social appeal and political utility.

The Church of England, in particular, was a formidable competitor for English Methodism, for it had a centuries-old parish system and deep traditions of popular devotion (and indeed a peculiarly English and Anglican lack of devotion) which helped balance its well-known structural and pastoral deficiencies.[60] Moreover, Anglicanism, in places such as Lancashire and the West Riding, displayed a capacity to recover from early shocks to become modest Anglican strongholds.[61] Patriotism, paternalism and privilege gave Anglicanism access to control mechanisms that were simply not available to any comparable church in North America.[62] At the other end of the scale of piety, Methodism also experienced formidable competition from an alternative parish structure, in the shape of a centuries-old alehouse culture which performed many of the same functions of sociability and management of information as American Methodism brought to western settlers. Americans were, of course, not free from the terrors of the demon drink and its institutional manifestations, but its role in the transmission of culture was not as powerful as it was in England. These external factors, together with the inexorable institutionalization of the English Methodist tradition, ensured that while Methodism was able to shake the old English denominational order to its foundations, it was unable to establish a nationwide hegemony of its own.

Methodism in the United States was also transformed from 'a socially despised sect of the poor, "the offscouring of all things", into a respected denomination of some power and influence', but by mid-century it was the largest single denomination in the country and had a truly national constituency.[63] Moreover, far from struggling for cultural survival among large sections of the population, Methodism was the most numerous, if not always the most influential, tradition within a rampant evangelical Protestantism which Richard Carwardine and Nathan Hatch have argued in their different ways was the principal subculture in ante-bellum America.[64] Methodism in both Britain and the United States, perhaps because of its populist origins, world-denying piety and suspicion of abstract theological debate, was more influential in shaping culture by stealth than by the display of a vigorous intellectual and social leadership.

However one accounts for the respective strengths and weaknesses of American and British Methodism, a dramatically less impressive pattern of Methodist expansion was evident in other parts of the North Atlantic world in the same period. This is particularly true of Ireland and France whose social and political conditions proved much less receptive to the same kind of evangelical Arminianism as made such sweeping gains in England and the United States. What accounts for the difference?

Methodism in Ireland, as will be explained in more detail in the next chapter, took root initially in southern market towns along the routes of Wesley's preaching tours, but it then began to develop more strongly in the north of the country and in two quite specific areas in the southern and south-western border counties of the province of Ulster.[65] The reasons given for Methodist growth by the preachers who produced it are the familiar Methodist cocktail of itinerant preaching, cell groups, love-feasts, hymn-singing, the spiritual influence of women, and manifold special providences which played a vitally important role in persuading Methodists that God was indeed clearing the paths before them.[66] The Methodist emphases on conversion and free association brought new features to the Irish religious landscape which until then had been dominated by churches – Roman Catholic, Church of Ireland and Presbyterian – minister-

18

ing to pre-assigned communities.[67] But such explanations of themselves do not do justice to the peculiar geographical and chronological pattern of Methodist expansion in Ireland. Growth was particularly rapid in the changing and expanding economy of southern Ulster in which a rough sectarian equilibrium between Protestants and Catholics led to increased competition for land, employment and, ultimately, for social and political power. These were also old centres of predominantly English settlement. Ward's statement that one of the reasons for the breakneck expansion of American Methodism was that it offered the English in America 'a way of affirming their Englishness without being Anglican' has an obvious application to the English settlements of southern Ulster (echoes here of Delmarva).[68] Thus in this part of Ireland a powerful mixture of economic competition, cultural and religious conflict and ethnicity all played their part in the remarkable growth of Methodism at the turn of the century.

The chronology of Methodist growth is as important as its geography. The main growth spurt comes in the period 1770–1830 after which date the pace of growth slowed quite dramatically due to population migration, political conflict and structural changes within the Methodist community itself. But the growth of Irish Methodism is also more volatile than that of English Methodism in the same period. A chart of annual growth rates shows intense pulses of revivalism at roughly twenty-year intervals, including a particularly dramatic surge in the years immediately after the Rebellion of the United Irishmen in 1798. As in England and the United States, there seems to be no very clear link between Methodist expansion and economic indices, and growth slows down after 1830 despite the increase of clerical manpower and the provision of more elaborate buildings.

In many accounts of Methodist growth in the British Isles and the United States, the so-called endogenous and exogenous features are usually kept quite separate, even when both are alluded to, but it is increasingly clear that there is a symbiotic relationship between the two. In Ireland, for example, there is a correlation between the religious ideals of evangelical Arminianism and the cultural ideals of an expanding society, and between notions of religious improvement and social progress. In frequent displays of popular enlightenment chauvinism, Methodists expressed their sense of superiority over those allegedly enslaved either to Romish superstition or to the spiritual mediocrity of the Established Church. More prosaically, the cheapness and flexibility of the Methodist system was well adapted to a society undergoing profound social changes, and the connexional system facilitated the transfer of resources from wealthier urban congregations to sustain pioneer work in poorer rural areas.

As the class membership lists for southern Ulster make clear, Methodism grew spectacularly quickly in one of the last frontiers of the European Reformation at a time of acute sectarian competition. This both opened up space for its growth and development in the short term, and ultimately closed it down in the long term, as Irish Protestants became more nervous about eroding their homogeneity through denominational fragmentation. This is essentially why a large proportion of Irish Methodists chose to remain within the Established Church, and why Irish Methodism could find little growing space within areas controlled by the Roman Catholic and Presbyterian churches.

Methodist growth in France, though on a much smaller scale, has some interesting parallels with the pattern in Ireland. In the second quarter of the nineteenth century Methodism grew almost exclusively in the department of the Gard, the region with the strongest concentration of French Protestants.[69] Although Protestants comprised almost a third of the Gard's population, the proportion was even higher in the cantons to the west and north of the city of Nîmes and higher still in the Garrigues and the hills of the Cevennes. Although primarily an agricultural region, the economic and social structure of the Gard was affected by major changes in the structure of its textile production and by the growth of mining and metallurgical industries. Demographic mobility further added to the capacity for social conflict, but despite these changes Gardois society was divided less by economic issues than by matters of religion. James Deming has shown that

> though the Reformed community of the Gard experienced the same social and economic stresses that placed the social question at the forefront of public debate, religious identification continued to unite the Protestant merchant, artisan, peasant and landlord, against the menace from the Catholic majority.[70]

The existence of old Moravian settlements in the Gard, a tradition of illuminism sustained through isolation and persecution, and the decline of Calvinism within the French Reformed Church all seemed to indicate that this region would yield significant fruit to the Methodist missionaries who fetched up there in the years after the Napoleonic Wars. Motivated in part by English chauvinist zeal to redeem the French from their secular excesses, and perhaps even from their residual Roman Catholicism, Methodist missionaries contributed valiantly to a spiritual awakening within Gardois Protestantism in the period from the mid-1830s to the mid-1850s. But when the dust settled 'four decades of Methodist preaching in France yielded a stagnant church of only 1200 members by 1857'.[71] Why then were the gains so modest?

As was the case in Ireland there was an initial desire to proselytize French Catholics, but this was never a practicable proposition. Many within the Reformed Church had no desire to antagonize French Catholics or to renew ancient hostilities. Moreover, as Methodism in France moved from a societary renewal movement with missionary support towards a more settled denomination, it created all sorts of tensions with the Reformed Church. As separatism bred denominational competition, it soon became obvious that the religious market was simply not large enough to accommodate new forms of Protestantism. A powerful combination of government restriction, French Reformed opposition and popular antipathy further eroded the space available for French Methodism. In a cultural sense the French Reformed Church was as much of a religious establishment as the Irish episcopal church or indeed the Irish Presbyterian Church in its cultural heartland of north-eastern Ulster. As one French Reformed pastor put it, 'he did not want to see French Protestantism fracture into small sects without strength or means of existence'.[72] In short, voluntarism and revivalism threatened the cultural homogeneity of French Protestantism which had been built up over centuries of determined opposition to Catholic assimilation and state persecution. The price of adopting Methodism was simply too high to pay. Methodism thus made a profound impact on the religious vitality of the Reformed Church, but it was able to carve out only a distinctly small niche for its own particular brand of religious enthusiasm.

Mark Noll, in his survey of evangelical religion in North Atlantic societies in the Age of Revolution, has written that 'it was the presence of social crisis – compounded of political, intellectual, and often military upheaval – that created the circumstances in which evangelicalism rose to cultural influence'.[73] Put another way, evangelical religion seemed to thrive in the expanding crevices and margins of societies undergoing profound change of one sort or another. In England, and more particularly the United States, in the period after 1780, the social, cultural and political space for Methodist expansion seemed almost unlimited. In England a complex of changes eroded both the social and cultural foundations of the confessional state and, crucially, its powers of religious coercion. In the United States a more flexible, demographically mobile and pluralistic society offered immense potential for any religion which could combine an egalitarian appeal with an efficient organizational structure. In both countries religious revival 'helped to create a situation of theological and religious pluralism, which was the minimum condition of any sort of progress'.[74] In both England and the United States, therefore, the margins which Methodism was able to exploit were expanding, but the reverse was the case in Ireland and France where the crevices were old ones left over from the Reformation and from the settlement patterns of the sixteenth and seventeenth centuries. These crevices were temporarily widened in south Ulster and in the Gard region, largely as a result of new social tensions grafted on to old confessional conflicts, but the sheer weight of inherited cultural hegemonies soon closed them up. The available space, if anything, narrowed, and Methodism emerged as no more than the religion of an exotic minority.

So far the analysis has concentrated on a comparative treatment of Methodist expansion in different parts of the North Atlantic world in the Age of Revolution. What is lacking in this, as in almost all historical accounts of Methodism, is some kind of investigation of the religious motives both of those who propagated it and those who committed themselves to it. There is no lack of interest in the careers of the great leaders of the Methodist revival, but this has not filtered down, with a few distinguished exceptions, to those energetic foot-soldiers of Methodist expansion, the itinerant and local preachers, and still less to the great mass of the laity.[75] Both the institutional historians of Methodism and their vigorous Marxist critics have shared a disconcerting diffidence in approaching the 'boiling hot religion' of early evangelical enthusiasm.[76] One can understand why the cultural interpreters of Methodism in its twentieth-century forms would have little interest in recovering a potentially embarrassing past, but professional historians have less reason to be so selective. The problem lies, I think, with the evidence, both in finding it, and in knowing what to do with it.

Methodism, although ultimately the bearer of literacy and self-discipline in almost all the geographical areas it penetrated, was, in its pioneering phase, a movement characterized more by orality and physical expression. It was also assiduous in its record-keeping, but the records it kept, for obvious reasons, had more to do with the stationing of preachers, the listing of members and the building of churches than with the chronicling of experience in class meetings, love-feasts or camp meetings. But experience, as Edward Thompson shrewdly observed a generation ago, is the heart of the matter. Thompson, to his credit, was intrigued by the conversion narratives of the Methodist faithful, but his conceptual framework was limited by his own presuppositions about the nature of religious experience. 'We may see here in its lurid figurative expression', he wrote of one conversion narrative, 'the psychic ordeal in which the character structure of the rebellious pre-industrial labourer or artisan was violently recast into that of the submissive industrial worker.'[77] In its distilled essence, this is what Thompson meant by the transforming power of the cross which serves as the title for his chapter on popular religion in *The Making of the English Working Class*.

It has to be admitted at the outset that the investigation of religious experience and motivation is fraught with difficulties. If Marxist historians have tended to promote notions of displacement and repression, historians with religious convictions have too readily assumed that there is a pure and consistent essence of religious experience regardless of time, place and culture.[78] The problem is compounded by the fact that most narratives of religious experience are based on borrowed language either from the Scriptures or from other forms of religious literature, including the spiritual biographies of predecessors. Many employ language rich in symbol and imagery drawn mostly from the Bible or from nature, and choose the most highly coloured and dramatic forms of expression. Recorded conversions, as with later public testimonies, were designed not only to reinforce the commitment of the recorder, but were also constructed with a wider audience in mind. The better the story, the more dramatic the effect.[79]

The recording of religious experience in Methodism's age of expansion deserves a much fuller treatment than is possible here. All I wish do to in the short space available is to highlight some common themes from the recorded experiences of the Irish itinerant preachers and make some connections with similar materials from other locations. The most striking feature of the Irish accounts is the space devoted to direct 'supernatural' interventions, not only in the drama of religious conversion, but also in the manifold special providences which protected the faithful from the evil intentions of the rich, the powerful and the lewd. This sense of direct divine interest in the affairs of the world helps explain the pietist enthusiasm for keeping spiritual journals and for maintaining historical records as authentic accounts of God's dealings with the community of faith.[80] The most complete collection of materials relating to the life of an itinerant preacher in this period is that of the Irish rural revivalist Gideon Ouseley (see Chapter 7) whose stated ambition was to preach to every human settlement in Ireland.[81] His career as an itinerant preacher stretching over some fifty years was rooted in a profoundly painful conversion experience during which he described himself as 'harassed, perplexed and hopeless'. His resultant release from fear and despair acted as the main psychological motor for his preaching career and was appealed to in virtually every sermon. It supplied him with an unshakeable faith in his status as God's messenger both to save the lost and to proclaim judgement against the wicked. He also jealously protected his right of private judgement and freedom of action even to the extent of refusing to sign Wesley's larger minutes as mere human compositions. He was remorselessly anticlerical, which manifested itself in an unremitting anti-Catholicism, and, on occasions, anti-episcopalianism. Above all he never doubted that a supernatural presence guided his every movement in every place in every day.

The experiences of Ouseley and the Irish itinerants closely match those of Methodist preachers in the United States in the same period. 'An unprecedented wave of religious leaders in the last quarter of the eighteenth century', states Hatch,

> expressed their openness to a variety of signs and wonders, in short, an admission of increased supernatural involvement in everyday life. Scores of preachers' journals . . . indicated a ready

acceptance to consider dreams and visions as inspired by God, normal manifestations of divine guidance and instruction.[82]

The same is true of the North American revivalists brought to life in the work of George Rawlyk, including the intriguingly named Freeborn Garrettson who brought religious revivalism to Nova Scotia in the 1780s.[83] Apart from the traditional conversion experiences, what is striking about these accounts is their sense of emotional ecstasy:

> the enmity of my heart was slain, and the plan of salvation was open to me. I saw a beauty in the perfections of the Deity, and felt that power of faith and love that I had been a stranger to. My soul was exceeding happy that I seemed as if I wanted to take wings and fly to heaven.[84]

Whatever psychological mechanisms are at work in these intense conversion experiences, mere repression or displaced sexuality do not seem to offer persuasive explanations. What is not in dispute is that such experiences, especially among those who then went on to become itinerant and local preachers, operated as great chain-letters of evangelistic transmission in Methodism's age of expansion. They not only require a more subtle psychological treatment than has frequently been the case, but they need to be rooted in the specific cultural settings that conditioned their expression.

The North American itinerants, given the distances that had to be covered, were a particularly remarkable collection of preachers. Primarily young white males from artisan backgrounds, their religious enthusiasm was unleashed by vivid religious conversions.[85] Mostly unmarried, with little formal education and on remarkably low pay, this energetic fellowship of preachers helped sustain one another's devotion and established an easy familiarity with their audiences. Part of that familiarity was based on a shared enthusiasm for direct supernatural interventions – from dreams and visions to prophecies and physical prostrations – and on bonds of mutuality cemented by hospitality and hymn-singing. The demands on body and spirit were exceptional, and many fell by the wayside, but the striking fact is that, despite almost no material rewards worth speaking of, supply more or less kept pace with demand until predictable pressures emerged to dilute the itinerant part of the preaching. The same had happened at an earlier stage in Britain and for roughly the same reasons: money, marriage and material comforts.[86] But at the peak of its efficiency, itinerant preaching was a remarkably effective device for Christianizing individuals and their communities, and for bringing a powerful combination of supernatural excitement and iron discipline to those who embraced both.

While it is now recognized, in some quarters at least, that the most basic prerequisite for religious revival was the existence of a corps of dedicated revival preachers, more attention also needs to be paid to the religious conversions of the rank and file in Methodist societies. The main problem again is lack of suitable evidence beyond the sprinkling of journals, diaries and obituaries which naturally contain their own built-in distortions. Nevertheless, a valiant attempt has been made by Julia Werner to analyse the religious conversions of the first generation of Primitive Methodists in England. Although they display a bewildering eclecticism of age, denomination and occupation, it seems that most had some sort of religious background on which to draw, most were servants, farm labourers or unskilled workers, and most converts – though not in the overwhelming proportions conventionally assumed – were likely to be female and relatively young.[87] However, regional variations clearly demonstrate here, as in other studies, that the pattern of Methodist recruitment was more likely to reflect the social and occupational structure of the regions in which it took root than to match the familiar monochromatic categories devised by social historians.[88] This alone should persuade us of the continuing value of micro-histories of Methodist growth in town and country to set alongside the burgeoning regional, national and international studies.[89]

What is striking, however, about Werner's sample is the proportion of Methodist converts who 'had had a premonition of death, had died within a year of joining, or had been in very poor health'.[90] In addition, she is able to relate pulses of Primitive Methodist revivalism to particular times and regions where outbreaks of disease and the predominance of hazardous occupations supplied an urgent social backcloth to religious enthusiasm. There seems little doubt that religious revivalism thrived on the perceived vulnerability of individuals and social groups when confronted by rapid social change or by threats to health and personal security. In such circumstances Thompson's 'chiliasm of despair' and Werner's emphasis on the dynamics of hope offered by Methodist revivalism are but different ideological sides of the same coin. What we need to know more about is the way in which fearful attitudes to death and uncertainty were capable of being alleviated by religious revivalism, both in the short term and over the life of a generation. On the one hand, appeals to the terrors of judgement and eternal punishment (more commonly made by the uncultivated rough diamonds than by the more educated revival preachers) increased anxieties, while, on the other, the deeply personal emphasis on the experience of assurance offered immediate release. The distinctive Methodist combination of assurance and perfection offered both emotional satisfaction, and, crucially, the means and the way to a better life in this world as well as the next. Moreover, religious conversion offered not only a degree of personal assurance of sins forgiven, but also a ticket, literally in the case of the Methodists, to new forms of community. Class membership tickets were collected and prized as tangible signs of new community identities at a time when old patterns of social and religious organization were no longer adequate.[91] In that sense, the Methodist quarterly ticket was as much a symbol of the demise of the English confessional state as the Toleration Act of 1812 or the constitutional revolution of 1828–32.

It is time to attempt some broad conclusions from this short excursion into the territory marked out by Thompson. In his valiant efforts to bring together Methodist *experience* and *methods* and to locate them in the social *margins* of industrializing England, Thompson was asking the right kind of questions, but he was predisposed by his Marxist assumptions and Weberian methods to give ideologically slanted answers based on selected evidence from selected regions of a selected country. In particular, his inability to conceive of a popular religion that was in any sense a radical expression of popular sentiment against educated and clerical elites restricted the scope of his historical imagination and resulted in the kind of 'condescension of posterity' he so vigorously opposed in his treatment of the English working class.

The tide of Methodist historiography on both sides of the Atlantic is slowly moving away from explanations based on social change alone, which was the intellectual fashion of the 1970s and 1980s, towards a more sensitive approach to the analysis of religious motivation and to a new awareness of the importance of the *supply* side of the equation of Methodist growth.[92] Recent local studies show that the intensity of religious investment in terms of human resources matters as much to the spread of Methodism as does the 'right' kind of economic and social climate. There is need for care here. My intention is not to shift the debate away from one kind of incomplete explanation in favour of another, equally incomplete alternative. Similarly, in the search for a convincing framework for understanding religious motivation in Methodism's age of expansion, the argument is not for some kind of decontextualized spiritual illuminism which no historian should tolerate, but for a sensitive exploration of religious experience and motivation within the mental and social landscape of populations in different parts of the world in the period 1750–1850. It is as pointless arguing that Methodism is a hermetically sealed creed of essentially identical characteristics wherever it appeared in the world in its great age of expansion as it is foolish not to accept that in its distinctive Arminian theology, organizational structure and religious rituals, Methodism offered a peculiarly attractive and distinctive form of religion to expanding societies breaking free from old patterns of confessional control.

Whatever one says about religious motivation, and the essence of Methodism, international comparisons of Methodist growth convincingly demonstrate that some kinds of societies were more receptive to this kind of religion than others. For a religion which itself chipped away at conventional boundary lines of clericalism, gender, age and education, the most conducive environments were those interstitial and marginal areas where traditional hierarchical structures were either absent or perceived to be antithetical to new interests. From the Kingswood collieries to the American frontier and from the border counties of southern Ulster to the Welsh valleys, Methodism offered individual assurance and community disciplines. As Noll has written of the great awakening in the Age of Revolution,

> Evangelicalism was at its most effective in revolutionary situations because, with unusual force, it communicated enduring personal stability in the face of disorder, long-lasting eagerness for discipline, and a nearly inexhaustible hope that the personal dignity affirmed by the gospel could be communicated to the community as a whole.[93]

Here is a more optimistic fusion of motivation, discipline and community than was offered by Thompson and one that does justice to a wider range of sympathy, evidence and geographical location than was available to Thompson some thirty years ago.

It has nevertheless been the argument of this chapter that Thompson, with all his prejudices about the baleful effects of popular religious enthusiasm, intuitively made the connection between the motives of the Methodist faithful, the methods they used to transmit their enthusiasm and the social margins they were able to exploit in Methodism's age of expansion. Moreover, as he well understood, these were not independent variables or separate exhibits, rather they were like fused chemical elements whose catalytic power operated on one another in a quite remarkable way.[94] In that respect, Methodism's inner tensions – between assurance and perfectionism, grace and works, liberty and discipline, and 'methodism' and spontaneity – manifested themselves in a kind of dialectical spiritual energy that leaps out from the pages of recorded religious experience. Conversely, wherever in the world Methodism took root, its disciplined and respectable piety inexorably eroded the primitive supernatural excitement that accompanied its own growth. As love-feasts and quarterly conferences departed from the inner dynamics of the old revivalism, and as class meetings and itinerant preaching were diluted in scope and intensity, neither motives nor methods quite had the old vitality.[95] Even so, the Methodist *system* held together and adapted itself to new social conditions with admirable realism. In both Britain and the United States, such adaptability did not bring denominational expansion to an end, but it did set more careful boundary lines beyond which it was deemed imprudent to go.

What then of the future for the study of Methodism in its great age of expansion? There is cause for optimism that the creative work of women and African-American historians in particular will further shift the balance of interpretation away from the ecclesiastical structures controlled by men to the religious experiences – however they are to be interpreted – of men, women and children of different ethnic origins in different parts of the world.[96] In the meantime it remains a sobering fact that there have been dozens more books on the various components of Methodism's ecclesiastical bureaucracies of one kind or another than there have been on the lives and experiences of those who paid for them.[97] There is also a growing awareness that the application of generic causal mechanisms without due sensitivity to the specifics of time and place has done more harm than good to the history of Methodist scholarship on both sides of the Atlantic. Only more sophisticated local studies showing what the Methodist message was and how it was heard and appropriated, together with more wide-ranging comparisons illuminating the variety of the Methodist experience in different places and at different times, can do justice to the complexity of the task in hand. Historians of Methodism could do worse than take to heart Natalie Zeman Davis' appeal for a more rigorously contextual (family, parish and locality), comparative (sex, social class and denomination) and relational (both inside and outside religious structures) history of popular religion in the late medieval and early modern periods.[98] Only then will it become clearer what exactly was distinctive about the peculiar Methodist branch of the 'Great Awakening' and what it was in the social, economic and political conditions of the eighteenth and nineteenth centuries that enabled popular evangelicalism to make such remarkable gains in so many different parts of the world.

2

METHODISM IN IRISH SOCIETY, 1770–1830

> The principal concern of many among you has long appeared to be about the increase of your own body. Numbers – numbers to be added to your Society.[1]

John Walker, sometime fellow of Trinity College Dublin and arch-critic of everyone's religious opinions but his own, wrote his *Expostulatory Address* to the Methodists in Ireland during one of the most remarkable outbreaks of rural revivalism in Irish history. Walker, who inevitably founded the Walkerites, not only condemned Methodist acquisitiveness, but also drew up a list of its Arminian sins after the style of the eighteenth-century Calvinistic polemicists.[2] He alleged that Methodists were idolatrous in their veneration of Wesley, hypocritical in their class-meeting confessions, irrational in their pursuit of religious experience, arrogant in their supposed claims of Christian perfection and heretical in their interpretation of the doctrines of justification and sanctification. The chief importance of Walker's pamphlet was not its polemical originality, but the reply it provoked from Alexander Knox, Lord Castlereagh's private secretary. As an admirer of Wesley's transparent piety and of the beneficial influence of Methodism on the labouring classes, Knox wrote a sensitive and sympathetic riposte:

> When therefore I consider the practical effects of Methodism especially amongst the working classes, I cannot view it, in any other light than as a gracious appointment of Providence, for evangelizing the poor. And the more so, because I cannot conceive any thing more indispensable to persons of that class, in order to their attaining serious religion than some institution of this nature.[3]

Unwittingly perhaps, the confrontation between Knox and Walker isolated two of the most intriguing aspects of Methodist history: why did it grow so rapidly in the British Isles in the period 1770–1830, and what exactly was its impact on the society in which it grew? Through the proliferation of local studies and the application of statistical methods, these questions have been addressed by historians of popular religion in England, but not in Ireland. As a result, students of Irish Methodist history have to rely on Crookshank's three-volume annual register of Methodist progress, or on the large number of preachers' biographies and the centenary histories of local chapels.[4] While these are indispensable quarries of information, they do not shed much light on Methodism in its social setting. Rather they tend to emphasize further the institutional and architectural dimensions of a movement which once prided itself on being free from such concerns. The aim of this chapter then is to work towards a social history of Irish Methodism by using three resources: the rich collection of statistics, printed works and manuscripts of the Irish Wesley Historical Society; the impressive body of new literature on the history of revivalism and pietism in western Europe;[5] and the pioneering work of Irish economic and social historians.[6]

In attempting to answer the apparently simple question, why did Methodism grow, one is immediately presented with a paradox. No religious denomination has left more statistical information on its growth and development than Methodism, yet predictably no subject has occasioned as much debate, often intensely ideological, among its historians. Thus, Methodist expansion in England has been interpreted in many different, if not mutually exclusive, ways. It has been seen as both a component of the psychic process of counter-revolution, and as a religious expression of popular radicalism.[7] Its success has been attributed to weaknesses in Anglican parochial machinery and to its creative interaction with English popular culture.[8] Its growth has been related to specific kinds of community, to certain occupational categories and to the booms and slumps of the economy.[9] More traditional Methodist historians still like to emphasize Methodism's theology and pragmatic organization, its standards of pastoral care and innovations in worship, its evangelistic zeal and its concern for education.[10] Since no religious denomination is either a mere product of social forces or a spiritual island entire unto itself, numerical growth must be the result of both endogenous and exogenous factors. In explaining Irish Methodist growth, however, the relative weight given to each of these categories, region by region, would be difficult to determine even if all the necessary data had survived. As it is, the problems are compounded by lack of information about the age, sex and occupation of early Methodists and, compared with England, the lack of regional research on Irish social and economic history before the famine. Against these difficulties must be offset the rare advantages of having a full set of Methodist membership figures for every circuit in Ireland after 1770, a good collection of Conference minutes from 1752, with details of preachers, chapel building and financial organization, and a large number of preachers' biographies, reminiscences and private letters.

Unsurprisingly, the overwhelming impression from such material is that Methodism grew rapidly through a combination of its own resources and divine favour. This explanation deserves serious treatment from the historian, not only to do justice to what contemporaries thought was happening, but also because the early Methodist organization is now the subject of admiration from church renewal movements.[11] The most striking features of eighteenth-century Methodism were its itinerant ministry, cell groups, outdoor preaching, love-feasts, hymn-singing and spiritual discipline. Even erstwhile critics could see the advantages of the connexional system:

> After all we think there may be something worthy of imitation among the Methodists ... they are more frequent in assembling together than any other people. Their classes serve as nurseries to exercise their members in prayer and admonishing. From these they can call out such as are likely to be popular men for preachers. ... It cannot be denied but the Methodist preachers are generally well chosen – of free utterance, good memory, warm and vehement. ... The frequent exchanging of their preachers affords constant variety to the people as well as a kind of breathing to the preacher. Their preachers are indefatigable not only in preaching but in inquiring into the progress of the classes, visiting the people, encouraging them, directing to proper books, warning them when they in the least deviate from Wesley's doctrine and entertaining them both in public and private with marvellous accounts of the success of the Gospel as they call it, extraordinary conversions and the like for which they are well furnished by that constant correspondence which they keep up with each other through the several parts of the British dominions.[12]

The itinerancy in particular was well suited to a pioneering religious movement with few financial resources. Even allowing for inevitable exaggeration and nostalgia, the autobiographical fragments of Wesley's early Irish itinerants tell a remarkable story of miles travelled, sermons preached, persecutions suffered and illnesses endured.[13] When Henry Moore, Wesley's literary executor, was appointed to the relatively poor Charlemont circuit in 1779, he left his new bride at a neighbouring parsonage and spent six weeks riding once round the circuit.[14] As money was scarce among such humble people, the travelling preacher depended on simple hospitality, and this cemented the links between preacher and people. Thus the itinerants serviced the small societies, which in turn collected a penny a week from their members to finance the itinerancy. This was remarkably cost-efficient and pastorally successful until the increase in married preachers and new chapels put the whole system under stress in the early nineteenth century. By then the rate of membership growth per minister had gone into an irreversible decline (Table 1). But in their pioneering phase, Methodist missionaries and itinerant

Table 1 Rate of membership growth per minister in Irish Methodism, 1770–1830[a,b]

	Total ministers[c]	Members[d]	Quinquennial increase of members per minister
1770	20	3,124	
1775	24	4,237	46.4
1780	34	6,109	55.1
1785	40	7,817	42.7
1790	67	14,106	93.9
1795	76	15,266	15.3
1800	88	19,292	45.8
1805	104	23,321	38.7
1810	120	27,801	37.3
1815	132	29,357	11.8
1820	169	36,529	42.4
1825	190	34,217	−12.2
1830	205	36,903	13.1

Notes:
[a] The average growth of members per minister for the period 1770–1800 is 49.9.
[b] The average growth of members per minister for the period 1800–1830 is 21.9.
[c] 'Ministers' includes full ministers, probationers, supernumeraries and missionaries, all of whom were supported by the connexion.
[d] The figures for the years 1820–30 include Wesleyan Methodists and Primitive Wesleyan Methodists.

preachers, disparagingly called Black Caps, Swaddlers and cavalry preachers, spoke wherever they could attract a crowd – at markets, fairs, wakes, pilgrimages, public executions, Volunteer meetings and Orange gatherings.[15] As a result a high percentage of Irish Methodists in the eighteenth century had their first contact with Methodism through the public preaching of Wesley and his itinerant preachers.

Many of the early itinerants in Ireland were brought from England, but as classes were established they acted as channels through which new preaching talent could flow. Described by one Methodist theologian as a 'sort of spiritual hospital', the class system was at the heart of Methodism.[16] In the classes mutual confession of sins brought psychological release, prayer meetings heightened revivalistic expectancy and the sharing of burdens encouraged companionship and commitment. The class was also the basic unit of pastoral care and the hub of Methodist finances. Of course its intense discipline must have scared away as many as it attracted, but for the Methodist faithful, especially women, it was at the very centre of their allegiance.[17] Moreover, as classes were home, rather than chapel, based they were easily subdivided in times of expansion.

Holders of Methodist class membership tickets also gained automatic entry to the love-feasts, which were simple fellowship meals held at least four times a year.[18] These times of hymn-singing, prayer and exhortation attracted large crowds and were often important catalysts of religious revival. In the midst of the Cavan revival of 1801, for example, James Rennick told Dr Coke, the father of Wesleyan missions, that 'shortly after the love-feast was opened, the cry of mourners arose; and it was thought no less than thirty were converted; and great were the rejoicings of the truly pious'.[19] Such accounts were common, not only from Ireland, but from contemporaneous Methodist revivals in Yorkshire and Cornwall.[20] The love-feast, in a special way, combined community solidarity with intense religious emotions.

All contemporary accounts of Methodist expansion in the eighteenth century mention the centrality of itinerant preaching, class and band meetings, love-feasts and hymn-singing, but lurking behind these distinctive features of Methodism there are other, even more personal, reasons for growth. The role of women in early Methodism, for example, needs fresh attention. The revealing memoirs of Margaret Davidson and Alice Cambridge, Crookshank's eighteen little portraits of 'memorable women' and occasional references to societies dominated by older women testify to the importance of this subject without providing a satisfactory analytical framework.[21] It seems that in early Methodism older unmarried or widowed women played an important part in Methodist growth, especially in the more remote areas. In the larger towns men were in the ascendancy, a position confirmed in the nineteenth century when the growth of chapel building, ecclesiastical bureaucracy and formal theological training thrust Methodism into the male world of financial and denominational management.[22] To a remarkable extent Methodist historiography has reflected this nineteenth-century institutional drift by concentrating almost exclusively on the chapels to the neglect of the cottage meetings. But at an earlier stage in its development Methodism was indebted to women for their hospitality, family influence and spiritual endurance. In many Methodist families the wife or daughter was the first to be converted, resulting either in family hostility or in the swift conversion of other members. So marked was this pattern that enemies of Methodism alleged that creeping into homes and making captives of 'silly women' was a speciality of the itinerant preachers.

The psychological impact of frequent 'special providences' is another factor in Methodist growth. As one would expect, many of the most extravagant examples were passed down by oral tradition or were associated with particularly flamboyant preachers.[23] One such was Lorenzo Dow, an American frontier preacher who arrived in Ireland after the '98 rebellion because he thought the journey would help his asthma. His unkempt appearance and odd ideas scarcely endeared him to the Dublin Methodist elite, but he found favour with some rural itinerants. His *Works: Providential Experience of Lorenzo Dow in Europe and America* is full of supernatural occurrences, some not without their humorous side; 'a few days since, as I was credibly informed, there was heavenly melodious music heard, from whence could not be ascertained: and at the same time a young woman died happy'. Instances of angelic music at the death of young women were often reported to Wesley himself and continued to characterize Welsh revivalism until the beginning of the twentieth century.[24]

More substantially, the biographies of the Irish itinerants show how special providences sustained their missionary zeal in what was otherwise a hostile environment. The *Life of the Rev. Mr Henry Moore*, one of Wesley's closest friends and a man of some learning, is full of providential interventions, including the story of his first open-air service in Dublin when he was mocked by a drunken sailor who subsequently drowned in the Liffey.[25] One of the most embellished of early Methodist providences was the sudden death in 1795 of J. D. Bourke, the Anglican Archbishop of Tuam, after he had threatened to take legal proceedings against the Methodists under the Conventicles Act. The main facts of the case are easily authenticated, but not the prophetical dreams of the Methodist faithful.[26] The wide circulation of countless providences gave an immediate spiritual authenticity to the Methodist message in a predominantly superstitious rural culture. Not surprisingly, many of the most remarkable providences were directed against the rich, the powerful and the scoffers. If God was indeed for the Methodists, who could stand against them?

Lack of space prevents a full investigation of all the endogenous factors in Methodist growth. Much could be said about one of the most creditable aspects of Methodism in Ireland – its widespread use of literature in evangelism, its establishment of Sunday and daily schools and the high levels of Methodist literacy compared to the rest of the population.[27] The Methodists also made a commendable contribution to a wide range of charitable institutions. Evangelical religion at its best was, therefore, educative, charitable and pious. It encouraged a sturdy sobriety and sense of responsibility, which attracted those with a small stake in the world, but who were anxious to increase it.

The first step then in understanding the growth of Methodism is to see it primarily as a religious movement that posed a radical challenge to the prevailing denominational orthodoxies of the eighteenth century, whether Catholic, Anglican, Calvinist or liberal. Methodism in its pragmatic structure, Arminian theology, innovations in worship, utilization of the laity and conversionist zeal, brought a new feature to the Irish religious landscape, which until then had been dominated by churches ministering to their own communities.[28]

If understanding the deeply religious nature of Methodism is the first step in the explanation of its growth, it is not, as is customarily the case in denominational histories, the only one. The distinctive regional and chronological characteristics of Methodist expansion cannot be explained merely in religious terms. For example, the most striking feature of Methodist growth rates in the period 1767–1830 is their irregularity (Table 2 and Figure 3 on p. 48), even by comparison with the equivalent figures for English Methodism.[29] The rate of Methodist growth in England during this period only once rises above 10 per cent per annum and a minus figure is recorded only three times. By contrast, the Methodist membership in Ireland grows more rapidly than 10 per cent per annum on twelve occasions, including extraordinary figures for the years 1769–71, 1785–9, 1800–2 and 1819–20, but a minus figure is recorded on sixteen occasions. Since the religious and organizational characteristics of the English and Irish connexions were broadly similar, the reason for such a major difference probably lies in the social, economic and political conditions of late eighteenth- and early nineteenth-century Ireland. That is not to deny that some membership fluctuations were caused by institutional frailties, either in the collection of figures or in the local circumstances producing them.

The geographical distribution of Irish Methodists is also remarkably uneven. As in England there are easily identifiable areas of Methodist strength. From an early stage there were Methodist communities in most of the large Irish towns such as Dublin, Waterford, Cork, Bandon, Limerick, Sligo, Athlone, Enniskillen, Newry and Londonderry. As most early Methodist expansion derived from the labours of itinerant preachers and from a network of private contacts, it is scarcely surprising that Methodism also made an impact on smaller market towns, which had the double advantage of being situated on major roads and of having a regular influx of people from the surrounding area. Indeed a recently constructed map of Ulster roads and market towns in 1783 bears a remarkable similarity to patterns of Methodist recruitment.[30] Moreover, there are examples of Methodist expansion in the rural hinterland of market towns, even if the towns themselves could not sustain Methodist societies.[31] Methodism also appealed to certain kinds of marginal communities with tight boundaries around them, such as the Palatine colliers of Tipperary and the soldiers in Irish garrisons.[32]

In terms of regional distribution there was a significant shift in Methodist strength in this period. In 1770, 53 per cent of Irish Methodists lived south of a line drawn from Sligo to Dundalk, whereas by 1815, 68 per cent lived north of that line. The main reason for this is that well-established societies in southern towns began to recruit more slowly at the same time as new opportunities opened up in the north, especially in two quite distinct areas – the 'linen triangle of Ulster' and in a rectangular area with Lough Erne at its centre (Figure 1). By 1830, 47 per cent of Irish Methodists lived within those boundaries. Methodism was, therefore, relatively strong in some southern Irish towns, especially Dublin,[33] in a range of

Table 2 Methodist membership and growth rates in Ireland, 1767–1830[a]

Year	Number	Percentage change	Year	Number	Percentage change
1767	2,801		1801	24,233	25.6
1768	2,700	−3.6	1802	26,700	10.2
1769	3,180	17.8	1803	24,605	−7.9
1770	3,124	−1.8	1804	22,954	−6.7
			1805	23,321	1.6
1771	3,632	16.3			
1772	3,792	4.4	1806	23,773	1.9
1773	4,013	5.8	1807	24,560	3.3
1774	4,341	8.2	1808	24,550	0.0
1775	4,237	−2.4	1809	25,835	5.2
			1810	27,801	7.6
1776	4,798	13.2			
1777	5,211	8.6	1811	28,194	1.4
1778	5,336	2.4	1812	27,823	−1.3
1779	5,940	11.3	1813	28,770	3.4
1780	6,109	2.9	1814	29,388	2.2
			1815	29,357	0.1
1781	6,175	1.1			
1782	6,512	5.5	1816	28,542	−2.8
1783	6,053	−7.1	1817	27,167	−4.8
1784	6,427	6.2	1818	27,147	−0.1
1785	7,817	21.6	1819	32,987[c]	21.5
			1820	36,527	10.7
1786	10,345	32.3			
1787	11,313	9.4	1821	37,100	1.6
1788	12,213	8.0	1822	35,643	−3.9
1789	14,010	14.7	1823	34,654	−2.8
1790	14,106	0.7	1824	33,969	−2.0
			1825	34,217	0.7
1791	14,158	0.4			
1792	15,018	6.1	1826	35,289	3.1
1793	13,974	−7.0	1827	35,833	1.6
1794	14,551[b]	4.1	1828	36,156	0.9
1795	15,266	4.9	1829	36,457	0.8
			1830	36,903	1.2
1796	16,762	9.8			
1797	17,004	1.3			
1798	16,630	−2.2			
1799	16,227	−2.4			
1800	19,292	18.9			

Notes:

[a] Figures are taken from the annual minutes of Conference and refer to the numbers of Methodists enrolled in societies. From 1817 onwards the figure given is the combined number of Wesleyan Methodists amd Primitive Wesleyan Methodists. Growth rates are calculated by expressing the annual net turnover of membership as a percentage of the total membership in the previous year.

[b] Figure is based on an estimate for the Newry circuit which sent no return.

[c] Since the Primitive Wesleyan numbers for 1819 are not available, the recorded figure is arrived at by adding the Wesleyan numbers to an estimate of Primitive Wesleyan numbers, calculated by averaging the figures for 1818 and 1820.

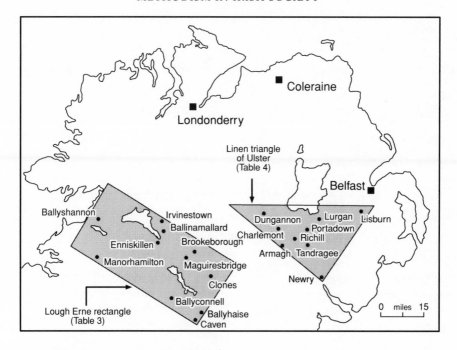

Figure 1 The 'linen triangle of Ulster' and the 'Lough Erne rectangle'

smaller market towns and in southern and south-western Ulster. It was correspondingly weak in central and western Ireland, in bog and upland areas and, to a lesser extent, in the Presbyterian heartlands of Antrim and Down. Generally speaking, Methodism took strongest root in areas with an existing Protestant, especially Anglican, population that was only loosely committed to an established denomination; and, apart from periods of wildfire rural revivalism, Methodism appealed more to literate and calculating urban dwellers than to the illiterate in rural communities. Finally, converts from Roman Catholicism or from raucous irreligion were more notable for the fuss made of them than for their quantity.[34]

Describing the geography and outlining the statistics of Methodist growth is one thing, discovering why it grew when and where it did is quite another. Since national figures disguise almost as much as they reveal, meaningful analysis must take place on a regional or local level, though the lack of surviving evidence sets its own limitations. For that reason the 'linen triangle' and the 'Lough Erne rectangle' have been selected for more detailed treatment.

The most notable feature of Methodist growth in the Lough Erne area is that it is more volatile than in any other part of Ireland (Table 3). Methodist growth in the nation as a whole only exceeded 20 per cent a

Table 3 Methodist membership and growth rates in the 'Lough Erne rectangle', 1770–1830[a]

Year	Number	Percentage change	Year	Number	Percentage change
1770	569		1800	5,413	37.0
1771	669	17.6	1801	8,412	55.4
1772	937	40.1	1802	9,079	7.9
1773	1,160	23.8	1803	8,426	−7.2
1774	937	−19.2	1804	7,293	−13.5
1775	990	5.7	1805	7,248	−0.6
1776	872	−11.9	1806	7,153	−1.3
1777	996	14.2	1807	7,103	−0.7
1778	972	−2.4	1808	6,661	−6.2
1779	1,175	20.9	1809	6,690	0.4
1780	1,184	0.8	1810	6,664	−0.4
1781	1,196	1.0	1811	6,750	1.3
1782	1,284	7.4	1812	7,190	6.5
1783	1,819	41.7	1813	6,829	−5.0
1784	1,861	2.3	1814	6,869	0.6
1785	2,059	10.6	1815	8,000	16.5
1786	2,968	44.2	1816	7,995	−0.1
1787	3,837	29.3	1817	7,503[b]	−6.2
1788	3,821	−0.4	1818	7,010	6.6
1789	3,995	4.6	1819	8,500[c]	21.3
1790	4,423	10.7	1820	10,201	20.0
1791	4,345	−1.8	1821	10,888	6.7
1792	4,541	4.5	1822	10,313	−5.3
1793	4,043	−11.0	1823	10,314	0.0
1794	3,891	−3.8	1824	9,915	−3.9
1795	3,771	−3.1	1825	9,834	−0.8
1796	4,291	13.8	1826	10,133	3.0
1797	4,116	−4.1	1827	10,958	8.2
1798	4,139	0.6	1828	11,227	2.5
1799	3,950	−4.6	1829	10,807	−3.7
			1830	10,883	0.7

Notes:
[a] See Figure 1 for the approximate area of the sample. Since Methodist circuits changed their boundaries through expansion in this period the actual geographical area is not absolutely precise. The circuits included in the sample are Enniskillen, Clones, Ballyconnell, Brookborough, Cavan, Ballinamallard, Manorhamilton and Killeshandra. From 1817 onwards the figures include Wesleyan and Primitive Wesleyan Methodists, though their circuits were not identical.
[b] Because of the chaos in circuit geography after the split of 1816, this figure is an average of those for 1816 and 1818.
[c] The recorded figure is arrived at by adding the Wesleyan numbers to an estimate of Primitive Wesleyan numbers, calculated by averaging the figures for 1818 and 1820.

year on three occasions, but this area has ten such years, including remarkable periods of growth in 1772–3, 1783, 1785–7, 1799–1802 and 1819–20. Predictably perhaps these years of rapid growth are often followed by periods of decline. The membership figure for 1802 is not exceeded until 1820, and the figure for 1830 is only marginally larger than that for 1820. How then can one account for such an erratic pattern?

Apart from a few forays by Wesley himself, the most important figure in the early penetration of Methodism into this area was an illiterate preacher called John Smith.[35] His father was a first generation Scottish Presbyterian who, as was customary in the Tandragee area, made a living as a small farmer and linen weaver. After a colourful youth, Smith was converted to Methodism in middle age by a Methodist preacher, and he subsequently graduated from the class meeting to itinerant preaching in 1766, when Wesley appointed him to the Fermanagh circuit. Smith claimed that his sermons were 'red hot from heaven' and, not surprisingly, soon reported scenes of religious revival and physical prostration in the farming country of north-west Cavan. Indeed two themes emerge from Smith's reminiscences to his son: the first is the regular recurrence of rural revivalism, and the second is the part played in Methodist success by respectable Protestant farmers, who benefited from the prosperity of the cattle trade with Britain in the second half of the eighteenth century. The economy of the Fermanagh area was based on profitable dairy farming, small-scale linen weaving and a rapid expansion of markets and communications. It was also one of the most rural parts of Ulster with an evenly balanced ratio of Protestants and Catholics.[36]

The most dramatic of all the revivals in this area occurred between 1799 and 1802 when Methodism more than doubled its membership and attracted huge crowds to outdoor meetings. After visiting Enniskillen on Christmas Day 1800, Charles Graham, an Irish speaking missionary, told his son that 'superstition and formal religion are flying like the chaff of the summer threshing floor'.[37] Dr Coke, chief organizer of the Irish Methodist mission, received a string of letters on the progress of the revival:[38]

> O! Sir, to see the fields covered with the spiritually slain, what a blessed sight it was. Husbands and wives, parents and children, all in a kind of regular confusion, weeping, exhorting, praying, and rejoicing alternately with and for each other. So graciously has God engaged the hearts of the people in quest of salvation, that at times I have had much to do to prevail on them to disperse and go home.[39]

> We have preached to thousands in the open streets and in the fields, in the fairs and markets, and in the principal towns of the North . . . the preachers and people thought it impossible that we could hold out, having not only the labours of the streets and fields, but a revival

almost in every part, that keeps us preaching, exhorting and praying for hours.[40]

The Methodists interpreted the revival as God's blessing on the newly appointed Irish speaking evangelists, together with the spiritual power generated by the cottage prayer meetings of the Methodist faithful. It would be unwise to ignore this explanation altogether, because the journals of the missionaries themselves and the reports on their activities from other sources testify to the unique role they played.[41] In his most productive period Gideon Ouseley travelled over 4,000 miles a year, preached about twenty times a week and generally found himself at the centre of intense spiritual excitement wherever he went. He understood this to be a sign of approval from the Holy Spirit, while his opponents made allegations of credulity and fanaticism.[42] Nevertheless, the novelty of preaching in both English and Irish to large crowds at markets, fairs and county assizes, along with an extensive distribution of literature, brought notoriety to the Methodist missionaries; and in the economy of rural revivalism all publicity is good publicity.

The Methodist explanation for their remarkable success in Fermanagh and Cavan from 1799–1802 is, however, inadequate. The Irish-speaking preachers made little impact on other parts of Ireland, and their record in the Lough Erne area after 1802 was much less impressive. Rather it could be argued that a well-established revivalistic tradition in south-west Ulster was given added urgency in the period 1799–1802 by the psychological impact of the '98 rebellion in an area of sectarian equilibrium. It was also a period of high food prices and serious scarcities. The missionaries were, therefore, both the conscious and unconscious catalysts of other profound emotions as they denounced 'the judgments of heaven against the crimes of a guilty nation'.[43] In such circumstances the old Methodist command to flee from the wrath to come had obvious temporal applications in the rural environs of post-rebellion Ireland.

Despite the remarkable Methodist growth in this period two cautionary notes should be struck. First, only a fraction of those who attended outdoor meetings actually committed themselves to the discipline of Methodist societies. Second, there was considerable leakage from those societies throughout the following decade (Table 3).[44] Facts like these from all over the British Isles persuaded influential Methodists of Jabez Bunting's generation that Methodist revivalism obeyed a law of diminishing returns.[45] Instead, they put their faith in denominational consolidation. The resultant tensions between denominationalists and revivalists led to division in England and to heated quarrels in Ireland between the wealthy Dublin Methodists and folk preachers like Ouseley, whose sermons were described as all 'nonsense and noise'.[46]

The almost rhythmic pattern of generational revivalism (Figure 3) did not die out in south-west Ulster at the start of the nineteenth century, but thereafter it was on a smaller scale and there was much less at stake. In this area Methodism emerged as a force to be reckoned with by the older denominations, but it never again threatened to supplant them altogether.

Methodist growth in the linen triangle of Ulster shows some similarity to that of the Lough Erne area (Figure 2). Both grew rapidly in the 1780s, 1800–2 and 1819–21, and in both areas expansion slowed down considerably in the 1820s. Against that the growth pattern in the linen triangle is much less volatile. Indeed one would not expect an exact correlation between the two areas because of their different social and economic structures. In the second half of the eighteenth century the economy of the

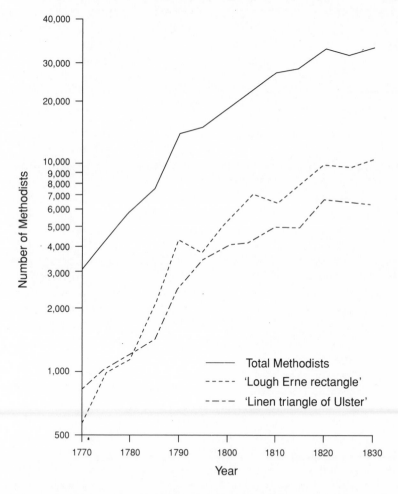

Figure 2 Members of Methodist societies in Ireland in the 'Lough Erne rectangle' and in the 'linen triangle of Ulster' at five-yearly intervals (hundreds: semi-log)

linen triangle was dominated by the expansion of the linen industry in all its phases, and by the subdivision of townlands into small farms of less than 5 acres accompanied by a weakening of landlord control. Moreover, by comparison with south-west Ulster this area had more market towns, a better communications system and a much greater diversity of occupations.[47] But perhaps the most important exogenous factor in Methodist growth was the interaction of economic fluctuations with religious sectarianism. Although Catholics were latecomers to the weaving trade in the eighteenth century, the relaxation of the penal laws and the prosperity generated by the linen industry soon attracted them into the land market.

> It was in such areas, where the protestant weavers were struggling to maintain their plebeian ascendancy against competition from the catholic weavers, that Orangeism was to thrive; and because these protestants were not entirely dependent on the land for their livelihood they could identify more easily with – and be mobilized by – reactionary landlords, creating a protestant sense of identity in contradistinction to the catholics.[48]

The linen triangle was, therefore, the focus of conflict between Protestant Orangemen and Catholic Defenders, especially during the slump of the mid-1790s when the Napoleonic Wars dislocated the linen trade.

Although early Methodist growth in the linen triangle can be accounted for in the traditional way by emphasizing the importance of itinerant preachers encountering an expanding and more independent population,[49] the period 1784–1800 can be understood only against a background of economic, religious and political competition. Methodism was, therefore, a beneficiary of, and partly a contributor to, the increased sectarian tensions of the last two decades of the eighteenth century. The biography of Adam Averell, the future leader of the Primitive Wesleyan Methodists in Ireland,[50] records impressive scenes of religious revival in the linen triangle in the aftermath of the conflict between Orangemen and Defenders in 1795 (Table 4).[51] But, as Averell realized, political excitement was a two-edged sword. Whereas Methodism benefited from a greater degree of Protestant solidarity in the mid-1790s, it suffered correspondingly in the acute political and economic crisis of 1798–9.

With the exception of a small group of 'Jacobin Methodists' in the Lisburn circuit,[52] the Irish Wesleyans were impeccably loyal to the British government in 1798.[53] In fact so many Methodists were recruited for the yeomanry that Averell was worried that drilling on the sabbath would lead them away from their first love.[54] Whether for this reason or, more likely, because of the widespread distress of these years, Methodism suffered serious membership losses in 1798–9 (Table 4). These were more than replenished in the following year when the linen triangle shared in the great Methodist revival of southern Ulster. Further gains were made

Table 4 Methodist membership and growth rates in the 'linen triangle of Ulster', 1780–1830[a]

Year	Number	Percentage change	Year	Number	Percentage change
1780	1,257	−2.3	1805	4,294	−0.1
1781	1,138	−9.5	1806	4,600	7.1
1782	1,126	−1.1	1807	4,574	−0.6
1783	1,108	−1.6	1808	4,299	−6.0
1784	1,125	1.5	1809	4,494	4.5
1785	1,463	30.1	1810	5,105	13.6
1786	1,750	19.6	1811	5,231	2.5
1787	2,104	20.2	1812	5,108	−2.4
1788	2,395	13.8	1813	5,119	0.2
1789	3,100	29.4	1814	5,096	−0.5
1790	2,614	−15.7	1815	5,066	0.6
1791	2,928	12.0	1816	4,913	3.0
1792	3,181	8.6	1817	4,896[b]	− 0.4
1793	3,004	−5.6	1818	4,875	−0.4
1794	3,071	2.2	1819	6,383[c]	30.9
1795	3,515	14.5	1820	6,906	8.2
1796	4,007	14.0	1821	7,267	5.2
1797	4,071	1.6	1822	7,335	0.9
1798	3,720	−8.6	1823	7,079	−3.5
1799	3,687	−0.9	1824	6,702	−5.3
1800	4,161	12.9	1825	6,639	−0.9
1801	4,145	−0.4	1826	6,282	−5.4
1802	4,488	8.3	1827	6,257	−0.4
1803	4,367	−2.7	1828	6,365	1.7
1804	4,300	−1.5	1829	6,498	2.1
			1830	6,512	0.2

Notes:
[a] See Figure 1 for the approximate area of the sample. Since Methodist circuits changed their boundaries through expansion in this period the actual geographical area is not absolutely precise. The circuits included in the sample are Armagh, Tandragee, Newry, Lisburn, Charlemont, Lurgan and Dungannon. From 1817 onwards the figures include Wesleyan and Primitive Wesleyan Methodists, though their circuits were not identical. Figures exist for the 1770s, but are unreliable for present purposes because of circuit expansion.
[b] Because of the chaos in circuit geography after the split of 1816, this figure is an average of those for 1816 and 1818.
[c] The recorded figure is arrived at by adding the Wesleyan numbers to an estimate of Primitive Wesleyan numbers, calculated by averaging the figures for 1818 and 1820.

in 1809–10 and 1819–20, but thereafter the evangelistic enthusiasm of Methodists in the area declined, until the 1859 revival brought a temporary reminder of old times.[55]

These brief glances at Methodist growth in two parts of northern Ireland show the complexity of the subject. The deeply religious motivation of early Methodism must not be neglected. Without the zeal of itinerant preachers, the commitment of class members and the liveliness of Methodist meetings there would have been no growth at all; but once Methodism was established, it is impossible to ignore the influence of social, economic and political factors in determining the pattern and extent of that growth. Of course endogenous and exogenous explanations are not mutually exclusive, nor even unrelated. The cheapness and flexibility of the Methodist system, for example, was well adapted to a society undergoing profound social changes. Moreover, itinerant preachers were able to take advantage of improved communications, and the connexional system facilitated the transfer of resources from wealthier urban congregations to sustain pioneer work in poorer rural areas.[56]

The recent historiography of European popular pietism and English Methodism has concentrated on their relationship with popular culture as one important, but neglected, reason for their growth. In England, for example, labour historians have drawn attention to Methodist success in mining and fishing villages allegedly because 'Wesleyan superstition matched the indigenous superstitions of tinners and fishermen who, for occupational reasons . . . were dependent upon chance and luck in their daily lives'.[57] In addition to matching popular superstitions, Methodism had the capacity to translate them into religious idioms. Thus, Cornish Methodists declared holy war on drink, hurling, wrestling, bull-baiting, cock-fighting and folk superstitions, but replaced them with revivals, love-feasts, providential interventions and colourful local versions of the cosmic drama between God and the devil.[58] However contentious such arguments may be, it is nevertheless essential to place religion in a proper social setting and not reduce it to its institutional manifestations.

Early Irish Methodists were at least partly aware of the difficulties of reaching quite humble people. The missionary preachers in general, and Ouseley in particular, were expert at explaining complex theological ideas in simple rustic parables such as the scutching of flax (stripping the husk from the fibre), and the cutting of peat in the summer for use in the winter.[59] The predominantly agricultural nature of biblical imagery also worked in their favour. Moreover, some Methodists were keen to understand the culture within which they operated. Adam Clarke, a native of County Londonderry and early Methodism's most eminent scholar, asked Ouseley for detailed information on the Irish Catholic poor, especially

> their *peculiar* civil and religious customs – their superstitions, legends, tales, belief in a spiritual world, and the agents employed in it, etc., etc., as from such things as these, the character and genius of a people may be more readily collected than from any philosophical reasonings.[60]

This may seem tame by contemporary anthropological and missiological standards, but it was unusually impressive for its time. Clarke also used his considerable influence on the British and Foreign Bible Society to get the scriptures printed in the Irish language. Indeed the concern of Methodists and evangelicals for the preservation of the Irish language, not only on grounds of missionary expediency, is an aspect of Irish social history that deserves more attention.[61]

The idea that Methodism, through its providences, folk preaching and concern for the Irish language, chimed in with Irish popular culture should not be pressed too far. The Methodists after all condemned a range of rural sports from cock-fighting to horse-racing and tried hard, not always successfully, to suppress smuggling, illicit alcohol production and sexual irregularities within their own societies. In fact the private minutes of Conference show that the preachers were themselves occasionally guilty of such misdemeanours.[62] Despite their own special providences, Methodists were opposed to most rural superstitions, bawdy rituals, feasts and festivals – whether Catholicized or not – and to the purveyors of local magic.[63] In short, the Methodists opposed the world of divinations and portents by offering what some might regard as the alternative magic of theology and the new birth. Ultimately, however, Methodism appealed as much to the mind as it did to the heart, and it both depended upon and encouraged a more literate approach to religion than was common in the Irish countryside. Indeed all the churches found it hard to penetrate the superstitious shield of Irish peasants, who were willing to use Catholic rites of passage without coming under the control of the Roman Catholic Church. Methodism experienced similar problems. It attracted thousands of curious Irishmen to outdoor meetings, but only a small proportion was willing to exchange rural entertainment for the discipline of class meetings. As this became evident, Methodism's mission to the disreputable gradually gave way to recruitment from the respectable.

Perhaps Methodism's most important contribution to Irish society was the stimulus it gave to a much wider evangelicalism, initially in the Dublin area and then later in the province of Ulster. Many Methodist characteristics, particularly itinerant preaching and the establishment of voluntary religious societies, were taken up by individuals, missionary organizations and eventually by the churches themselves. When William Gregory toured Ulster in the summer of 1800 under the sponsorship of the Evangelical Society he found new evangelical enthusiasms among all denominations, even in the most obscure corners of rural Ulster.[64] In a landscape still bearing the scars of the 1798 rebellion and in an atmosphere dominated by political uncertainty and a strong military presence, crowds unlimited flocked to outdoor meetings. As in England, the Irish Methodists did not create this religious enthusiasm single-handed, nor were they necessarily the dominant force within it, but by pioneering more flexible religious forms and structures they opened up new possibilities which others were able to exploit. To begin with, this upsurge of interest in 'serious religion' transcended ecclesiastical boundaries, even those between Catholics and Protestants, but inexorably denominational lines were hardened by the need to maintain discipline and control in the face of religious innovations which threatened the old denominational order.[65]

In the eighteenth century the major Irish denominations – Anglican, Presbyterian and Roman Catholic – had generally kept within their own ecclesiastical boundaries; 'each was a church ministering to a pre-assigned community – none was a sect seeking converts'.[66] Methodism's early relations with these churches were ambivalent. Although they were under strict instructions to say nothing against the Established Church, Methodists were generally frowned upon by Anglican ecclesiastics. The most common Anglican criticisms were that Methodism's class meetings resembled Catholic confession, its extempore prayers and testimonies were exhibitions of religious vanity, its 'enthusiasm' was an offence against reason and its meetings interfered with Anglican services.[67] Some of the more astute Anglican leaders feared that sooner or later Irish Methodism would imitate its English counterpart and become a separate dissenting denomination. On the other hand, some Anglican clergymen welcomed the religious seriousness of the Methodists, along with the life they brought to otherwise limp congregations.[68] Provided their enthusiasm was kept under control and they did not draw people away from the Established Church, Methodists were tolerated, if rarely embraced, by the Anglican clergy. Ironically, just as the growing evangelical presence within the Church of Ireland promised better relations with the Methodists who inspired it, the majority of Irish Wesleyans formally separated from the Church in 1816.[69]

Methodist relations with the Presbyterians were similarly ambivalent. Whereas Irish Presbyterians emphasized reformed doctrine and polity, the godly community and a sense of their own historical tradition, Methodism was pragmatic, conversionist and experiential.[70] In Ulster some Presbyterians, notably Seceders and Covenanters, had a brief flirtation with itinerant and field preaching through the Evangelical Society of Ulster (1798), but most orthodox Presbyterians had nothing to do with such innovations and the Synod of Ulster explicitly condemned the Methodist system in 1804.[71] Nevertheless, Presbyterian meeting-houses, unlike Anglican or Catholic churches, were frequently made available to Methodist preachers who were told to say nothing that might undermine evangelical growth within Irish Presbyterianism.[72]

The precise impact of evangelicalism on Ulster Presbyterianism before the infamous Arian controversy of the 1820s is still unclear. Henry Cooke, who later emerged as the champion of the evangelical cause, told the Irish education commissioners that

I was ordained in 1808, I believe I succeeded an Arian: another friend was ordained in 1808, and he succeeded an Arian ... until in one whole district which was twenty years ago entirely Arian, I don't know of one single minister you could suspect of Arianism, except one.[73]

Cooke attributed this to the influence of Bible and missionary societies, and to the growing popularity of evangelical preaching, which gave orthodox ministers a new sense of purpose. Judging by the frequency of references to Presbyterian congregations in the biographies of Irish Methodist preachers, there is no doubt that Methodism played an important catalytic role in the spread of Irish Presbyterian evangelicalism at the turn of the century. Moreover, Methodism's emphasis on personal conversion against the kirk's stress on the conversion of the whole secular order, within the scope of God's providence, toned down Presbyterian millenarianism, and helped prepare the way for the great Ulster revival of 1859.[74]

If Methodism's relations with Anglicans and Presbyterians were ambivalent, its dealings with the Roman Catholic Church were more straightforward. Although early Methodists had never intended to provoke Catholic hostility, it soon became clear that Methodist preachers were not acceptable to the Catholic hierarchy or to parish priests.[75] The early reports of the Irish-speaking Methodist missionaries contained tales of hardship and persecution caused by 'Catholic intolerance and bigotry'.[76] Initially these were suffered in silence, but their frequency persuaded Ouseley in 1807 to appeal directly to Dr Bellew, the Roman Catholic Bishop of Killala.[77] After that Ouseley became a prolific anti-Catholic pamphleteer, carried the fight to northern English cities, joined the Orange Order and became intimate with ultra-Protestant aristocrats like the Earl of Roden and Lord Farnham.[78] Ouseley is merely the most colourful example of how Methodist evangelicalism was politicized in the years after the '98 rebellion.[79] This process gathered pace in the 1820s when the demand for Roman Catholic Emancipation reached more popular levels, and when the folk preaching of early Methodism gave way to denominational self-interest. Thus, Methodism's objective of forming an interdenominational association of religious societies foundered on the rocks of Irish sectarianism, and on its own upward social mobility. Methodism was, therefore, both victim and instigator of an increase in Irish religious competition which inevitably had political consequences. Moreover, the political consciousness of Irish Methodists rose in inverse proportion to the decline of their religious enthusiasm. The Methodist contribution to anti-Catholic politics was, however, merely a symptom and not the cause of the slowing down of the revival. The severe economic and political problems of pre-famine Ireland, whatever their value as short-term stimuli of religious revival, relentlessly eroded Methodist resources, both financial and personal. The steady stream of Methodist emigrants to North America, running at about 1,000 a year by the 1830s, denuded the movement of its most youthful and energetic members.[80] Thus, emigration and the cataclysmic effects of the Irish famine in the 1840s severely curtailed Methodist growth. But in the same way as eighteenth-century Irish Methodism gained recruits from displaced European minorities, its nineteenth-century successor exported prime talent to North America, Australasia, South Africa and India.[81] Popular Protestantism for all its denominational sectarianism is therefore engagingly internationalist in its recurrent folk migrations.

In Ireland, however, the graph of annual growth rates between 1770 and 1830 (Figure 3) shows an unmistakable decline, and the generational pulses of revival were both less frequent and less pronounced. A perceptive religious cardiologist would have diagnosed a serious illness, for which the Methodist medicine of more preachers and more chapels offered little prospect of a lasting cure.

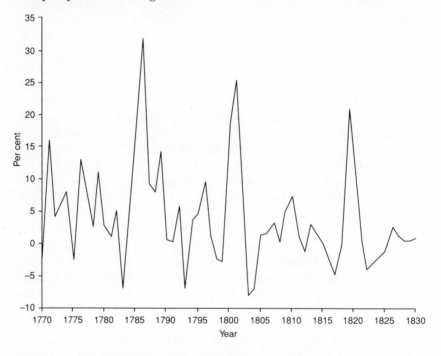

Figure 3 Growth rates of Methodism in Ireland at annual intervals, 1770–1830

3

POPULAR RELIGION IN MODERN BRITAIN

Popular religion adheres to no one definition; in different settings, in the hands of different people, the amalgam of belief that makes up its theology constantly changes.[1]

Concepts like 'popular religion' eliminate the line between past life and death and the specifics of time and place.[2]

This popular expression of religiosity was based upon different definitions of religious duty, belief and association and it arose from distinctive ideals and images of goodness and morality. The characteristic feature of this kind of religious response was its defiance of institutional categories and definitions and its combination of various types of religious expression. . . . Popular religion was neither church-based religion nor folk religion but nor was it divorced from either type of religious discourse.[3]

When the editors of *History Today* asked the question, 'What is religious history?' an eminent array of respondents found it unexpectedly difficult to give an answer. Although the study of theology and religious institutions was deemed worthwhile, there was widespread agreement among the contributors that religious history ought also to include the beliefs, motivations, experiences, rituals and practices of ordinary people in specific locations at particular times.[4] This is no easy task. Not only do historians disagree quite fundamentally about the nature and social function of religion, they are also aware of the formidable obstacles in the way of reconstructing 'popular religion', with all its behavioural and psychological complexity, from the scraps of surviving evidence. Indeed the term 'popular religion', as with its close relative 'popular culture', is easier to use than to define. It is not merely the antithesis of 'official religion', nor is it a systematic and unified alternative to it. Moreover, the traditional polarities used by historians and sociologists to get to the essence of popular religion – Christian and pagan, traditional and modern, rational and irrational, religious and irreligious, internal and external –

have proved to be insufficiently flexible to cope with the sheer diversity of popular belief and practice.

Religious cultures are not static, nor are they isolated from their social setting, rather they are made and remade by the people who live them, and therefore hardly ever conform to the fixed boundaries commentators have designed for them. The lost worlds of popular religious cultures can only be recovered by suspending our contemporary presuppositions about the role of religion in modern life, marginalized as it now is, and by making an imaginative leap into a very different past. To aid this process one early modern historian has urged a degree of 'profanation' to eliminate modern reverential and ideological bias, and to convey the earthiness of religious belief and practice in ordinary communities.[5] Another has suggested a rigorously contextual (family, parish and locality), comparative (sex, social class and denomination) and relational (both within and without religious structures) approach to the study of popular religious behaviour so that light comes from as many sources as possible.[6]

The aim of this chapter, then, is to build on the creative insights of early modern European historians and sociologists, who have pioneered this field of study, by trying to recapture, in however limited a degree, the flavour and texture of British popular religion in diverse locations since 1800. Since anything approaching an exhaustive treatment of this theme is clearly impossible in such a short space, a secondary and more realistic objective is to introduce some of the new methods and approaches employed in the past two decades to illuminate the dark corners of popular belief and practice. As we shall see, the corners are dark because the religious behaviour of the great majority of men and women in the British Isles, especially after 1900, only rarely conformed to the institutional structures devised for them.[7]

It is perhaps appropriate to start where the Victorians themselves started in trying to understand the impact of industrial and urban growth on their civilization – with numbers. Indeed this Victorian obsession with statistical information, expressed in census reports, Blue Books and statistical societies unlimited, and which was satirized with such effect by Dickens in *Hard Times*, has been reawakened by religious historians searching for contours and perspective in their study of past religious behaviour.[8] The quantitative methods pioneered by Alan Gilbert and others have indeed plotted the major religious landmarks of the modern period: the remarkable resurgence of popular evangelicalism and Roman Catholicism from about the 1780s; the relative weakness of the Church of England between 1780 and 1835, its suburban-led recovery in the Victorian era and its sorry decline, especially in inner cities in the twentieth century; the rise of evangelical Nonconformity which virtually took control of culture and society in Wales and Cornwall as did the Free Church in the Highlands and islands of Scotland; the astonishingly high mass attendance figures in the towns of post-famine Ireland; and the significant post-Second World War growth rates of Jehovah's Witnesses, Latter Day Saints, Adventists and a range of pentecostal and charismatic groups.[9]

Further refinements of the quantitative approach have shown a higher proportion of women, rural dwellers and upper- and middle-class people attending churches than their male, urban and working-class counterparts.[10] As with women, so with children, for Professor Laqueur has estimated that by 1851 over 2 million working-class children between the ages of five and fifteen (around 75 per cent of the total) were enrolled in Sunday schools.[11] One does not have to accept Laqueur's inference that the primary divide in nineteenth-century society was between the religious and the irreligious, not the middle and working classes, to conclude that Sunday schools played a substantial role in popular religious culture in town and country. For ordinary people the benefits of cheap literacy and self-improvement ensured that the Sunday school 'was the only religious institution which the nineteenth-century public in the mass had any intention of using'.[12] Regrettably from the churches' viewpoint only a tiny minority of pupils later made their way into full church or chapel membership.[13] Statistical methods have not only helped confirm some old hunches and stimulate some new observations, they have shown too that religious practices do not operate in a social vacuum. It has been suggested that 'a church's power of recruitment arises from its proximity to, congruity with and utility for those whom it recruits', with the clear implication that patterns of church growth cannot be isolated from economic and social changes or from ethnic migration and cultural identity.[14] Early Methodism, for example, grew fastest in areas of Anglican parochial weakness, where the supervision of squires and parsons was at its most rudimentary, and appealed also to particular occupational groups in closely knit communities such as small industrial, mining and fishing villages.[15]

Similarly, ethnicity as a compelling force in religious adherence is only now receiving its due attention in Ulster Protestantism and Irish Catholicism, and among Irish Roman Catholics in Britain and nonconformists in Wales.[16] As these examples show, religious allegiances based largely on ethnic and cultural congruities are the most durable and the least susceptible to socio-economic fluctuations. Indeed this highlights a wider European phenomenon in the modern period, that attachment to the churches remained strongest in those areas, urban and rural, in which the pressures of political, social and ethnic conflict tended to reinforce rather than undermine religious loyalties.[17]

Statistics, maps and graphs are indispensable tools for social historians of religion, but we worshippers of the computer terminal need also to recognize our god's limitations. Tables and graphs create an illusion of certainty, even inevitability, about historical processes that are infinitely complex. Moreover, they set up boundaries between denominations, and between the 'religious' and the 'irreligious', which are in reality less clearly defined, and thereby diminish the importance of life cycle changes and of variety in people's intensity of religious commitment. More prosaically in the context of the British Isles, the way in which Anglican, Roman Catholic, Presbyterian, Methodist and nonconformist figures are constructed makes comparisons invidious. It is, for example, difficult to compare figures based on episcopalian communicants, Presbyterian communicants, Methodist and nonconformist membership and either the estimated Roman Catholic population or mass attenders, since they clearly measure different aspects of religious adherence and commitment. In particular, the conventional assessments of Anglican strength by numbers of Easter Day communicants seriously undervalues the relative importance of the Church of England in English society, at least before the First World War. Flora Thompson, in her evocative reminiscences of rural religion in *Lark Rise to Candleford* towards the end of the nineteenth century, estimates that nine out of ten Lark Rise inhabitants would have declared themselves members of the Church of England, having been christened and married in the parish church.[18] In addition, they buried their dead at church, attended festivals at Christmas, Easter and harvest time, visited the rectory on May Day, qualified themselves for the valuable charities dispensed by clerical families, paraded their finery and singing voices on Sundays and could even be roused under certain circumstances to exhibit half-hearted displays of anti-Catholic sentiment. The majority, of course, never darkened the church's door outside festival time, unless closely bound by deference to squire or clergyman, and most of them, especially the men, resented clerical visits, particularly if the subject of religion was mentioned. According to Flora Thompson, most Lark Rise residents were also perfectly at home in the world of folk-tales, ghosts, haunted places and devil's stories, but from the point of view of rural entertainment rather than from dread of unfriendly supernatural visitations.[19] The kind of religion etched in by the author is a delicate mixture of social utility, rural entertainment and moral consensus in which the parish church was closely enmeshed, albeit within certain defined limits set by the community.

Quantitative methods were, of course, never intended to yield up the dark secrets of popular religion in rural Britain which until recently had been virtually ignored by social historians, despite the creative insights offered by Victorian novelists, topographers and folklorists. No doubt stimulated by the pioneering investigations of Keith Thomas into English popular religion in the sixteenth and seventeenth centuries,[20] the subject has been opened up in the modern period by Obelkevich's fine local study of South Lindsey in Lincolnshire and Connolly's equally suggestive work on rural Ireland.[21] Obelkevich defined popular religion as 'the non-institutional religious beliefs and practices, including unorthodox conceptions of Christian doctrine and ritual prevalent in the lower ranks of rural society' and boldly concluded his study by advocating a 'Copernican revolution' in our understanding of nineteenth-century rural religion: 'It is hard to avoid the conclusion that paganism was dominant and Christianity recessive in popular religion. Paganism was rarely Christianized but Christianity was often paganized.'[22] The evidence for this interpretation is, at least on the surface, impressive. Among Lincolnshire labourers there was scarcely a Christian observance that was not surrounded with superstitious beliefs and practices, or else ignored altogether. They were armed instead with a complete set of beliefs about the supernatural designed to bring good luck, to cure people and animals, to foretell the future and to cope with fear and death. There was also a subcultural world of witches and wise men, oracles and folk healers in which belief in the devil, humorous or otherwise, was more prevalent than knowledge of Jesus Christ. Obelkevich thus corroborates the brooding impression conveyed by George Eliot in *Silas Marner* that popular rural religion was overwhelmingly pessimistic – designed more to fob off misfortune than to appropriate the remote abstractions of salvation:

> Such strange lingering echoes of the old demon-worship might perhaps even now be caught by the diligent listener among the grey-haired peasantry; for the rude mind with difficulty associates the idea of power and benignity. A shadowy conception of power that by much persuasion can be induced to refrain from inflicting harm, is the shape most easily taken by the sense of the Invisible in the minds of men who have always been pressed close by primitive wants. . . . To them pain and mishap present a far wider range of possibilities than gladness and enjoyment.[23]

It is a weakness in Obelkevich's study that the terms Christianity and paganism are accepted as the respective poles within which religious belief and practice should be studied, when the words themselves inadequately describe the complex patterns of religious inheritance, ecclesiastical penetration, community solidarity, primitive security and rural entertainment which all contributed something to rural religious life. As McLeod has stated, his 'three worlds of church, chapel and popular religion appear too much in isolation from one another'.[24]

Flora Thompson, on the other hand, suggests that most Lark Rise residents could combine devotion to Anglicanism with rather less orthodox beliefs and their morality was similarly complex. Illegitimacy was looked upon with a mixture of sympathy and disapproval, with the latter giving way to the former after the birth of a child, but adultery was subject to community hostility expressed in rough music and skimmington rides, while lying and stealing were repudiated without benefit of ceremony. Social utility and social consensus were therefore more important determinants of Lark Rise religion and morality than were church dogmas or popular superstitions. This is at the root of the suggestion made by both Flora Thompson and George Eliot in *Silas Marner* that too much religious enthusiasm by way of churchgoing and religious devotion was regarded as antisocial behaviour by those who wished not to be placed at a disadvantage in their dealings with the Almighty.[25] Popular rural religion was therefore predominantly syncretistic in belief and inextricably bound up with community morality in practice. The traditional labels of Christianity and paganism are thus insufficiently flexible to describe historical reality.

Another boundary highlighted by Victorian fiction is that between Anglicanism and Nonconformity, church and chapel. The sharpness of this division and the degree of hostility occasioned by it depended largely on local social and economic circumstances. The tensions of an emerging class society were commonly translated into religious forms, which accounts, for example, for the close links between agricultural trade unionism and Primitive Methodism in Lincolnshire and East Anglia where anti-Anglican sentiment and the political objectives of farm labourers were two sides of the same coin.[26] With regionality and chronology all important in assessing the relationship between church and chapel in rural communities, there is little value in broad generalizations from fictional fragments. Nevertheless, literature, especially of an autobiographical kind, suggests that denominational allegiances and conflicts were often more complex than mere tables of membership statistics would allow. Edmund Gosse's *Father and Son*, for example, shows how the little Devonshire Plymouth Brethren assembly was built on the foundations of earlier Wesleyan Methodist and Bible Christian evangelism. In such small communities the denominational label counted for less than the simplicity of the religious forms and the social bonds of the membership. What is particularly valuable about Gosse's portrait is that it restores a sense of the dignity, albeit tinged with comic absurdity, of humble rural religion, which is all too rare in ideologically committed histories. 'I wish I could paint', he writes,

> in colours so vivid, that my readers could perceive what their little society consisted of, this quaint collection of humble, conscientious, ignorant and gentle persons. In chronicle or fiction I have never been fortunate enough to meet with anything which resembled them. The caricatures of enmity and worldly scorn are as crude to my memory, as the unction of religious conventionality is featureless.[27]

This is in the same spirit as Flora Thompson's treatment of Lark Rise Methodists, or 'Devil dodgers' as they were called for their practice of attending parish church on Sunday morning and their own cottage meetings in the evening. The author shows how the Methodists, and the

Roman Catholics for that matter, drove a thin wedge into the Anglican uniformity of village religion, but they were relatively easily accommodated so long as they refrained from overtly attempting conversions. Similarly the Methodists accepted the centrality of the parish church in village religion until a ritualistic vicar offended their evangelical sensibilities. Flora Thompson's account of Methodist meetings rings with the authenticity of mingled sympathy and gentle criticism. She captures the warmth of religious enthusiasm transmitted through extempore prayer, lively singing, fervent preaching and mutual confession. The weekday reserve and godly discipline of the Methodists gave way on Sunday evenings to shining eyes and loving expressions. On the other hand, she pokes fun at the exaggerated and highly coloured testimonies of the Methodist faithful, the religious equivalents of public house yarns and at the uneducated preachers basking so self-consciously in their religious limelight. The exemplary lives of the Methodists in Lark Rise earned community respect, but there is evidence to suggest that Methodists were singled out for harsh treatment if their moral pretensions failed to match their moral practice.[28] Hypocrisy was therefore more resented than religious enthusiasm.

Other boundary areas of rural religion still awaiting proper historical treatment are those of age and gender. Several surveys of religion in town and country have shown that women were more faithful in performing their religious duties than men and that changes in the forms of worship during the century, if anything, further contributed to this pattern.[29] For example, the great upheaval caused by the replacement of the village band's rough music by the more polished tones of Miss Day's organ in Thomas Hardy's *Under the Greenwood Tree* was a frequent occurrence in Anglican parish churches. The organists who succeeded the parish clerks and village bands were chiefly the wives and daughters of parsons, squires and farmers and were much less independent than their predecessors and far more likely to be subservient to the clergyman. Paradoxically, therefore, the 'improvements' in religious worship instigated by reforming Anglican clergy may have done as much to alienate the Church of England from male village culture as it did to improve the fortunes of the Church within the wider community. 'Whatever the wishes of the villagers', Obelkevich concludes, 'anglican services became more dignified, more feminine, and more clerical.'[30] The most insightful account of this transformation is in Samuel Butler's *The Way of All Flesh*, which, although not published until 1903, is based on the author's acute social and religious observations of the early and mid-Victorian periods. In particular, Butler gives his impression of the changes in worship in the parish of Battersby-on-the-Hill (really Langar in Nottinghamshire where Butler's father, Thomas, was rector), a small village of 500 inhabitants. At the beginning of the period the old Norman church was falling apart, but it was reasonably well attended by the village faithful, including the agricultural craftsmen and labourers. The worship was accompanied by a doleful gallery choir with rudimentary musical instruments. Butler described their efforts as 'discordant, but infinitely pathetic', and he detected a wild and haunting strain which reminded him of pre-Reformation litanies, psalm-singing on emigrant ships and Welsh Methodist camp meetings. Some of this is mere nostalgia for primitive rural religion which seemed to take hold of the mid-Victorian intelligentsia in reaction to cities, ritualism and red-brick conventicles. Butler's opinions, moreover, need careful handling because many of them are filtered through intense hatred of his father's religion.[31] Butler's account of Battersby parish church half a century later is nevertheless revealing. The church had been carefully restored, which, according to Butler was the most distinctive and character-istic feature of the Victorian age, and in it

> there was a harmonium played by a sweet-looking girl with a choir of school children around her, and they chanted the canticles to the most correct of chants, and they sang Hymns Ancient and Modern; the high pews were gone, nay, the very gallery in which the old choir had sung was removed as an accursed thing which might remind the people of the high places. . . . But in the evening later on I saw three very old men come chuckling out of a dissenting chapel. There was a look of content upon their faces which made me feel certain they had been singing; not doubtless with the old glory of the violoncello, the clarinet and the trombone, but still songs of Sion and no new-fangled papistry.[32]

The supporters of this effete worship were of a higher social level than their predecessors, but otherwise not much had changed. Butler describes them as good sensible folk whose ideal was the maintenance of the status quo and who 'would have been equally horrified at hearing the Christian religion doubted, and at seeing it practised'.[33]

Another dimension to the inequality of the sexes was the way in which clergymen were perceived by men and women in small communities. The fragmentary literary evidence suggests that women accepted the refine-ments of the clergy, both Anglican and Wesleyan, as an attractive ex-pression of cultivated gentlemanly values, whereas men with an emerging, if still inchoate class-consciousness, were more resentful. In Thomas Hardy's short story, *The Distracted Preacher*, Stockdale, the young Wesleyan fresh out of theological college, is interestingly called 'an old woman' by the village smugglers,[34] and similar tensions of class, age and manliness are evident in the confrontation between the new vicar and the village band in *Under the Greenwood Tree*.[35] Flora Thompson is explicit in *Lark Rise to Candleford*, as is D. H. Lawrence in his autobiographical novel, *Sons and*

Lovers, that men resented clerical interference in their households much more than women.[36]

These literary references in themselves prove nothing, but they do at least raise interesting questions about Anglican attempts to put its own house in order after 1835 by building and restoring churches and parsonages, increasing the percentage of university trained clergy and having more cultivated services. These reforms, laudable though they were in terms of energy and zeal, may not have contributed as much to the restoration of Anglican fortunes as their advocates assumed. Ironically the Church's most successful innovation, the harvest thanksgiving service, was in reality a symbolic concession to popular paganism.[37] Nonconformist denominations were not immune from the complex cultural problems faced by the Church of England, but their more enthusiastic religious atmosphere and, crucially, the wider number of acceptable religious (and political) jobs for men to do, delayed the seemingly inexorable processes that were confining religion to the young, the old and the female.

In measuring religious adherence age is yet another flexible boundary which does not show up well in churchgoing statistics. It is now well known that the Christian churches, at least in an institutional sense, exercised more influence over the young, through Sunday and day schools, than over any other age group in Victorian England. Moreover, research on a narrow selection of working-class biographies has shown that definite conversions to Christianity were most common among the age group fourteen to seventeen, and were most prevalent in the context of a revival meeting.[38] A high proportion subsequently lost their faith in mature adulthood, possibly to return to it in old age. The point is that a single life could consist of various phases of faith and doubt, and that the common division between the religious and the irreligious is far too rigid. This is well illustrated in the heroine of George Moore's *Esther Waters* who experiences a Plymouth Brethren upbringing, gives birth to an illegitimate child, marries the owner of a public house cum-gambling den (though she very nearly married a Brethren preacher), is on the receiving end of religious disapproval most of her life, yet still manages to return to a simple faith in older age as much out of nostalgia and consolation as conviction. Esther's life has parallels with her Brethren mistress and companion in old age who likewise found the pressures of life difficult to square with the simplicities of faith. Esther's mistress, Mrs Barfield,

> loved to hear Esther tell of her father and the little shop in Barnstaple, of the prayer meetings and the simple earnestness and narrowness of the faith of those good brethren. Circumstances had effaced, though they had not obliterated, the once sharply marked confines

of her religious habits. Her religion was like a garden – a little less sedulously tended than of yore, but no whit less fondly loved.[39]

Moore's fiction, indirectly supported by oral evidence, suggests that for the old the influence of nostalgia for their religious past, the need for companionship in the present, and fear of a bleak future all coalesced to revive the dying embers of personal religion. Thus, the early Victorian churches' Herculean efforts with the young probably bore unquantifiable fruit in the religious faith of the aged up to half a century later. Victorian literature shows, therefore, that the categories constructed by historians to make sense of rural popular religion need to be sufficiently flexible to incorporate the manifold complexities of human behaviour, but fiction must never be allowed to determine typicality or causality. What it can do is to show that popular religious belief and practice are indissolubly linked to other social frameworks within which people's lives are located.

The mining communities of early industrial Britain afford excellent illustrations of how the allegedly separate worlds of popular politics, religious affiliation, work, leisure and domestic life were integrated into a coherent set of communal values. In the mining villages of England and Wales, evangelical Nonconformity, particularly of the Methodist or Primitive Methodist variety, helped create a sense of community and reassurance for people experiencing profound economic and social changes, and for whom scarcity and disaster were ever present threats. Choirs, classes, chapels and Sunday schools were not simply imposed from above, but were appropriated from below, by people searching for cohesion, security and a lively alternative to local tavern culture.[40] According to Robert Colls, Methodism built 'a cocoon of seriousness in a pub and coursing-path world of careless enjoyment and self-mockery. The cocoon provided its own reason and reward for self-improvement – so dearly won by the miner'.[41] It is well to be reminded that the inhabitants of this cocoon were always in a minority in English pit villages, but not so in South Wales where nonconformists of various denominations turned the valleys into remarkable strongholds of popular evangelicalism. Welsh Nonconformity was particularly successful because its opposition (part religious and part political) to Anglicans and landowners was more intense, its congruence with the world of work and popular leisure was more all-embracing, and its capacity to offer meaningful social institutions in a frontier landscape was more conspicuously welcomed in Wales than in England.[42] The result was a remarkable religious harvest which transformed cultural life in Wales in the century before the First World War.

Popular religion in rural Ireland in the nineteenth century presents an interesting comparison with what has been said about England and Wales. Before the Great Famine in the 1840s, popular adherence to the formal observances of the Catholic Church was relatively low, but there was widespread attachment to the rites of passage, especially baptism and extreme unction which were almost universal. As with the Lincolnshire labourers described by Obelkevich, the inhabitants of rural Ireland subscribed to a whole range of beliefs and observances only tenuously related to orthodox Catholicism. These included superstitious interpretations of historic Christian festivals, a wide range of magical practices from calendar customs to charms and omens, belief in fairies, banshees and witches, and an Irish propensity for squeezing the maximum amount of raucous entertainment from festivals and wakes which the church struggled valiantly but unsuccessfully to control.[43] Although the Irish rural poor were not short of religious devotion, 'what they were devoted to, however, was a popular religion, diverging from orthodox Catholicism in a range of important respects'.[44] As in England, the labouring poor valued the social and psychological utility of religion more highly than confessional orthodoxy, but the apparent similarities of English and Irish versions of popular syncretism should not obscure some important differences. For example, although there was a substantial gap between the worlds of official and popular religion in Ireland, it was probably not as wide as in England, and there was rather more overlap and mutual accommodation between the two. Indeed the relationship between Catholicism and popular religion was immensely complicated. On the one hand, ancient Celtic celebrations, such as the pilgrimage to Croagh Patrick, were Catholicized, just as ancient magical springs were turned into holy wells dedicated to saints, while, on the other, a whole series of quasi-superstitious beliefs and practices surrounded Catholic priests, the Virgin Mary and the relics of saints. One possible interpretation is that Irish popular beliefs in this period were closer to those held in Elizabethan England than to those of nineteenth-century English rural labourers.[45] Obelkevich in fact suggests that one of the reasons for the wide gulf between Christianity and paganism in rural Lincolnshire was the long-term success of the Reformation in undermining the sacramental framework of the medieval church.[46] This negative achievement of the English Reformation is not applicable to rural Ireland which was relatively untouched by both the Reformation and the Counter-Reformation.

In Ireland the reforming energy of bishops, priests and wealthy laity, as with the evangelicals and Tractarians in England, probably widened the gap between official Catholicism and popular customs in the first half of the nineteenth century, but unlike England, the decimation of rural Ireland by famine brought unexpected opportunities to the Catholic Church. The so-called 'devotional revolution' was underway before the famine but it achieved its most striking successes among the reduced population of the post-1850 period.[47] Professor Corish's most recent estimate of mass attendance in this period is 50–75 per cent in the four Irish cities, almost 100 per cent in towns, 37–75 per cent in English-speaking rural areas and 25–50 per cent in Irish-speaking rural areas.[48] Such figures should give pause to those British and European historians who have assumed too readily that urban living was the nemesis of organized Christianity. Irish Catholicism had, it is true, special advantages. There were closer links between priests and people, religion and education, religious and political aspirations and church and national identity than could be achieved anywhere else in western Europe. As a traditional society dragged into the modern world on the coat-tails of an expanding British economy, Catholicism in Ireland offered important symbols of culture and identity to a population determined to preserve its ties with the past.[49] Similar patterns are to be found among migrants from rural and conservative societies to the United States in the period 1850–1917.[50]

The nature of popular Catholicism in Ireland is of interest not only to Irish historians, but also to those who wish to uncover the religious experiences of Irish migrants to English and Scottish cities. By 1860 there were some three-quarters of a million Irish-born inhabitants living predominantly in the industrial towns of Lancashire and western Scotland, and in London. Most were at least nominally Catholic, but it was a Catholicism 'rooted in an ancient Gaelic-speaking tradition of native Irish spirituality and in a pre-Tridentine popular peasant culture of the home and the pilgrimage, rather than in Mass-going in a new shrine church'.[51] The ethos and atmosphere of this humble Irish culture of 'belligerent fidelity' has been vigorously brought to life by Sheridan Gilley and Raphael Samuel in England and by Bernard Aspinwall and John McCaffrey in Scotland.[52] Separated by their nationality, race, religion and poverty, the Irish clustered together in tight slums in which survived a patriotic religiosity 'which was heartily popular because it was heartily vulgar'.[53] Primitive violence was rarely far from the surface in such communities, but there existed, too, warmth and generosity, humour and faith. There was, moreover, a gregarious familiarity between priests and people, in marked contrast to the prevailing relationship between clergy and laity in Protestant denominations. Just as important in cementing community solidarity were the valuable welfare and educational facilities offered by the Catholic Church and its lay organizations. Despite these advantages, however, and despite the emotional power of the close relationship between Celtic nationalism and Catholicism, only a minority of Irish migrants conformed to the prescribed devotions of official Catholicism. The Catholic Irish were nevertheless better church attenders than their English working-class counterparts, for as McLeod's study of late Victorian London has shown, Roman Catholicism was the only form of religion that integrated its adherents into a working-class environment instead of making them stand out from their neighbours.[54]

The migration of the Irish to Victorian towns and cities is but an ethnically distinctive example of a much wider social pattern in nineteenth-century Britain. The census of 1851 appeared to show, for the first time, that more people were living in urban than in rural communities and that almost half of the inhabitants of every large town had been born outside its boundaries.[55] The questions of what happened to the religious beliefs and practices of rural migrants and of what impact urban living had on the subsequent evolution of British religion have occasioned as much controversy among historians and sociologists as they did with the Victorians themselves.[56] It was after all the much analysed 1851 Religious Census with its shocking revelation – to middle-class Victorians at least – of alleged working-class defection from organized religion which has been the basic starting-point of much historical enquiry into religion in urban Britain. More recently these tired old debates have been given fresh life by a variety of new methods and approaches which have exposed the complexity of popular behaviour so often masked by mere statistics. My approach, therefore, is intended to be part chronological and part methodological: the period 1790–1840 will be reassessed in the light of creative new work by women historians; the early Victorian years will be viewed through the lens of literature; the later Victorian period has been illuminated by economic and structural analysis, as has the period 1890–1920 by oral evidence; finally, the modern period has been subjected to a range of sociological techniques, including participant observation, the results of which almost certainly have a bearing on earlier periods of popular religion.

Those who attended the History Workshop on religion and society in London in 1983 could not fail to have been impressed by the substantial proportion of papers given by women on the role of women in the history of religion.[57] Given that many statistical surveys of religious adherence have shown a preponderance of women, and the fact that they have been virtually absent from the pages of traditional ecclesiastical histories, any readjustment along these lines is to be welcomed. Regrettably much of this history, for reasons of evidence, is irrecoverable, but valiant efforts have been made by the American scholars Gail Malmgreen and Deborah Valenze in the period of the early Industrial Revolution in Britain.[58] Valenze's stated aim in *Prophetic Sons and Daughters* was to uncover the sacred world-view of English labourers of both sexes and relate it to the profound economic and social changes of the period 1790–1850. More realistically, her chosen terrain is the popular evangelicalism of cottage meetings which proliferated far more widely in the period of the French Revolutionary Wars than the more publicized radical political clubs. Initially, Wesleyan Methodism was the vehicle through which these popular religious energies were expressed but by the 1790s its increasing formalism and notorious connexional discipline alienated some of its more humble supporters. Thereafter, sectarian Methodism became the dominant, but not exclusive, expression of cottage-based religion. Such religion

61

threw up a kaleidoscope of practices from prophecies and healing to trances and dreams, and brought forth a sturdy independent leadership, the most striking aspect of which was the relatively high proportion of women. This was facilitated by the domestic setting of cottage religion, the sense of autonomy women gained from their labouring experiences and the receptivity of men to female leadership when social and economic changes threatened to dislocate families and kinship networks. Moreover, the women brought to life in Dr Valenze's study are far removed from the idealized domestic angels we encounter in Victorian fiction. Acquainted with grief and hardship from an early age, and made even more independent by geographical mobility and late marriage, these women were remarkably young – around eighteen years of age – when they started their preaching mission and were not easily controlled by any authority. Indeed they were the embodiment of a 'world turned upside down' which repudiated the formalism of churches and chapels and the disciplines of economic and social control. There is much here that is reminiscent of the millenarian groups of the French Revolutionary period described by Professor Harrison and of the Civil War and Interregnum puritanism brought to life by Christopher Hill.[59] In several insightful case-studies Dr Valenze shows, too, how popular evangelicalism could re-create the world of cottage industry, village familiarity and household unity in an increasingly urban and factory dominated environment. Successive waves of rural migrants into manufacturing towns eschewed employer-sponsored Anglican churches and nonconformist chapels in favour of a more intimate and informal religious atmosphere in which the professional preachers had no part. This era of home-based religion declined rapidly from the 1850s when towns, institutions – including churches – and railways spread into most corners of British society, and cottage religion virtually disappeared with the household economy which had sustained it.

Aside from pointing up the importance of women in this humble culture, before they were shuffled aside in the 1840s by a Nonconformity dominated by theologically educated preachers, respectable laymen and chapel trustees, Dr Valenze also touches on themes of wider significance. For example, it is still not clear how much of the urban-based popular evangelicalism of Victorian Britain had its roots in the rural revivalism of the previous half century.[60] Davies has shown how much of nineteenth-century Welsh Nonconformity had its origins in the religious and social protest of tenant farmers and smallholders in the countryside and among the proto-industrial workers of Glamorgan and Monmouthshire against predominantly Anglican landowners and entrepreneurs. Similarly, the remarkable strength of the Free Church in the northern Highlands and islands of Scotland was built around a population living in near destitution by engaging in a subsistence agriculture with the minimum of tenurial security. Moreover, the Church of Scotland had become associated in many minds with landlordism, clearances and cultural supremacy.[61] Thus revivalism, social change and poverty lived in a symbiotic relationship. In England, too, early Wesleyan and later Primitive Methodist revivals were part religious, part social protest against Anglican paternalism. Even in Ireland much of the popular evangelicalism, which has exercised such a profound influence over the northern part of the country, had its origins in the rural revivals among the small tenant farmers and outworkers of southern and south-western Ulster between 1780 and 1820. Here the story is yet more complex, for much of this rural revivalism was directed not so much against the episcopal Established Church but against Roman Catholics who were competing for land and commercial advantage in the linen markets.[62] This rural sectarianism was brought into Belfast by migrant workers in the early nineteenth century and has done much to set the tone of politics in that resilient but unhappy city.[63] Religion, it seems, sinks its deepest roots into popular culture when it helps give expression to the social, economic, ethnic and cultural homogeneity of populations facing rapid change or oppression. But to take the additional step, as some socialist historians do, of suggesting that religion is primarily a form of social control is to minimize the way in which humble people make and remake the religious traditions to which they give their allegiance.[64]

If, as has been suggested, popular evangelicalism achieved its greatest successes in British society in the period of transition from community to class and from traditional recreations to the advent of mass leisure, there has also been widespread agreement that Victorian towns and cities hastened these changes and produced a working class whose apparent religious apathy was in marked contrast to the institutional religiosity of the middle and upper middle classes. Indeed, virtually every statistically based analysis of Victorian religion, from Horace Mann's reflections on the Religious Census of 1851 to Hugh McLeod's and Jeffrey Cox's treatment of London at the turn of the century, have drawn attention to a class differential in religious practice in modern Britain (though it is well to be reminded in such discussions that, owing to the pyramidal structure of British society, the majority of churchgoers was almost certainly working class).[65] Why this was the case and, more particularly, what kind of religion, if any, survived among the urban working classes, both churchgoing and non-churchgoing, are difficult questions to answer. There is as yet no study of popular urban religion, with the possible exception of some recent work on South London,[66] to match the quality of Obelkevich's rural insights, and working-class Anglicanism in particular has been strikingly under-researched by comparison with the work done on the nonconformist and Catholic churches.[67] So peripheral is religion alleged to have been in the lives of working-class Britons, outside the regional exceptions already mentioned, that some social historians have virtually dispensed with it altogether in their descriptions of popular life before the First World War.[68] Two recently exploited sources, literature and oral evidence – with all their attendant flaws – have shed a glimmer of light on urban popular religion.

Nineteenth-century novels, because of their quantity and quality, have been irresistible quarries of information for social historians, especially those, who like the Victorians themselves, are interested in religion.[69] Quarrying is, of course, rough work and is generally more concerned with extracting raw materials then in appreciating the landscape within which they are found. Literary critics have therefore been rightly suspicious of certain kinds of historical approaches to literature – most notably the cuckoo method – which has been described by E. M. Forster as a kind of pseudo-scholarship. Conversely, empirically minded historians have often had their nerves set on edge by the amateurish historical methods employed by some literary critics. Interdisciplinary study, to borrow Michael Wolff's phrase, seems to teeter on the brink of becoming anti-disciplinary study.[70] Nevertheless, despite the effects of distorting lenses, both deliberate and unintentional, of much Victorian fiction, novelists are, on the whole, sensitive observers of the society in which they lived. Even their misconceptions can be revealing, as are the features of their society that they unconsciously took for granted. Disraeli's fiction, for example, which was strongly influenced by the view of English history propagated by R. H. Froude and other early leaders of the Oxford Movement, exaggerated the religiosity of England's medieval past and thus over-reacted to the popular infidelity of the early Victorian period.[71] By isolating the problem of religious decline, romantic medievalists were partly responsible for creating new problems of explanation which have dominated the historiography of religion in this period.

Conversely, George Eliot in *Silas Marner* creatively inverts the conventional pattern of a historically religious countryside contrasted with the new irreligious towns which seemed to have been irrefutably demonstrated by the census of public worship in 1851. What is hinted at through Silas, however, is that the religion of the countryside was a rather pale mixture of deference, dependency, custom and community solidarity whereas popular urban religion, albeit a minority taste, was based more on voluntary commitment to religious associations. The local studies of social historians have indeed shown that although churchgoing was a vulnerable habit of rural migrants to Victorian towns and cities, many of those who came from large 'open' villages had already little to lose, while others brought their religious enthusiasm with them. The point is that Victorian towns and cities reflected the religious characteristics of their rural hinterlands more closely than is sometimes appreciated.[72]

What then does Victorian literature reveal about the beliefs and practices of those who lived in urban Britain in the nineteenth century? The so-called industrial novels of the 1840s and 1850s suggest that the relative absence of formal religious observances did not necessarily mean that religion was redundant in popular life. Religious belief, according to these sources, could be important in facing up to death and disaster, in establishing a rudimentary moral code, in developing neighbourly concern in times of economic hardship and depression, in nurturing a sturdy respectability in family life and in providing a biblical justification for attacking the oppression of the rich and the lack of justice in labour relations.[73] Conversely religion was more likely to be repudiated when it concentrated on eternal rather than temporal objectives,[74] when it condemned popular leisure activities,[75] and when it introduced unnecessary tensions into the family and the workplace. Above all, and this has been corroborated by working-class autobiographies and city mission reports, any form of religion which reinforced rather than diminished class distinctions was unpopular with the urban poor.[76] Indeed, the sheer 'respectability' of much pre-First World War religion with its sabbatarianism and temperance, its clerical professionalism and opposition to popular recreations, excluded as many as it attracted. What was left has been described as 'proletarian parochialism', which was founded on community solidarity and a homespun morality of not doing anybody any harm.[77] Such religious apathy was largely beyond the reach of both the plebeian ultra-evangelicalism of Brethren, Baptists, Salvationists and city missioners, and the more colourful rituals of High Church Anglicanism and ethnic Catholicism. In short, popular adherence to Victorian churches was to some extent limited by a combination of class and culture conflict with which readers of Dickens and Samuel Butler will already be familiar. But churches were still widely used for rites of passage, watch-night and harvest thanksgiving services, and outright scepticism was remarkably rare. In a recent local study of the London borough of Southwark, Sarah Williams has wisely cautioned against treating popular enthusiasm for the rites of passage as an unimportant manifestation of the polite and respectable conformity of working-class Londoners. Rather, 'the pattern of occasional and conditional conformity to church-based rituals and practices was based upon different definitions of religious duty, belief and association', and testify to a vibrant popular religiosity based upon 'a coalescence of a range of religious narratives'.[78] What is required to penetrate to the heart of this popular religiosity is not the crude application of a predominantly middle-class definition of religious commitment based on regular churchgoing, but an imaginative grasp of the importance of beliefs, symbols, values and memories in the texture of life in working-class communities. The popular religion Williams has uncovered cannot be accurately described as mere folk religion, or as some kind of pre-urban religious survivalism, but was rather an integrated and cohesive framework of religious beliefs and practices which was entirely appropriate to popular life.

> It was a dynamic and vibrant system of belief which retained its own autonomous existence. It drew on elements, images and ideals of church-based religion, but these were appropriated, reinterpreted and internalised in a distinctly popular manner in combination with a folk idiom. Hymns, religious phraseology and forms of private religious devotion continued to hold an evocative power within popular culture.[79]

Here is yet another timely reminder of the danger of appropriating middle-class Victorians' own judgements of the state of religion in British cities, but perhaps Williams' optimistic assessment of the strength of popular religiosity is partly attributable to her interest in women who were the main initiators of popular participation in church-based rituals. For many working-class men, especially those with an emerging political con-sciousness, religious institutions seemed to be antithetical to their lifestyles and indifferent to their interests. Nevertheless, even from this source, criticisms of the churches 'often reflected not so much irreligion or indifference as disappointed expectations'.[80]

The impression conveyed by Victorian novelists that the religion of the people could have a whole range of private and social meanings, quite apart from institutional adherence, is supported by a relatively new source available to students of popular religion in the late nineteenth and early twentieth centuries: taped interviews with controlled samples of old people who were brought up in that period. The pioneering work of Elizabeth Roberts, Paul Thompson and Thea Vigne, and Stephen Humphries has been helpfully synthesized and reinterpreted by Hugh McLeod in *Oral History*.[81] Oral evidence helps to do justice to the complexity and fluidity of the religious outlook of ordinary individuals, but however well chosen are the samples and the questions put to respondents, this method, as with any other, has its limitations. Samples probably overrepresent the more respectable elements of the working class and may reflect life cycle changes, exaggerated by nostalgia, of greater religiosity among the young and the aged. Samples are also too small to be conclusive and questions tend to focus more on habits and affiliations than on beliefs and experiences. The results nevertheless confirm the impressionistic evidence from literature that religion was not confined to the institutionally religious. Even non-churchgoers sent their children to Sunday school, dressed up on Sundays, used religion to get jobs and welfare relief, sang hymns as a means of cementing community solidarity, extolled 'practical Christian' virtues, relied heavily on Christian sexual ethics (not least as a point of departure), derived comfort from religion in times of suffering or disaster, accepted that church and chapel or Protestant and Catholic were fundamental social divisions and used the churches' social facilities without feeling any need to attend more overtly 'religious' activities.

One important, but often neglected, aspect of popular religion amplified by oral evidence is the emotional resonance achieved by the religious music of hymns and choirs, and the happy memories of church- or chapel-organized seaside treats and social gatherings. None understood the raw edge of nostalgic emotionalism in popular religion more than the predominantly American-technique revivalists of the late nineteenth and twentieth centuries unless it be those more recent producers of mellow religious pop on Sunday television.[82] But not all religious emotion was artificially produced. In the late Victorian era churches and chapels, even within the same denominations in different parts of the same town, produced 'atmospheres' of attraction or repulsion, warmth or stiffness. Much depended on the personality of the preacher, the architectural style of the building, the attractiveness or otherwise of the music and the singing, the social class and degree of familiarity of the attenders, and the impression conveyed by a full congregation, on the one hand, or a half-empty church, on the other. Sensory perceptions were as important as the verbal content of Victorian sermons, even if the latter have proved more accessible to religious historians. Nothing could be clearer from nineteenth-century novels, spiritual autobiographies and the ubiquitous Victorian hymns, however, than that the emotional power of religious feeling was at the heart and centre of all genuinely popular religious assemblies. The hymns and their equally important tunes, states Obelkevich, were 'earnest, self-absorbed, and incurably sentimental', revealing 'the soft centre at the core of Victorian Protestantism'[83] Lest Victorian nostalgia take over, it is well to be reminded, however, as David Clark has done in his study of a Yorkshire fishing village, that popular religion could also be crass, bigoted, sectarian and disruptive of human relationships.[84] 'These cramping cults', wrote H. G. Wells in *The New Machiavelli*, 'do indeed take an enormous toll of human love and happiness . . . they make frightful breaches in human solidarity.'[85] Religious emotions can be characterized by aggression as well as nostalgia.

Before leaving the oral evidence of pre-First World War working-class religion it should be pointed out that it does make a contribution to the current debate of whether or not it makes much sense to divide the urban working classes into the 'rough' and the 'respectable'. Here the evidence is predictably inconclusive. Regular and devoted pub-goers did not attend churches and vice versa, but there were, unsurprisingly, various shades of commitment in between. The real value of oral evidence, however, has been to show that religion was important to non-churchgoers in a variety of ways. It frequently intersected with other social frameworks including politics, employment, leisure, values, emotions, ethics and community identification and differentiation. It shows too that secularization, however it is to be defined, was a more gradual and complicated process than is sometimes supposed.

Just how closely religion could interact with other social frameworks has been the subject of a number of outstanding local studies of religion in British industrial towns and cities in the period 1850–1930. Although not specifically concerned with the characteristics of popular beliefs and practices, MacLaren, Joyce, Foster and Yeo have tried to relate religious cultures to much wider economic and structural changes in Victorian Britain.[86] Indeed industrial Britain, and its by no means ideologically uncommitted historians, has thrown up a bewildering range of religious patterns from Joyce's description of orange-coloured popular Protestantism in Lancashire to Foster's treatment of petit bourgeois nonconformist liberalism in Oldham; and from MacLaren's portrayal of sturdy Scottish Presbyterian respectability in Aberdeen to Yeo's picture of religious organizations in Reading, in common with other voluntary associations, coming in and going out with the tide of liberal capitalism. What they have in common is a conviction that religion in industrial society is inseparable from the class, employment, community, ethnic and cultural interests of its adherents. This is no mere reductionist argument, however, for religion was itself an active agent in the creation of wider cultural frameworks. The Methodist miners of Durham, for example, developed a style of politics, trade unionism and wage negotiations with their nonconformist employers which owed more to their religious beliefs than to the pursuit of narrow class interests as such. Similarly, class antagonism in late Victorian Lancashire was overlaid by religious and ethnic identities which often resulted in an 'unreasoning sectarianism in popular politics'.[87] This pattern survives in an even more acute form in twentieth-century Ulster.

Despite the proliferation of excellent case-studies of urban religion in the late nineteenth and early twentieth centuries, including a remarkable concentration of work on south London, the actual beliefs of the urban working classes remain tantalizingly opaque. Indeed oral and literary evidence, combined with the decoding of popular adherence to the rites of passage, for all their methodological problems, are generally more insightful than the recorded impressions of clergymen, city missioners and autobiographers. A number of consistent themes do nevertheless emerge from such sources. Although thoroughgoing scepticism was rare, most working-class Londoners had only the dimmest perceptions of Christian doctrines or of eternal life, whether heavenly or hellish. Strictly speaking they were neither unbelievers nor anxious doubters, and the churches, according to Cox, were still able to promote a 'diffusive Christianity' through education, welfare relief, clubs and rites of passage, at least until the state spread its collectivist tentacles. Notwithstanding such competition the churches were able to further diffuse a 'diffusive Christianity' through religious broadcasting and services at school assemblies.[88] Here indeed, as consumers of such religion will testify, is religious diffusion to the power of infinity. Working-class Londoners could still urge their womenfolk to set decent religious standards for their children, and they could still be roused to displays of religious patriotism during wars and royal jubilees, but McLeod is right to emphasize the further erosion of working-class religiosity in twentieth-century London as ever more puritanical restraints were cast off and the terrors of hell were seen as nothing compared to the sins of social inequality.[89]

London is, of course, far from typical of the nation as a whole, and there remain in the twentieth century higher levels of popular religious adherence in other parts of the British Isles, particularly in the Celtic fringes. Understandably, but regrettably, there has been far more written by both historians and sociologists of religion on the reasons for, and characteristics and consequences of, secularization than there has on the content of the popular religion which has survived. One recent and entertaining exception is David Clark's *Between Pulpit and Pew*, a study of folk religion in Staithes, a North Yorkshire fishing village. The method employed is participant observation and the author set out with clear distinctions between 'official' and 'folk' religion which proved easier to define in theory than to observe in practice.[90] For villagers, the two cultures, popular and sacred, became a seamless web in the personal cycle of birth and death, and in the annual community cycle of Sunday school and chapel anniversaries, and the New Year, Easter, harvest and Christmas celebrations. In addition, the occupational dangers of a fishing community spawned its own subculture of superstitious practices which were adhered to with a mixture of embarrassment and deadly seriousness. The inhabitants of Staithes could also display local cantankerousness in their opposition to that familiar triad of twentieth-century religion, ecumenism, bureaucratic centralization and ministerial professionalism. Ironically, local chapels came to mean more to the villagers when threatened with amalgamation or extinction than they did as going concerns. Staithes religion then was composed of a complex mixture of local custom, half-belief, occupational superstitions, cyclical rituals and rhythms, chapel loyalties and nostalgic religious emotions. Many of these features co-existed not only within the same small community but also within the minds of the individuals who composed it.

Staithes is, of course, a most unrepresentative sample of modern popular religion. Although not immune from modernizing trends, including the hospitalization of birth, sickness and death, its geographical location and economic function have partially cocooned it in a time warp. As Clark suggests, what is needed now are more studies of folk religion in an urban setting to see how far popular culture has been demystified by the secularizing forces of the twentieth century.

It is tempting to get embroiled in the prolific debates on secularization, but in the limited space available it would be impossible to add anything fresh to the historically based work of Yeo, Gilbert, McLeod and Brown or to the sociological approaches of Berger, Martin, Wilson and Bruce.[91] Besides, the problems with the term itself are well known, since religion is not amenable to precise definition, and the baseline from which secularization is assumed to have proceeded constantly shifts with the impressive body of new research on late medieval and early modern popular religion.[92] Yet with all the attendant difficulties of using the term properly it is clear that both institutional religion and popular religiosity, of whatever hue and texture, has declined significantly in the twentieth century. It may have been partly diffused into other channels as Cox suggests or partly replaced by sacralized alternatives as Lyon has it,[93] but outside Ireland and pockets of Scotland and Wales much of the intensity of Victorian religion has simply ebbed way. The speed, characteristics and extent of 'secularization' have varied considerably in different communities, among different social classes and in specific regions. Indeed its causes and effects have been as complex as the religion it has undermined. It would be a mistake, moreover, to suggest that 'secularization' is either unilinear or irreversible. International pentecostalism, charismatic renewal and new religious movements, whether epiphenomenal and culturally marginal as some suggest, or major new landmarks on the world's religious landscape, testify to the stubborn refusal of religion to move quietly aside, even in technologically-advanced western societies.[94] Here, the 'strange gifts' of the charismatic renewal may indeed be examples of 'the incoherence of confused enthusiasm' as one critic has called it,[95] but such language is uncannily similar to the remarks of Anglican bishops and clergy on early Methodist revivalism in Devon and Cornwall in the 1740s.[96]

A century later a worldwide Methodism with several million adherents was still regarded as a heresy by some Anglican High Churchmen,[97] but it was no longer perceived by anyone to be a localized and transitory phenomenon. There are, of course, substantial dissimilarities between early Methodism and the charismatic renewal, not least in their social constituencies, but they do suggest that popular enthusiasm for the raw edges of spiritual authenticity, however irksome to those with more traditional views of the role of religion, is remarkably resilient to secularizing forces.

What conclusions then can be drawn from this rapid survey of almost two centuries of popular religion in the British Isles? The first and most important, as the introductory quotations suggested, is that the concept 'popular religion', like its cousin 'popular culture', is potentially misleading. There was in fact no such thing as a distinctive and definable popular religion in Britain in this period. Rather there were many complex individual and communal expressions of belief and practice among the mass of people in different settings and at different times. More local studies, especially of non-metropolitan urban religion, are therefore desirable, but they are not of themselves sufficient, for as Professor Ward has rightly pointed out:

> The consequence of the increasing precision of local studies is to force attention upon the fact that the major international movements in Protestant (and for that matter, Catholic) history are not to be explained upon a local basis, any more than they are upon the institutional presuppositions which ecumenical historians share with denominational ones. There will be no explaining the shared responses to shared perceptions until historians recognize that such things exist.[98]

In the same way as Obelkevich has stated that religious life cannot be 'reduced' to its social foundations, but is unintelligible without them, so too popular religion cannot be 'reduced' to its local setting however necessary it is to explore its proper context and social meaning.[99] Ward's own work on the international dimensions of popular pietism in the eighteenth and nineteenth centuries, transatlantic comparisons of evangelicalism, and McLeod's forthcoming comparative study of religion in major western cities are welcome attempts to investigate modern religion on a much wider canvas than has been the recent fashion.[100] If done sensitively, to avoid either a crude form of historical dispensationalism or social and economic determinism, such an approach opens up the way for far more creative analytical frameworks than is possible from the growing mountain of empirical local studies by themselves.

Second, the boundaries and categories constructed by historians to make sense of religion – official and popular, Christian and pagan, religious and irreligious, secular and sacred, rough and respectable, traditional and modern, imposed and indigenous – are insufficiently flexible to describe a much more complicated and integrated reality. There must be enough scope to include life cycle changes, distinctions between male and female religiosity and the survival of religious frameworks and meanings in communities, ethics, even politics, long after formal and institutional religious adherence has declined. In particular, more needs to be said about the role of women and children, and the importance of class and ethnicity in the development of religious cultures.[101]

Third, and perhaps most difficult of all, more comparative and relational studies are required to highlight both the massive continuities of 'popular religion' and the important periods of change and adaptation. The religious geography of the British Isles, and of large parts of continental Europe for that matter, shows clearly enough the historical continuities of belief and practice over several centuries. Equally important are the profound changes of the periods 1730–50 when popular evangelicalism took root in the British Isles; 1790–1850 when English and Welsh nonconformists and Irish Catholics substantially undermined the Anglican confessional supremacy at popular if not at elite level; and 1890–1920 when it became clear that Victorian religion, at least outside the Celtic fringes, was a declining, if far from spent, force. The developments of the twentieth century, especially the ethical solvents of the 1960s, further undermined both institutional and popular religion. Only time will tell if the pentecostal, charismatic and new religious movements, on the one hand, and the resilience of conservative Protestantism and Roman Catholicism, on the other, can arrest the general demise of British Christianity.

Finally, as Trexler has pointedly suggested, we commentators and interpreters need to divest ourselves of a whole range of twentieth-century perceptions about the nature of past religion and its social function.[102] Both the older denominational historians and the more recent sociologists and social historians of religion, through lack of imagination, have been guilty of minimizing the complexity and diminishing the humanity of the religion of quite humble people and their communities.

PART II

PEOPLE: POWER AND PIETY

In the furious search for structural causes and contexts in the expansion of Methodism and popular Protestantism it is easy to overlook the fact that religious traditions are built by people for people. What follows, therefore, is a set of short biographical essays on important figures in the early history of Methodism in the British Isles. The subjects and the themes to which they relate were not chosen randomly. John Wesley was, of course, the founder of Methodism and is a man not to be ignored. As he wrote so much himself and has had, in consequence, even more written about him, it is with some trepidation that I have addressed the subject at all. My aim has been to look again at Wesley's political theology in relation to the eighteenth-century state. Dr Clark's influential representation of Wesley as a part of the mainstream Anglican tradition was both the stimulus and the point of departure of my short chapter. By trying to move away from the conventional approach to Wesley's politics in terms of how he fits in to the supposed great party divide between the Whigs and the Tories and the ecclesiastical divide between Church and Dissent, I have laid greater emphasis on his opinions about the constitution, the Established Church, property and law, which offer a more rounded consideration of his approach to public affairs than is sometimes the case. What emerges is a rather more ambiguous and pragmatic portrait than is immediately self-evident from some of Wesley's more robust writings.

Wesley's death in 1791 left the Methodist connexion in sore need of government. The next generation not only had to work its way through many of the ambiguities of the Wesleyan tradition, but also had to interpret that tradition in the most troublesome of times. The French Revolution, periods of European warfare, severe economic depression and the emergence of a vigorous popular radicalism all combined to make the task of governance no easier for the Wesleyan Methodists than for any other contemporary institution in Church and State. In this most important of all the periods of post-Reformation religious history, two figures within the Methodist tradition are particularly worthy of attention. One is obviously Jabez Bunting who achieved an unparalleled ascendancy among

73

his peers within the Wesleyan pastorate in the first half of the nineteenth century. As much is already known about Bunting's period of supremacy between his first appointment as President of the Methodist Conference in 1820 and his retirement from the full-time work of the ministry in 1851, I have concentrated instead on his much more interesting formative years in the quarter century after his religious conversion in 1794. An awareness of the pressures and processes which helped turn the eager young revivalist preacher and friend of religious liberty into the connexional brontosaurus of the Victorian period may not make this frankly unlikeable man any more likeable, but it will at least bring to the surface one striking illustration of how the generation that came of age at the turn of the century had to pick its way through social, political and religious issues of immense complexity. My hope, therefore, is that Bunting, if not more liked, will at least be better understood as a result of my trawl through his private correspondence. In that respect, I wish to record my thanks to Professor Ward for entrusting into my care his immaculate transcripts of the Bunting correspondence without which my chapter could not have been written.

By comparison with Bunting, Thomas Allan has been indeed a 'man forgotten by history', notwithstanding the fact that he has left the largest collection of papers of any Methodist layman in the half century after 1790. That he has attracted so little attention is a sad commentary both on the intellectual consequences of the development of a high view of the pastoral office within Wesleyanism, from which Allan himself received not a few slings and arrows, and on the surprising lack of interest among those who have written about Methodism and politics in this period in the layman who did most to shape the politics of the Wesleyan connexion. Of course the perspective from the metropolitan lay elite of Methodism is not the only one worth having, nor is it in all probability the most important one, but it is nevertheless worthy of attention for its own sake and for what it reveals about the increasing pluralism of religious life in the British Isles at the turn of the century. The rise of pluralism and its relationship to increased toleration and constitutional change has not had the same tasty historiography devoted to it as the growth of class consciousness, but that reflects more the presuppositions of historians than the nature of the evidence itself. Retrieving Allan from the immense condescension of the Wesleyan pastorate and from the lack of interest among social historians of religion is the chief aim of my chapter.

In the welter of membership statistics and structural analyses of industrial processes which have shed much light on the history of Methodism, it is a regrettable fact that almost nothing has been done, until comparatively recently, to bring to life those worker bees of the Methodist revolution, the itinerant and local preachers. Why would men, and not a few women, subject themselves to hardship, abuse and ridicule for a career which, in the main, offered few material rewards and almost nothing by way of comfort? That most basic of all questions about Methodist growth has curiously excited little curiosity. My essay on Ouseley is therefore a modest attempt to bring to life one of the myriads of Methodist itinerants who tramped around, or rode around, vast acreages of the North Atlantic world in the period 1750–1830. Ouseley was chosen, not because of his peculiar zeal, but because of the peculiar richness of the sources which he has left behind. Itinerant evangelists by their very nature travelled light and were, in general, no great hoarders of private correspondence. Thankfully, special circumstances intervened in Ouseley's case.

I am all too aware that this section on people does not contain a single woman, or a Methodist local preacher, class leader or chapel attender, but a start has to be made somewhere and I have chosen the safe historical route of selecting individuals who have left extensive records of their lives over those who are more silent. What the chapters nevertheless illustrate is that the counter-attractions of power and piety, at whatever social level they are encountered, are rarely far from the surface of those at the heart of religious communities.

4

JOHN WESLEY AND ENGLAND'S
'ANCIEN RÉGIME'

Eighteenth-century British history so long illuminated and shaded by the work of Sir Lewis Namier has witnessed a remarkable resurgence of historical enquiry in the past decade. In particular, there have been important studies made of the aristocracy, political ideology, Anglican and dissenting religion, criminality and the law, urban growth, commerce and consumerism and the growth of manufacturing.[1] Much of this research was understandably compartmentalized, and the time was clearly ripe for a major new work of synthesis and interpretation. This was provided by Dr Jonathan Clark, whose book *English Society 1688–1832* has occasioned almost equal amounts of criticism and praise. The wider merits and demerits of Dr Clark's important book have been exhaustively debated elsewhere,[2] but for present purposes it is what he said about John Wesley and the Evangelical Revival that is of most interest.[3] As part of his wider scheme of presenting eighteenth-century English society as pre-industrial, hierarchic, aristocratic and confessional, he states that Wesley inherited almost intact the political theology of mainstream Anglicanism. As against those who regard Wesleyan Methodism as essentially a liberal, egalitarian and progressive ideology, Clark emphasizes Wesley's belief that God, not the people, was the origin of all civil power and that obedience to the king was the duty of all citizens of Britain and its colonies. Stung by dissenting criticism of his views and fearful of Wilkesite radicalism and American rebellion, Wesley wrote a clutch of loyalty tracts between 1772 and 1782 in which he eulogized the monarchy, castigated rebellious Americans and disaffected Englishmen, rejected the libertarian rhetoric of radical dissenters and developed a full-blown English patriotism against foreigners and papists.[4] Some dissenters detected in all this a return to 'the good old Jacobite doctrines of hereditary, indefeasible, divine right, and of passive obedience and non-resistance'.[5] A new Sacheverell seemed to be on the loose and even Burke repudiated Wesley's court-inspired propaganda. Dr Clark stresses that Wesley's 'loyalty tradition' was also the official ideology of early nineteenth-century Methodism, enabling Methodists, evangelical Anglicans and the Church of England as a whole to make common cause against revolutionaries, radicals and republicans. 'This conclusion was all the more remarkable', suggests Clark, 'in that Methodism was deliberately directed towards the poor.'[6] Clark thus finds himself as an unlikely supporter of E. P. Thompson in stating that Wesleyan Methodism, though numerically insignificant compared to the wider Church of England, stoutly defended the old order in both Church and State against attacks from secular and religious radicals of all persuasions.[7] This conclusion is all the more noteworthy from Clark's viewpoint because it indirectly shows that religious populists were at least as conservative as Anglican bishops and that genuine religious radicalism made its presence felt through a small but influential coterie of rational dissenters and the great numerical weight of Irish Roman Catholics.

The interpretation just outlined has, of course, many merits, not least its attack on a growing tradition of Methodist scholarship more interested in what Wesley anticipated than in what he did, but its main drawback is a lack of subtlety in exploring Wesley's motives, assumptions, inconsistencies and wider principles, which not only help to explain, but add important conditions to his bold public statements. In saying this one is mindful of Henry Adams' remark about that other complex and elusive eighteenth-century octogenarian, Thomas Jefferson. Almost every other statesman, he wrote, could be portrayed with 'a few broad strokes of the brush', but Jefferson 'only touch by touch with a fine pencil, and the perspective of the likeness depended upon the shifting and uncertain flicker of the semi-transparent shadows'.[8] Wesley too requires careful etching and for some of the same reasons. Men of principle who live long enough to become men of affairs, and who write more than is entirely wise, are rarely models of consistency. The aim of this chapter then is not to set up a radical Wesley in opposition to the conventional establishmentarian portrait, but merely to draw attention to aspects of Wesley's life and work which are not so easily encapsulated by Dr Clark's broad brush strokes. Of particular importance are Wesley's attitudes to those four cornerstones of British society and ideology in the eighteenth century: the constitution, the Church of England, property and the law. These issues have been selected, not because they conveniently suit my interpretation of Wesley's views, but because of their centrality to the theory and practice of the eighteenth-century state, and are therefore a proper test of Wesley's attitudes in the round. In each of these areas Wesley's principles have important radical elements within them and his views are generally more instrumental and pragmatic than his more colourful dogmatic statements would suggest. As with most writers of trenchant prose what is most quotable in Wesley's works is not always the most representative of his actual opinions in so far as they can be determined.

The High Church Toryism of Wesley's family background and Oxford connections is well known and has been justifiably re-emphasized by his most recent biographer who locates the central consistencies of Wesley's political views in the scriptural principle of

> obedience to the powers-that-be, which could be glossed by the old High Church and Tory views of divine right, suitably adapted to the Hanoverian dynasty. Loyalty, as he said in 1777, was for him a branch of religion; but it was also a family tradition. . . .[9]

Not only did Wesley inherit a strong Tory tradition from his parents, who were themselves divided on the legitimacy of the Hanoverian regime, but he clearly flirted with Jacobitism (later vigorously denied) in his early Oxford days and in the surprisingly Jacobite circles in which the early evangelical awakening was located.[10]

> Wesley, in short, was born of the Jacobite issue, and born into a rabidly Tory circle which damned foreigners, foreign relations and foreign entanglements, kept up Jacobite sentiment far down the eighteenth century, united it with country-party principles to form a wide-ranging critique of British society and government, and persuaded themselves that the Restoration had not led merely to the reconstruction of the Church of England, but to a revival of morality, had been indeed a cosmic event modelled on the resurrection.[11]

It was 'the sordid thirst for lucre' associated with the government and society of Walpolean England, combined with a sense of exclusion from influence in both Church and State, that brought about an 'ideological congruence' between some of the early Methodists and some disenchanted Anglican Tories, at both elite and popular levels.[12] In a comparison between Doddridge's dissenting endorsement of the Whig ascendancy and Wesley's jibes at Walpolean stockjobbing, for example, Ward states that 'Doddridge writes with the complacency of a man comfortably protected by the second-class establishment created by the Toleration Act, Wesley with the radicalism of a party defeated in the struggle for the control of the first-class establishment'.[13] The chief reason for early Methodist flirtations with the fringes of Tory disaffection was not so much a well-considered enthusiasm for the religion and politics of the later Stuarts as a sincere conviction that the 'Robinocracy' was corrupting the national church and national morals in a disgraceful way.

Wesley's alleged Jacobite flirtations ought not to be pressed too far however. Although he occasionally spoke ill of Walpole, he never, to my knowledge, spoke against the king. Moreover, once Wesley had launched his religious movement in the late 1730s support for the king offered a more realistic prospect of securing basic toleration than would ever have been delivered by the old Laudian High Churchmen who hated the revival with a consuming passion. Furthermore, the war with Spain in 1739 brought the Roman Catholic threat closer to the centre of the stage and made it more unlikely that Wesley would drift any nearer to the Jacobite cause, which in any case always contained more 'floating voters' than committed activists within its ranks.[14]

Wesley's rejection of the Jacobite cause and acceptance of the Hanoverian dynasty was influenced also by the work of the repentant non-juror William Higden and by Wesley's own quirky interpretation of the English monarchy's dynastic lineage; but there is more to it than that. Wesley's enthusiasm for the Hanoverian monarchy was based not only on the continuation of his old Tory belief in loyalty to the sovereign, but also on the settled conviction that the Glorious Revolution had ushered in an unprecedented era of civil and religious liberty in British society. In his *Thoughts Upon Liberty*, Wesley set out to defend *both* liberties as fundamental to humankind. 'Religious liberty', he wrote, 'is a liberty to choose our own religion, to worship God according to our own conscience, according to the best light we have. Every man living, as man, has a right to this, as he is a rational creature.'[15] Since religious liberty is based on God's creation of a rational humanity it is 'an indefeasible right' and superior to all other rights, including those of property. It is precisely because Hanoverian monarchs turned out to be better protectors of religious freedom than their Stuart predecessors that Wesley is so fulsome in praise of them. The same is true of civil liberty which Wesley, after Blackstone, defined as 'a liberty to enjoy our lives and fortunes in our own way; to use our property, whatever is legally our own, according to our own choice'.[16] The threat to such liberties, and to the social stability contingent upon their maintenance, in the England of the 1770s, according to Wesley, came not from king or parliament but from mobs and misguided patriots. This judgement, whatever its merits, should not detract from the fact that Wesley supported limited monarchy in eighteenth-century England as the best way of defending civil and religious freedom; hence his support for it is purposeful and instrumental as much as it is theoretical or dogmatic. A similar concern for the liberty of the person characterizes Wesley's *Thoughts Upon Slavery*. Borrowing from Blackstone once again, he states that slavery is 'against the plain law of nature and reason' and is thus inconsistent with 'any degree of natural justice'.[17] But Wesley's opposition to slavery goes beyond Blackstone's strictly legal rebuttal to embrace higher notions of racial equality and human compassion.[18] Moreover, he subjects the commercial, climatological and necessitarian defences of slavery to remorseless criticism, even stating that slave islands would be better 'sunk in the depth of the sea, than that they should be cultivated at so high a price as the violation of justice, mercy and truth'. In a spirited defence of natural rights Wesley concluded that 'liberty is the right of every human creature, as soon as he breathes the vital air; and no human law can deprive him of that right which he derives from the law of nature'.[19]

Every person then, according to Wesley, regardless of creed, colour or social status, had the right to civil and religious liberty and to the protection of the law. Equally, Wesley saw no theoretical or practical justification whatsoever for extending such freedoms into the political sphere. He flatly rejected Lockean ideas of popular sovereignty and subjected Richard Price's *Observations on the Nature of Civil Liberty* to withering criticism.[20] He countered Price's statement that government originated from the people and was dependent on their consent by employing the historical argument that the enfranchised had always been a select minority (adult propertied males) and that there was 'not a single instance in above seven hundred years, of the people of England's conveying the supreme power either to one or more persons'.[21] A year later in his *Calm Address to the Inhabitants of England* Wesley followed up his attack on the radical dissenters:

Do you imagine there are no High Churchmen left? Did they all die with Dr Sacheverel? Alas, how little do you know of mankind! Were the present restraint taken off, you would see them swarming on every side, and gnashing upon you with their teeth. There would hardly need a nod from that sacred person whom you revile, or at least lightly esteem. Were he to stand neuter, in what a condition would you be within one twelve months! If other Bonners and Gardiners did not arise, other Lauds and Sheldons would, who would either rule over you with a rod of iron, or drive you out of the land. Know the blessings you enjoy.[22]

No clearer statement could be made of Wesley's rejection of the 'persecuting' tradition of English religion and his defence of the Hanoverian monarchy as the custodian of religious liberty.

If religious liberty in England was threatened by irresponsible dissenters (Unitarian or Calvinist) provoking a High Church reaction, and by Roman Catholics with their 'intolerant persecuting principles',[23] civil liberty was equally in danger from Wilkesite radicals, American revolutionaries and the chronically disaffected. Jonathan Clark has convincingly shown how this 'contagion of disaffection' in the 1770s drew out Wesley's conservatism in the same way as the French Revolution influenced the evangelicals in the 1790s, but even here Wesley's conservative reaction is based on a distinctive view of liberty. The libertarian rhetoric of ribald Wilkesites he repudiated as bawling cant, the American cry for liberty was in his opinion a cry for independence and the liberties demanded by the mob he dismissed as mere licentiousness. Above all, he did not see how English liberties could be improved by alternative forms of government, especially those instigated by violence or dependent upon the will of the people.

Putting labels on Wesley's political theology, whether Tory, Whig, mainstream Anglican, conservative, progressive or whatever, ultimately conceals as much as it reveals. He believed that God was the origin of all power and that the Bible was his revealed will. He loved his king, his country and the constitution, but above all he had an exalted view of civil and religious liberty which he sought to defend against violence and anarchy. Like Burke, Wesley was more concerned with duties than with rights and with God's providential ordering of society than with the collective wisdom of democracy. Therefore an emphasis on obedience to established authorities and on reciprocal duties in all human relationships promised greater rewards of happiness and security for humankind than could be guaranteed by revolutionary enthusiasm. Although opposed in principle to revolutionary change, however, he retrospectively endorsed the Dutch revolt against Catholic Spain in the sixteenth century, and by 1784 he had accepted the American Revolution as a *fait accompli*. But Wesley's position was no mere adaptation of Pope's phrase that 'whatever is, is right', because his approval went only to changes that in his opinion resulted in more, not less, civil and religious liberty.[24] This fundamental concern for human liberty, absent in Dr Clark's treatment of Wesley, has led Leon Hynson to the conclusion that over a period of fifty years Wesley's political theology underwent a subtle change in emphasis from a primary focus on divine right, passive obedience and non-resistance to a primary concern for human liberties as ushered in by the Glorious Revolution and maintained inviolate by the Hanoverian dynasty.[25] Thus, Wesley's support for the established order in the period 1772–82 was based not only on his residual and suitably amended Toryism, but also on his appreciation of the rights enjoyed by the free-born Englishman. This is also the framework within which his anti-French and anti-papist sentiments, especially evident in 1778, are best understood.[26]

Wesley was generally careful not to allow his innate sympathy for some popular causes to manifest itself in public opposition to the king and his ministers which he regarded as both irreligious and dangerous. His Toryism, though tinged with the kind of anti-Whig radicalism described by Linda Colley, was never allowed to spill over into overt support for the Jacobite cause.[27] Similarly, his early sympathy for the plight of the American colonists was almost embarrassingly subjugated to a full-blown defence of the mother country amidst understandable allegations of plagiarism (Wesley borrowed some of Dr Johnson's ideas and prose) and of being a weathercock.[28] With such evidence in mind Dr Clark states that Wesley inherited almost intact 'the political theology of mainstream Anglicanism', but Wesley's political observations, as has been shown, also follow a more tortuous path than some of his more propagandist writings would suggest. It also seems to be the case that the later Wesley became more stridently loyal and obedient to the Hanoverian regime as it became ever clearer to him how radical was the departure of Methodist ecclesiology from mainstream Anglicanism or Dissent. Wesley's vigorous defence of loyalty, therefore, as with the Methodists of the period 1790–1820, was combined with the most serious erosion of the Church's authority since the Civil Wars of the mid-seventeenth century.

Unsurprisingly, therefore, Wesley's attitude to the Established Church is as ambiguous as some of his political ideas.[29] The conventional view of the relationship between Church and State in the eighteenth century was expressed with characteristic vigour by Edmund Burke. 'In a Christian commonwealth', Burke told the House of Commons in 1792, 'the church and the state are one and the same thing, being different integral parts of the same whole'.[30] Burke's high view of the church–state connection as Jonathan Clark has shown was neither original nor out of step with a substantial corpus of Anglican literature thrown up in the period of the French Revolution.[31] Wesley, as is well known, lived and died within the Established Church, and maintained a profound veneration for its forms, liturgies and doctrines. But Wesley's support of the Church of England, always more impressive in thought than in deed, was neither static nor entirely unconditional. Indeed there is a profound ambiguity at the heart of his opinions on religious establishments. On the one hand, he valued the ecclesiastical discipline, historical traditions (including the writings of great Anglican churchmen) and social utility of the Church of England, while, on the other, he regarded state patronage of religion as one of the 'mysteries of iniquity' that destroyed the spirituality of the early church. The greatest blow against 'the whole essence of true religion', he wrote, 'was struck in the fourth century by Constantine the Great, when he called himself a Christian, and poured in a flood of riches, honours, and power upon the Christians; more especially upon the clergy'.[32] The connection between establishment, wealth and corruption was never far from Wesley's mind and he reserved his severest remarks for those 'indolent, pleasure-taking, money-loving, praise-loving, preferment-seeking Clergymen' whom he regarded 'as the pests of the Christian world; a stink in the nostrils of God'.[33] To overcome the inconvenience of devotion to the Established Church while disapproving of many of its bishops and priests, Wesley stated that the essence of the church was to be found in its articles and homilies, not in its personnel. Consequently he rejected the divine right of episcopacy as a Tudor innovation and the doctrine of apostolical succession as historically unsustainable.[34] His defence of the episcopal church was therefore essentially devotional and pragmatic, leading Maldwyn Edwards to the conclusion that Wesley was 'a rebel in thought as well as in action, and only a sleepy, loosely disciplined Church would have tolerated his shock tactics so long'.[35]

Since Wesley viewed the Church of England as primarily an instrument of the gospel, not a divine right institution of state, he worked out quite early on what his sticking-point would be if ecclesiastical discipline was used against him. In 1755 he told the Cornish evangelical, Samuel Walker, that he *meant* no separation from the Church:

> It is from a full conviction of this that we have, (1), preached abroad; (2), prayed extempore; (3), formed societies; and (4), permitted preachers who were not episcopally ordained. And were we pushed on this side, were there no alternative allowed, we should judge it our bounden duty rather wholly to separate from the Church than to give up any of these points. Therefore if we cannot stop a separation without stopping lay preachers, the case is clear – we cannot stop it at all.[36]

Henry Rack has shown that whereas Charles Wesley's self-declared 'chief concern on earth was the prosperity of the Church of England; my next, that of the Methodists; my third, that of the preachers', his brother's priorities were almost the reverse.[37] For John Wesley, the cause of vital religion and the need to sustain his holy mission took precedence over the laws, forms and discipline of the Church of England. Wesley was nevertheless aware that connexionalism might easily degenerate into congregationalism, and he used Methodism's position within the Established Church as a defence against the atomization of his societies. 'I see clearer and clearer', he wrote, that, 'none will keep to us unless they keep to the Church. Whoever separate from the Church will separate from the Methodists'.[38] Indeed one of the most persistent of the early Anglican attacks on Methodism was that its breaches of ecclesiastical order would result in the same sectarian avalanche as overwhelmed the puritans. Taking the Elizabethan Presbyterian, Thomas Cartwright, as his example, John Smith told Wesley that despite his best intentions 'strict order once broken confusion rushes in like a torrent at a trifling breach'.[39] Wesley's response was to draw a distinction between the anabaptist enthusiasts and the learned and pious puritans whom he greatly admired: 'Nor did they separate from the Church, but were driven out, whether they would or no.'[40]

At the root of Wesley's ambivalence about the Church of England was his biblically inspired belief that the true church in England was 'the congregation of English believers' and his experience told him that such a body was by no means coterminous with the Established Church.[41] One possible strategy available to him therefore was to bring together the evangelicals within the Church of England in an alliance with the Methodists, but once this had failed by the end of the 1760s it was clear that Wesley's desire to follow his own version of authentic Christianity overrode his scruples about church order. In that respect he was a reluctant rebel, never seeking confrontation with the Church, but always prepared to implement ecclesiastical innovations for the greater good of the gospel as circumstances dictated. Thus, even before the turning-point in relations between Anglicans and Methodists effected by the Deed of Declaration in 1784,

> John Wesley had effectively separated from the Church of England by founding a closely-knit connexion of preachers and societies administering vast properties subject to no Anglican oversight except that of one priest with no official cure of souls and sitting very loose to episcopal authority.[42]

For as long as the Methodists continued to attend Anglican worship and sacraments, and as long as the bishops declined to enforce church discipline, Wesley's affection for the Church remained unaltered, but it was the filial affection of a child with a mind of its own rapidly approaching separation from the parental home.

Wesley's views on the ownership and distribution of property were perhaps the most radical of his challenges to eighteenth-century conventions.[43] 'The chief end of political or civil society', wrote Locke, 'is the preservation of property', and while most of Locke's political ideology went unread or unheeded by practising politicians in eighteenth-century England, his defence of property rights was admirably suited to a governing elite composed of a tight privileged ring of landowners. With power based on the ownership of large estates, legal privileges and a remarkable degree of political control of elections and high offices of state, English magnates have been described as 'the most confident, powerful and resilient aristocracy in Europe'.[44] This social elite was neither easy to penetrate from outside nor entirely closed to fortunes made elsewhere. Not only did English landowners facilitate commercial development by exploiting their mineral resources, taking responsibility for roads and laying down ground plans for urban building projects, but they also contributed to a 'consumer revolution' through their demand for fine decorative goods such as furniture, porcelain and silverware.[45] Thus, eighteenth-century England has been regarded as both an 'aristocratic society' and as a great age of commercial expansion and consumer demand.[46] Into this kind of society Wesley brought a distinctive and remarkably radical attitude to property and commerce which for convenience may be divided between his injunctions to his own followers and his attitudes to the wider economy.

Most interpretations of Methodism's economic teaching and influence published in the last quarter of a century have drawn attention to Wesley's emphasis on thrift and hard work. 'Without industry', he wrote, 'we are neither fit for this world, nor for the world to come.' Hence it has been suggested that Methodist discipline and acquisitiveness were symbiotically linked to the early development of industrial capitalism.[47] Wesley and his followers are thus portrayed as exemplars of the Protestant ethic – old puritans made new. Whatever the merits of this argument in relation to the Methodist movement as a whole during the Industrial Revolution, it will simply not do for Wesley's own teaching and example. Both W. J. Warner and John Walsh have drawn attention to the fact that Wesley's economic teaching was scarcely a model of acquisitive capitalism.[48] After providing for necessities, Wesley repeatedly urged Methodists to give away the rest, otherwise they would be guilty of robbing God and the poor, corrupting their own souls, wronging the widow and the fatherless and of making themselves 'accountable for all the want, affliction, and distress which they may, but do not remove'.[49] In addition, Wesley told his followers to think nothing of the future, to demand no more than a fair price and to make sure that excessive wealth was not passed on to their children.

There is yet another dimension to Wesley's economic opinions, for Walsh has drawn attention to Wesley's early attraction to the primitive church and its practice of the community of goods. Wesley's 'idealized image of the primitive Church provided stark contrasts with the acquisitiveness of Walpole's England, of which, as an old-fashioned Tory, he disapproved strongly'.[50] In contrast to conventional Anglican teaching, he did not think that the sharing of goods was of necessity confined to the apostolic period, though he was realistic enough to recognize that material altruism was doomed unless it was based on Christian love and koinonia of the highest quality. But as with much of his economic teaching, Wesley found that persistent human acquisitiveness was against him and he was forced to retreat into the medieval solution of voluntary poverty for a self-denying spiritual elite. Even so, his sermons never lost their anti-materialistic bite – at times close to desperation – as he viewed with dismay the first fruits of Methodism's upward social mobility.[51]

Wesley's rigorous teaching to his followers on the spiritual dangers of acquisitiveness and conspicuous consumption was carried over into his general attitudes to economy and society in eighteenth-century England. In his *Thoughts on the Present Scarcity of Provisions*, Wesley blamed the country's economic ills on luxury, waste, engrossing, distilling and taxes. With opinions based more on empirical observations than on economic theory, Wesley's pamphlet is a thinly veiled attack on what Edward Thompson has called the 'theatrical materialism' of the rich. Horses and carriages, useless pensions, extravagant waste and an insatiable thirst for luxury are all condemned as 'thousands of people throughout the land are perishing for want of food'.[52] As Outler has shown, Wesley also repudiated Adam Smith's view that surplus accumulation was the basis of economic well-being.[53] Wesley's intensely ethical and biblicist stance, combined with a conviction that all great spiritual movements surged from the poor, left no room for the complacency of the country house. This is made clear in a remarkable letter to Sir James Lowther, owner of substantial estates in Cumberland, director of the South Sea Company, colliery and harbour developer, extensive borough patron and one of the wealthiest and most parsimonious men in England. Wesley's point by point rebuttal of an earlier letter from Lowther is a classic statement of his social and economic philosophy:

> (2). It is true men of fortune must mind their fortune – but they must not love the world. (3). It is true, likewise, you can't go about to look for poor people – but you may be sufficiently informed of them by those that can. (4). And if some of these are never satisfied, this is no reason for not relieving others. (5). Suppose, too, that some make an ill use of what you give – the loss falls on their own head. You will not lose your reward for their fault. (8). I rejoice likewise that you have given some hundreds of pounds to the hospitals, and wish it had been ten thousand. (9). To the support of the family I did not object, but begged leave to ask whether this could not be done without giving ten thousand a year to one who had as much already.[54]

Herein is encapsulated Wesley's spiritual distrust of riches, his characteristic refusal to distinguish between the deserving and undeserving poor, his advocacy of a *sacrificial* charity and his suspicion of hereditary wealth. All this was within a framework of belief which held that the bounty of the earth was a God-given responsibility of stewardship and that eternal rewards were immeasurably more valuable than worldly luxury. Wesley was, of course, no philistine and on occasions he was attracted by the aesthetic trappings of wealth, but in general terms he was as opposed to the conspicuous consumption of the landed elite as he was to the growing consumerism of English society. To conclude, Warner is probably correct to suggest that Wesley's twin emphases on industriousness and charity was 'incapable of mass realization',[55] but that should not distract from the genuinely radical elements in both his instructions to his followers and his wider reflections on eighteenth-century English society.

'It was a shibboleth of English politics', state Brewer and Styles, 'that English law was the birthright of every citizen who, unlike many of his European counterparts, was subject not to the whim of a capricious individual but to a set of prescriptions that bound all members of the polity.'[56] Wesley's belief in civil and religious liberty and his opposition to all forms of violence resulted in a high regard for the law in so far as it was properly applied and administered. But he also recognized perfectly well that early Methodism teetered on the brink of legal irregularities with respect to the penal legislation of Charles II's reign. A detailed analysis of how Methodism stood in respect of the penal legislation of the Clarendon Code is supplied in Chapter 8, but suffice to say that Wesley, by claiming fidelity to the Established Church, refused to accept that either he or his followers were technically dissenters. As such, in his opinion, Methodists were subject neither to the penalties of the penal laws nor to the relief offered to Protestant Trinitarian dissenters by the Toleration Act of 1689. Wesley was nevertheless forced by intimidation and lack of legal protection in the localities to accept that, under duress, it was legitimate for Methodist preachers and owners of meeting-houses to apply for certificates under the Toleration Act. Characteristically, Wesley refused to accept the dissenting logic of such actions; rather he defended them as a legal device to protect life and property from the licence of the crowd.

Despite the registration of preachers and meeting-houses, the extent of toleration enjoyed by Methodists in English localities depended less upon known laws, which were seen to be ambiguous and subject to confusing jurisdictional disputes,[57] than on the degree of social acceptance accorded to the Methodists themselves. Wesley found this inconvenient, but not intolerable, despite periodic splenetic outbursts about the inadequacy of religious toleration accorded to his followers. In a letter to Wilberforce he bemoaned the fact that Methodists were neither accepted as Anglicans nor afforded relief as dissenters under the Act of Toleration.[58] But behind the spleen Wesley knew well that he had at times used Methodism's ambiguous position under the law as a device to keep potential separatists in check. The truth is that Wesley recognized the fact that the Methodist structure created peculiar legal problems, but so long as his societies were not unduly restricted he was content to put up the best possible legal defence and cope with the consequences. As in his relationship with the Church of England, what Wesley could not accept was any interpretation of the law which would threaten Methodist rights, not only to the passive toleration envisaged by the authors of the Toleration Act, but also the right to propagate religious opinions on a nationwide basis without intolerable restrictions.

Whatever the complexities of the law with regard to preachers and conventicles, the great majority of cases against early Methodism which came before local courts was concerned with associated offences of public order, assault, riot and damage to property. Opponents of the Methodists alleged that they disturbed the peace by breaking known laws, while Methodists in turn claimed they were victims of mobs unrestrained by those responsible for protecting civil and religious liberties. Wesley frustratingly discovered that since there was 'no law for the Methodists', mobs were virtually indemnified against prosecution, costs and damages, and local constables and quarter sessions could not be relied upon to protect his followers against popular clamour.[59] But unlike the confusing legal debates surrounding the implementation of the Clarendon Code, Wesley was unequivocal in his repudiation of mob violence and unstinting in his efforts to seek legal redress. His strategy was to attempt to overcome local prejudices by taking as many cases as he could afford to the Court of King's Bench to establish that there was 'law for the Methodists'.[60] As case-law built up, Wesley used it to warn future protagonists and to remind local officials that their tenure in office depended upon their ability to maintain public order. In general terms, therefore, Wesley had confidence in English law and its interpretation by metropolitan courts, but he had correspondingly little confidence in local justice, especially when animated by violence and prejudice. As with his defence of the Hanoverian dynasty and the eighteenth-century constitution, Wesley valued English law primarily as a bulwark against the licence of the crowd and the curtailment of civil and religious liberty. In that respect, as in many others, Wesley shared Blackstone's patriotic view of English law as the very essence of freedom in 'the only nation in the world where political or civil liberty is the direct end of its constitution'.[61]

Allowing for the fact that Wesley's views were neither static nor entirely consistent, the striking feature of his attitude to the constitution, the Church of England, property and the law is that in each case his veneration for institutions was dependent on their achievement of certain ends. His primary concern, as in the creation of Methodism's connexional structure, was not with theory but with performance. Thus the constitution and the Hanoverian dynasty defended civil and religious liberties against radicals, revolutionaries, anarchists and mobs. The Church of England, notwithstanding its carnal and worldly clergy, was, through its homilies, articles and traditions, the custodian of the religion, pure and undefiled, of the English. The ownership of property conferred duties more than privileges, so that Wesley's preoccupation was more with the distribution of resources than with their acquisition. Finally, English law was not only the birthright of every English citizen, but the ultimate protection of the security of the person against intolerance, prejudice and violence.

In addition, Wesley had a lifelong dislike of human exploitation, whether of Caribbean slaves or the English poor. The corollary to all of this was that he profoundly disliked any ideology or system which in his opinion contributed to human bondage, including Roman Catholicism,[62] high Calvinism,[63] popular sovereignty and inhumane commercialism. Much of the radicalism – as well as the conservatism – inherent in Wesley's thought stemmed from his willingness to obey biblical injunctions and Early Church practices with unremitting rigour even, as was the case with his teaching on the community of goods and celibacy, when they were inappropriate to the circumstances confronting him.[64]

The ambiguities of the Wesleyan tradition have an even deeper foundation in the easily forgotten fact that 'the organization of Wesley's "Connexion" was strikingly different from that of most other eighteenth-century churches and religious associations, at least in its fully developed form'.[65] There is in Wesley's indebtedness to Enlightenment emphases on empiricism, contractualism and individualism, together with early Methodism's forging of a novel ecclesiology (based more on continental

European influences than on the plain English religious tradition) that threw up inevitable tensions between Wesleyan pragmatism and prevailing notions of faith and order in the eighteenth-century Church and State. For Wesley, the religious priorities of converting and perfecting souls made him impatient with any man-made forms of order which militated against his higher purposes. The radical implications of such a view were psychologically, ecclesiastically and politically mediated through Wesley's deep-seated Tory affection for order and obedience. The result was not schizophrenia, but neither was it a cosy sojourn in the womb of the mainstream Anglican tradition.

Jonathan Clark has performed a useful task in re-emphasizing Wesley's conservative political theology, particularly in his period of polemical warfare against the disaffected at home and abroad in the 1770s and 1780s, and in challenging those who would place Wesley too neatly in the tradition of the inexorable advance of Enlightenment liberalism. He may even be correct to state that the *affect* of Methodism in the generation overshadowed by the French Revolution was to reinforce the passive obedience of the poor, though that is another story altogether.[66] But, as the preceding pages have shown, Wesley could hardly be regarded as an impeccable exemplar of the mainstream Anglican tradition in the eighteenth century. Perhaps the point at which he most obviously departed from that tradition is the greater weight he gave to the writings of the primitive church, the Early Church Fathers and the continental pietists in constructing his ideology of authority in Church and State. Wesley's lifelong devotion to primitive Christianity and vital religion imbued his opinions with a degree of pragmatism and radicalism which can only be ignored at the cost of historical credibility. If certainly not a self-conscious rebel, Wesley was far from a comfortable conformist.

5

JABEZ BUNTING: THE FORMATIVE YEARS, 1794–1820

Jabez Bunting was converted in 1794 at the age of fifteen and became President of the Methodist Conference for the first time in 1820. For the next thirty years his 'eyes were on everything' as he ruled the connexion with almost papal authority until he retired from the full-time work of the ministry in 1851 with his policies in tatters and with the connexion in serious disarray.[1] Thanks largely to Ward's scholarly editions of Bunting's papers between 1820 and 1858[2] there remains little new to be said about his contribution to Methodism's great 'age of disunity',[3] but what emerges most clearly from Bunting's voluminous correspondence is the fact that his operating principles and style of leadership were already well in place by 1820. For Bunting, as is the case with most men of affairs, the years between fifteen and forty were the most significant in the shaping of attitudes that were to characterize his exercise of ecclesiastical power. It was Bunting's misfortune that these years coincided with the most turbulent period in the modern history of religion, not only in Britain but in most of the rest of Europe as well. The aim of this short biographical chapter, then, is to offer a fresh interpretation of Bunting's life as a Methodist preacher in the years overshadowed by revolution in France, war in Europe and unprecedented social and economic changes in Britain.[4] From these pressures neither Bunting nor Methodism emerged unscathed.

Bunting was received into full connexion as a Methodist itinerant preacher at the Conference of 1803 when he stood with twenty-eight other young hopefuls in the gallery of Oldham Street Chapel in Manchester: 'the place where Wesley had blessed him; to which his mother had taken him, Sabbath after Sabbath, when a child; and where, probably, he had formed his first wish to serve God'.[5] His preparatory years as a preacher on trial had been accompanied by the kind of enthusiastic aspirations appropriate to the Methodist itinerancy at the turn of the century:

As a Methodist preacher, I consider myself to be emphatically a stranger & a pilgrim upon earth; and have buried all hopes & desires of worldly prosperity. My wants are few and simple; and I am happy serving a people, whose regular & ordinary provision comfortably supplies them.[6]

When you and I finally lose the spirit of preaching, there will be room to fear that we have lost also the spirit of piety & zeal; a loss of all others the most to be dreaded.[7]

I trust the cause of pure & undefiled religion is likely to prosper among us. We have considerable expectations of a gracious revival; and many think they 'hear the abundance of rain'. May our hopes be blessedly realized.[8]

But behind the pious enthusiasm and the conventional advice offered to him to beware of 'rich' and 'lukewarm' Methodists and seek not 'the approbation of the world', there were some more unusual aspects to Bunting's early career.[9] The son of a radical Methodist tailor, Bunting was educated by Unitarians,[10] was nurtured in French theological classics, both Catholic and Protestant,[11] and was almost obsessed with the various connexional disputes, including the Kilhamite agitation, which rocked Methodism in the decade after Wesley's death.[12] Unsurprisingly, there was in evidence at this early stage of his career a number of unresolved tensions: between the 'supremacy of the pure reasoning faculty' enjoined by the Unitarians and the desire for 'the spirit of revival' urged by Methodist itinerants; between recognizing the 'value of a godly ecclesiastical order' in response to endemic connexional disharmony and being willing to let God work in his own way 'however contrary that may be to our own preconceived notions of order and propriety'; between a devoted attachment to the principles of religious toleration, including the right both to hold religious opinions and to propagate them, and a fear of ecclesiastical democracy; and between a desire to see the Methodist cause prosper and a deep-seated fear of the consequences of unrestricted enthusiasm. In the same period as he was attending medical classes under the tuition of the cultivated Unitarian, Dr Percival, he was attending prayer meetings at the house of a mad Methodist mechanic, who tried to demonstrate the strength of his faith by thrusting his hand into a fire, and who was later hanged for murdering two women. Nor was Bunting free from more common evangelical ambiguities: he strove earnestly for sacrificial piety yet craved the public recognition of his gifts; he married a vivacious and attractive woman and then tried to bend her will to Methodistical discipline; he believed in the providential ordering of events yet he schemed relentlessly to influence them; and he urged pan-evangelical co-operation at the start of his ministry while describing himself privately as 'a bigoted Methodist'.[13]

If the years before 1803 left an ambiguous legacy, the events of the year itself brought some resolution. For the first half of the year Bunting was stationed in Macclesfield where he encountered in a raw form the phenomenon that overshadowed the first decade of his public ministry – revivalism. It seemed that right across the north of England a band of Methodist revivalists including William Bramwell and James Sigston were poised to form a party and break away from the main connexion. Bunting was not only kept informed of the impact of revivalist methods on the northern circuits, but had to watch at first hand a painful separation in Macclesfield itself. He told a friend that

> Mr Bramwell's conduct has been strange indeed; & I cannot account for it but in the way you mention. Alas! 'all is not gold that glitters' ... he preached in the Room occupied by the Christian Revivalists last night, to a Congregation larger indeed than their ordinary one, but not numerous in proportion either to the size of the Town, or to the pains which had been taken to induce the people to attend. I am told he was uncommonly flat and low-spirited. They will not be able, I am pretty sure, to do much harm, if any, in Macclesfield. The people in this town are tired of parties & divisions: & in general equally tired of the rant and extravagancies of what is called revivalism.... Divisions *from* the Church, though awful, are perhaps after all less to be dreaded than Divisions in the Church, which, I fear, would have been perpetuated, if these men had remained among us. I therefore hope that their separation will be over-ruled for good. Revivalism, as of late professed & practiced was [likely if] not checked, to have gradually ruined genuine Methodism. [I am] glad, however, that they have been first to draw the sword. But as they have drawn it, I earnestly wish that our Preachers would take the opportunity of returning fully to the spirit & discipline of ancient Methodism, & with that resolve to stand or fall. The temporary loss of numbers would probably be more than recompensed by the increase of real, scriptural Piety, the restoration of good order, & the establishment of brotherly love.[14]

It was characteristic of Bunting to speak so self-confidently of Methodism as a church (still relatively unusual by 1803), and to emphasize discipline, good order and tradition to buttress his case. He contrasted the noisy and transient enthusiasm of the revivalists with an alternative vision of how to secure the future well-being of Methodism: sound finances, the careful selection of preachers, the assiduous application of Conference rules, the erection of new chapels and the vigorous exploitation of a connexional system of church government so that the weak could be helped by the strong.[15]

Bunting's altercations with the Christian revivalists in Macclesfield were not the end of the matter, for the problem arose again in different guises in many different parts of the country over the next decade. Bunting's correspondence makes clear that the main connexion slowly evolved strategies for combating the influence of the revivalists. Pastoral discipline was more firmly imposed, leaders were more carefully selected and revivalists were deliberately shunned.[16] By 1808, Bunting found Sheffield, one of the most disturbed of all the circuits, to be

> the most deeply pious society I have yet seen in any large town. The extravagancies of revivalism are nearly extinct; the congregations, for the population of the place, are good; and the distresses of the times appear to be sanctified to the spiritual good of the many.[17]

He told his friend James Wood that he was surprised that Methodists in Sheffield were so free from 'the follies of enthusiasm' because 'so few of them have attained to any considerable degree of mental improvement, or possess much general intelligence'.[18] For Bunting revivalism was not only a problem of connexional discipline, but was also a sign of the social instability and lack of mental cultivation of the English working classes. The former was an offence against his interpretation of ancient Methodism while the latter betrays obvious traces of his rationalist Unitarian education. Unsurprisingly, Bunting was equally contemptuous of the more bizarre manifestations of popular millenarianism which also took root in areas worked by the Methodists at the turn of the century:

> Mr Sadler tells me that the notorious Joanna Southcote, late of Exeter, is now at Leeds. She has abandoned the system of Richard Brothers, and set up for herself. She says that she is the bride, the Lamb's wife mentioned in the Revelation; and such as believe her testimony, she seals, by means of red wax, to the day of Redemption. Some hundreds in Leeds have thus been sealed of late. 'Anything,' said a good man, 'does with the Devil, and anything with the world, except faith and repentance.'[19]

Bunting, it is clear, preferred the patient refinement of the Methodist system to the fast results of revivalistic or millenarian enthusiasm. In future years he noted with interest, but with little comment, any extravagant numerical success in Methodist circuits. In one of his last references to the subject he defended his stance on 'systematic revivalism' by stating that 'everything I see & hear' and 'the longer I live' confirmed his opinion of its deleterious effect on the Methodist system.[20]

Nor was Bunting much impressed with other 'popular' causes. On the contentious issue of female preaching he proudly reported to a colleague the minutes of the Sheffield district meeting that 'we think the practice is contrary to the New Test., productive of more evil than good, disgraceful to our character, & injurious to our success'.[21] On this issue the connexional tide was running inexorably in his favour, but he faced a more formidable task in trying to impose Methodist discipline over the burgeoning Sunday school movement. In origin these schools were undenominational in character, and paternalistic in intention, but their offer of the prize of literacy without having to pay the price of committed church or chapel membership soon made them equally attractive to the urban working classes and to denominational imperialists. A clash between the two was inevitable, and, as with many of the class tensions of the revolutionary period, it was fought out within the Methodist polity itself. Bunting initially extolled the virtues of interdenominational co-operation and popular education to the genteel subscribers to the Sunday School Union in 1805, but his tone began to change a few years later.[22] His papers show that Methodists were finding it hard to subscribe to interdenominational societies when their own finances were close to collapse, and were beginning to see that interdenominational Sunday schooling promised no great harvest for the Methodist chapels themselves. Pious Bunting was also against the teaching of writing on the sabbath. He told Richard Reece in 1808 that

> the evil resulting from it, on the whole, (an evil silent & secret, but I fear exceedingly mischievous, in its operation & influence) is so strong, that if I thought my feeble voice had any chance of being heard with effect, I would conscientiously publish to the connexion my objections & my protest against it.[23]

Bunting thought that 'writing on the Lord's Day' violated the sanctity of the sabbath and he began to use his 'feeble voice' to put a stop to it. Even those who agreed with him urged caution, not only because some of the most successful of all the Methodist Sunday schools taught writing, but because the wise could see that there was much more bound up with this issue than mere sabbatarian propriety.[24] The subsequent battle for control of the Sunday schools reflected many of the tensions of early nineteenth-century society, including class conflict, anticlericalism, anticentralization and sectarianism. Bunting persuaded the Sheffield district to propose a minute of Conference recommending

> to the Teachers of all Methodist Sunday Schools to teach writing & arithmetic on the week-day evenings only, so that the whole of the Lord's Day may be devoted to Reading, Public Worship and religious instructions & exercises. And the Conference direct that in all *new* schools this plan shall be strictly enforced.[25]

Bunting's characteristic tactic of employing the authority of Conference to overcome local sensibilities was not entirely successful, and contests for control of the Sunday schools disturbed most of the northern circuits in the first quarter of the nineteenth century.[26]

While Bunting's strategy of removing all secular instruction from the sabbath was scarcely popular among the urban working classes and many of their local preachers and teachers, his attempts to undermine inter-denominational co-operation by establishing purely Methodist Sunday schools did not endear the connexion to the rest of the religious world. In 1814 Bunting received an angry letter from Joseph Butterworth, the Methodist MP and evangelical philanthropist, complaining that Method-ists all over the country were applying for books from the inter-denominational Sunday School Society without ever making reciprocal gestures:

> Churchmen & Dissenters in London are willing to give their money to Methodist schools in the Country. But it seems so ungracious and illiberal for the Methodists to be making continual applications for books, without any apparent cordiality in making a collection in return.[27]

As with many of Bunting's most contentious opinions, the passage of time merely confirmed him in his original wisdom. Not only did he believe that careless Sunday school education contributed to the wider social and political agitations of the Peterloo years, but he became ever more convinced that a specifically Methodist system of Sunday school education was vital to the long-term health of the connexion. He repudiated interdenominational Sunday schools because they were neither subject to pastoral control nor likely to produce good Methodists.[28] By 1840 Bunting had won both his battles over the Sunday schools: the teaching of writing on Sundays was forbidden and the Methodists had their own schools. Moreover, all was subsumed under the pastoral oversight of the preachers. Methodism had thereby become more disciplined, more clerical and more sectarian, but a price had to be paid. The history of every northern circuit in the period 1810–30 is riddled with angry clashes between those who saw the education of the people as an authentic expression of working-class culture and social aspirations, and those who were determined to harness those aspirations for the benefit of a particular religious de-nomination. Methodists came painfully to learn that winning denomina-tional battles did not alone advance the war effort against popular infidelity.

Before leaving this subject it is worth pointing out that Bunting's enthusiasm for the sabbath was no mere self-interested posture for defeating connexional radicals, but was as sincerely held as his near ruthless zeal for connexional discipline. A bizarre case in 1812 illustrates the point. Bunting was appealed to by a circuit superintendent from Horncastle about the case of a local class leader, one Mr Richardson, who insisted on using his windmill on the sabbath for 'grinding corn & dressing flower'. The cause of this 'evil to the cause of God' defended himself by stating that

1. There have been less wind on the weekdays this summer than other summers hence he has ground more on the Sundays than formerly. 2. The people *say* they want flower or bread & must have the corn ground. 3. That Jesus Christ nowhere forbids it in the New Testament. If we plead the moral law he seems to think it is done away by Jesus Christ, if not, he says we Methodist preachers break it, in Travelling on horse back & making collections on the Sabbath Day. If we speak of works of necessity & acts of mercy being allowed to be done on the Sabbath Day, he thinks it is *necessity* & *mercy* that justifies his grinding when there is *wind* on the *Sunday*, if there is corn wants grinding as there may be no wind on Monday, Tuesday, etc.[29]

Whatever the merits of the issues at stake, it is clear from this defence that there was a hidden agenda of resentment against the regular preachers and their financial exactions, and against the alleged indifference of the connexion to the material needs of the people. Zachariah Taft, the circuit superintendent, offered the recalcitrant class leader the arbitration of the quarterly and district meetings, or, if necessary, the Conference itself. Failure to submit to judgement would result in the miller's dismissal from his position as class leader, but not expulsion from the Methodist society. This case, as were many such cases which required the interpretation and application of connexional law, was taken to Bunting, who, equally predictably, devoted no small efforts to its resolution. His reply to this inconsequential case is a sacramental illustration of his later approach to more serious matters:

Mr. Richardson's conduct is absolutely unlawful, and that if he persists in it, he is not a proper person even for *Membership*, and much less for *office*, in our society. We think that a case of such necessity as would justify his grinding on the Lord's Day is very unlikely to occur. It must be a necessity of the most urgent & inevitable kind. Now the necessity he pleads is neither the one nor the other. It is not urgent, for if a poor family were starving, they might make a tolerable shift for one day to live upon other kinds of provision besides grain; or they might, in almost every supposeable case, either beg or borrow bread for Sunday, even if bread alone could support them . . . sooner than break the sabbath, or let the people want food, the mill should grind by night as well as day, & if that would not remove the evil, *another* mill should be erected. . . . The argument in defence of Sunday grinding built on the possibility of there being no wind on Monday etc., betrays a criminal distrust of Providence & would equally justify, *mutatis mutandis*, the practice of Sunday Hay-making or reaping.[30]

Bunting finished with a resolute defence of the fourth commandment and of the preachers' rights to do whatever they thought appropriate on the sabbath. The law-giver had spoken, ironically, at precisely the time when the Methodists were celebrating a major extension of religious freedom and toleration in the shape of the new Methodist-inspired Toleration Act of 1812. This apparent paradox would not have troubled Bunting in the least, such was his capacity for fine distinctions in the interpretation of connexional law.

It was suggested earlier that 1803 was a particularly significant year in Bunting's life because of his encounter with the potentially disruptive forces of 'Christian revivalism', but it was also the year of Bunting's first appointment to the London circuit which inevitably introduced him to the higher echelons of connexional politics and to a much wider circle of evangelicals interested in public affairs. Fortuitously, it was also the period leading up to his marriage, and the prolific correspondence with his future wife gives a more complete picture of his private thoughts than is available for any other period of his life.[31] Although only twenty-four years old when he arrived in London, Bunting, on the basis of his preaching ability and his knowledge of public affairs, was clearly a connexional star in the making and was treated as such. Bunting was not a natural orator, but he worked relentlessly at his preaching style throughout his early years of ministry. During his four years on trial he preached 1,348 times from a portfolio of 100 sermons and when he got to London he sat at the feet of all the most renowned London preachers and subjected their style and discourse to his perfectionist analysis.[32] It was his chief entertainment. Bunting's own sermons

> surprised no one by their novelty or ingenuity; but were always most natural, and such as would have suggested themselves to any thoughtful mind; while the discourses themselves were such as partook of all the sermonizing peculiarities of the period. There were divisions and sub-divisions, with formal exordiums and perorations, which yet were redeemed from everything like tameness and in-sipidity, by the distinctness and energy of the thoughts and expressions. You saw no deep emotion in the speaker, no enthusiastic bursts of passion, nor brilliant strokes of imagination; but you perceived a marked attention riveted upon him while he spoke, which never flagged nor decreased in its intensity till he closed and sat down.[33]

This observer seems to have captured not only Bunting's preaching style, but the essence of his personality. Novelty, ingenuity, emotion, passion or imagination were never much in evidence, but he had a remarkable ability to dissect a problem and command widespread respect as he delivered his judgements. He could not rouse an audience, but he knew how to impress them. If short on visionary leadership, no one could more methodically plot a course to arrive at a chosen destination. He was unexciting, but remarkably exact. His soul was cultivated not by warmth and affection, but by law and discipline. Unfortunately, he required the same from those around him.

While in London Bunting gained an early entry into the elite circle of Methodist laymen headed by Butterworth and Thomas Allan, and through them he made contact with Wilberforce and other members of the Clapham Sect. It is worth pointing out to those more familiar with the sterner strains of Bunting's political conservatism in the 1830s and 1840s that his early political inclinations, as befitted his Unitarian education, were more on the Whiggish and liberal side.[34] The issues which most affected him in his early career in London were the military persecution of Methodist soldiers stationed in Gibraltar, the preaching restrictions imposed on Methodists in Jamaica by the slave interest and the long-running legal disputes with the Kilhamites over the ownership of chapels. He wrote to his friend James Wood that

> we have just received accounts from Gibraltar, that some of our pious soldiers in that garrison are suffering grievous persecutions for attending Methodist Preaching, when not on duty. Two of them, for this only crime, have received two hundred lashes. . . . This matter is likely to be very seriously taken up by several Gentlemen in London; as such military tyranny is completely illegal. In Jamaica also they continue to pass & enforce penal laws against us. If the Government here wink at these attacks upon Religious Liberty, I shall begin to fear for the safety of the country. God will avenge his Church on all her oppressors, wherever he find them.[35]

What is interesting about this letter is that Bunting, in common with many other zealous churchmen of all traditions in the early nineteenth century, was forced on to a higher plane of speculative divinity to counter the state's unwillingness, or inability, to defend their respective versions of 'religious freedom and truth'. Less than a decade after Bunting first encountered the limits of religious toleration in Jamaica, Lord Sidmouth's Bill against itinerant preaching in Britain brought the problem much nearer to home. Bunting drew up a protest on behalf of the Methodists of the Manchester district, the first article of which stated

> That liberty of conscience, comprehending the freedom of public assemblies for religious worship and instruction, in such forms and under such teachers as men shall for themselves approve, is the inalienable right of all men; and that in the peaceable exercise of this right, as well as of the further right of peaceably communicating their own religious views and opinions to all who are willing to hear them, they are not justly amenable to the authority of the civil magistrate.[36]

Bunting's biographer, who on the whole was not given much to insight, made the astute observation that the Toleration Act of 1689 gave the nonconformists 'a season of repose after sore persecution and strife', but that it was the Methodists who 'were the first in this country to give the principle full sweep and play'.[37] In short, Bunting's methodistical claim to the 'further right of peaceably communicating their own religious views' if accepted by the state, was, in principle, nothing less than the de facto demolition of the old hierarchical, territorial and coercive framework upon which Church and State had relied for centuries. Unitarian rationalism and Methodist enthusiasm, it seems, had arrived at the same destination from very different starting-points, and Bunting, who refused to accept the 'inalienable rights' of political radicals, defended their religious application in uncharacteristically Painite language.

Just how uncharacteristic was soon made clear when Bunting so vigorously opposed Luddism while stationed in Halifax that his life was continually threatened in anonymous letters and he was unable to travel alone at night. Bunting was genuinely shocked to discover that six out of the seventeen Luddites hanged at York were the sons of Methodists. This 'aweful fact' confirmed him in his 'fixed opinion' that the progress of

> Methodism in the West Riding of Yorkshire has been more swift than solid; more extensive than deep; more in the increase of numbers, than in the diffusion of that kind of piety, which shines as brightly & operates as visibly *at home* as in the prayer meeting and the crowded lovefeast.[38]

Bunting was an equally resourceful opponent of the political radicalism of the Peterloo years when he supported every attempt – from London to Manchester and from Merseyside to Tyneside – to expel from the connexion Methodists who got involved in radical political associations of whatever hue and colour.[39] In a similar vein, when he was asked to rule on the propriety of Methodists joining the Burnley Odd Fellows, Bunting delivered the uncompromising judgement that

> if these clubs have any *political* object or business, then, as *secret*, they are, I believe unlawful, and certainly very dangerous. If, on the other hand, they are merely *convivial*, which I suppose to be the case, still it is *highly* improper and unscriptural that religious persons should join themselves with carnal and careless persons in such associations.[40]

Bunting was under no illusions that such a firm disciplinary crackdown on the radicals would result in serious membership losses and much unpopularity against the Methodists in the industrial districts, but the price had to be paid. Nevertheless, how the price should be calculated was a subject of much contention at the time, and among historians ever since.

John Stephens, who presided over the notoriously ungovernable Manchester circuit and who expelled radicals with unprecedented rigour in the aftermath of Peterloo, cheerfully told Bunting a year later that 'the people are growing tired of radicalism, and as that dies religion will revive. Our congregations are good. Methodism stands high among the respectable people. We have had some awakenings and conversions. Nearly every seat is let in the New Chapel'.[41] The advantages of recruiting among the aspirantly respectable rather than the impoverished and disaffected were borne triumphantly home to Stephens when the missionary collections of 1821 amounted to 'several hundred pounds above any former year'.[42] Having suffered the ferocious blandishments of the radicals in 1819–20, Stephens emerged in 1821 in an ebullient, almost ecstatic, mood:

> Can you pardon me, if I feel a little too much the exhillaration [*sic*] at such a result of a meeting, which I considered a sort of *popular* approval, or disapproval, of our moderate but firm, and steady conduct, in times the most trying, which Methodism has endured in Manchester for, at least, a quarter of a century. . . . I have been obliged to spend hour after [hour] with Kilhamites and Ranters wanting to come to us for the sake of *order*, and *liberty*, and *protection*! – We have nearly all that was respectable among the former; and it seems likely we shall have all who are worth having among the latter.[43]

Those 'worth having' had, of course, two meanings: they were those who could help solve Methodism's acute post-war financial problems and they were those whose respectability separated them from the radicals and enthusiasts. One who was certainly not worth having was Samuel Bamford who was imprisoned for high treason for his part in the events surrounding the infamous Peterloo Massacre. His encounter with Bunting in Lincoln jail triggered off a bout of religious nostalgia during which he informed Bunting that his grandfather, Daniel Bamford, had helped the Wesleys introduce Methodism to Middleton and that he himself had often sat under Bunting's ministry. Bamford wrote whimsically,

> One thing, however, struck me as a falling off from the good old apostolic customs of the preachers in my younger days. The reverend gentleman [Bunting] went away with his company without vouchsafing a blessing or a word of advice to me – not that I cared much about it – but I thought old John Gaulter, or little Jonathan Barker, would not have done so.[44]

Bunting's correspondence with circuit superintendents in the Peterloo years offers some support both for E. P. Thompson's view that those who encountered political and temporal defeat turned to Methodism by way of consolation,[45] and for W. R. Ward's opinion that 'Peterloo had for ever severed official Methodism from urban revivalism'.[46] But Thompson's view almost presupposes that there was a fixed group of people who oscillated back and forth like water in a tilting bucket, when, in reality, changes within the Wesleyan style and polity effectively closed it off from some sections of the population while opening it up to others. This transaction was related to social class, but it was not coterminous with it. Similarly, Ward probably exaggerates Methodism's capacity ever to act as a mass religion for the urban proletariat, but he is right to draw attention to the fact that while the connexional machine could, over time, repair membership losses, it 'could never evoke old expansiveness. The years 1819–20 were the moment of truth for the Wesleyans, as the years 1792–3 had been for the Church; Wesleyanism was never going to be a popular urban religion'.[47] The connexional administrators, among whom Bunting had emerged by 1820 in the pre-eminent position, were simply not prepared to cope with the many inconveniences that would have resulted from Methodism sinking deep roots among the more politicized sections of the urban working classes.

As with social class and political consciousness, so with religious denominationalism. When Bunting arrived in London in 1803 he soon became involved in an interdenominational scheme to establish the *Eclectic Review*, in which 'the wisest representatives of metropolitan Nonconformity, together with a section of the Evangelical party in the Church of England, united, for the first time, with the Wesleyans, to defend and to promote religion, upon the basis of a common creed'.[48] Bunting's enthusiasm for the new venture, in which he took the leading Wesleyan role, failed to survive the first issue when the evangelical Arminians felt themselves impugned by Anglicans and Calvinists. Bunting was further frustrated when the editor refused to print his rejoinder signed 'an Orthodox Arminian'.[49] Once the pique had settled down, Bunting was forced to recognize not only that interdenominational co-operation was more limited than he had hoped, but that the Methodists, notwithstanding their numbers, were still the Cinderellas of the metropolitan religious world.

> On Theological or Literary Subjects in general *we* have very few writers, to whom they could advert. This strikes me as one of the great defects of modern Methodism. It makes very little use of *the Press*, that powerful engine for promoting its tenets, or advancing its interests. That mode of influencing public opinion, & saving souls from death, we grossly neglect; a neglect, however, which is one out of many evils resulting from an *uneducated* ministry. Do not mistake me. I am no friend to colleges or academies. But I do think that some regular & systematic plan ought to be adopted, with respect to the young preachers, during their four years of probation, which, without interrupting their pulpit labours, would make them more accur-

ately & thoroughly acquainted with *Divinity as a Science,* and qualify them for more extensive and permanent usefulness.[50]

In this unlikely way, interdenominational co-operation occasioned further denominational definition. Bunting did not give up altogether, however, for he continued to patronize the Eclectic Society, the Society for the Suppression of the Slave Trade and the London Missionary Society, but not until the days of the Evangelical Alliance in the 1840s was Bunting ever again quite so enthusiastic about interdenominational co-operation.[51]

What dulled Bunting's interdenominational ardour, however, was not so much brickbats from Anglicans and Calvinists, unpleasant though they were to him, but the fact that Methodism itself could not properly be financed and propagated so long as scarce resources were being siphoned off by the great evangelical voluntary societies. The crunch came over the financing of Methodist overseas missions, which had been kept in a state of suspended benign chaos by the venerable and opinionated Dr Coke. Attempts to impose some control were thwarted by Coke's mercurial evasiveness and by internecine squabbles between senior laymen and the preachers about the connection, or lack of it, between fund-raising and the determination of policy. In 1810 Thomas Allan told Bunting that the financing of Methodist missions was a legal and moral disgrace, since the bulk of the money raised was expended not on foreign missions, as the connexion had been led to believe, but on making good the serious financial deficiencies at home.[52] The problem came to a head in 1813 when Coke announced his intention to leave England for India at precisely the same time as the London Missionary Society was using Methodist chapels to raise funds for its own missionary efforts. The situation had become intolerable and Bunting, with the support of other preachers and laymen in Leeds, launched a local society for the exclusive supply of Wesleyan missions. In terms of connexional proprieties – since the authority of the Conference was effectively circumvented by a district meeting – it was probably the most radical action Bunting ever took. It nearly went off at half cock, because a representative of the London Missionary Society, aware of what was at stake, tried to restore the interdenominational ideal by telling the audience that the 'missionary cause was but one cause, and that the various societies, though, like ships in harbour, they might now seem to crowd each other, would have room enough when they put out to sea'.[53] Bunting seized on the metaphor with a vengeance:

> The Methodist missionary ship is one, among others of the grand fleet, by which it is intended to carry to the ends of the earth the blessings of the Gospel; that this ship, like the rest, must be manned, freighted, and provisioned for the voyage; and that our most strenuous efforts and those of our friends are necessary to fit it for the sea, and to prepare it for the service on which it is destined to proceed.

Other denominations are particularly concerned for their own respective ships; and we must particularly care for ours.[54]

The financing of Methodist missions, as with the issue of control over the Sunday schools, was part of a much wider denominational self-awareness, which, as much as class-consciousness, is one of the great themes of British social history in the first quarter of the nineteenth century. What they each have in common is that the breakup of the old social controls in Church and State inexorably produced new attempts to impose discipline and control. Both the old ideal of an organic society and the evangelical attempt to Christianize the people on a shared religious basis fell victim to the structural pressures of class conflict and denominational competition. In fact the former partly supplied the dynamic for the latter.

It has been suggested that the Methodist enthusiasm for financing foreign missions in 1813–15 was part of a much wider missionary mania in British society stimulated by the demise of Napoleon, the growth of patriotism, the cultivation of an imperial mission of Christianity and civilization, and the influence of evangelicalism on all the major British denominations.[55] In the case of Methodism the argument has been taken one step further in the suggestion that the real motivation behind the formation of the new district missionary societies in the north of England was a self-conscious attempt to shift the energies of evangelical Arminianism away from the evangelization of the urban proletariat (because it was by then regarded as too dangerous) towards a new emphasis on the conversion of heathens abroad.[56] This interpretation is inherently implausible, not only because the connexion had devised any number of strategies to control the style and content of the domestic mission, but also because most of those involved in the establishment of Methodist missionary societies thought that domestic and foreign missions were not mutually exclusive but mutually reinforcing. Bunting wrote that

> I do not believe that Missionary exertions will lessen our home-resources. Zeal, once kindled, will burn in every direction at once. The pains taken in Missionary Meetings to evince the value & necessity of a Christian Ministry & of Christian Ordinances will shew our people *their own privileges*, as well as the wants of others. They will estimate the Gospel more highly, & of consequence be more ready to support it. Besides on the new plan, a large proportion of the Mission Fund will be raised among persons not in Society, & even among persons who are not so much as stated Hearers. This will set us more at liberty in our applications to our own members for our own particular collections. In Leeds, we have a private regulation, that no Leader shall allow a member to subscribe to the Missions, unless such Member previously subscribe to the Class-Money; & some have actually begun to pay class-

money, in order to purchase the privilege of giving an additional penny per week to the Missions.[57]

It is difficult to know what exactly lies beneath the surface of this letter. Much of it was devoted to a nationwide scheme for reordering Methodist finances to meet the needs of preachers and their families, but Bunting also commented positively on the remarkable folk revivals in Redruth.[58] It is nevertheless clear from his correspondence in the wake of Luddism at home and British military victories abroad that Bunting's vision for the future development of Methodism had less to do with the striking revivals in Cornwall and in the Durham coalfields and more with a financially stable and well-supplied federation of imposing chapels which would save the respectable at home and then finance the Christianization of the peoples of the Empire. Thus, a few months after the founding of the first Methodist missionary society, Bunting opened a subscription account for a splendid new chapel also in Leeds, 'and the contributions – not solicited, but voluntarily offered – already exceed our hopes. The missionary business has taught the poorer and middling classes the dignity and privileges of giving'.[59] Clearly the era of cottage meetings was beginning to give way to the building of great preaching houses in the towns and cities of industrializing England. The erection of a new chapel in Hull, for example, persuaded Bunting that it had inaugurated

a sort of new era in Methodism, and to have given it an impulse, a publicity, and a popularity such as it never had before. The very largeness of the chapel excited curiosity; and curiosity, there is reason to hope, will be so over-ruled in numerous instances, as to terminate in the production of genuine piety.[60]

Here was a philosophy of expansion far removed from the band-room revivalism of Macclesfield and Manchester at the turn of the century. Mechanics were giving way to mahogany.

Bunting's 'new era in Methodism' required the financial resources not only to build the chapels, but also to sustain the preachers and their families. The task ahead was formidable. The root of the problem was that Wesleyan itinerant preachers were paid expenses instead of a stipend or salary. This was remarkably cost-effective, as Wesley had found, when infused by moral excellence, generous hospitality and, preferably, celibacy, but it was virtually index-linked to the growing aspirations of many preachers. Wives, children and appropriate accommodation were all expensive, and the rise in Methodist membership did not keep pace with the rise in expenditure. The problem became even more acute during the post-war price deflation when Methodist chapel debts became more difficult to finance. The inevitable result of these financial pressures was more frequent appeals for help to the beleaguered membership. Responding to news of yet another new collection, one preacher told Bunting that they already had 155 collections each year:

> Was there ever such a begging system in existence before? Almost *every other day* we have our hands in the pockets of our people. . . . You speak of *prudent retrenchment of expenditure* – where will you begin? You have 181,710 members – 736 preachers, 400 wives = 1137 persons besides children to provide, for: so that you have 159 members to each person, which at one pence per week &c. is 66. 5. 0. Here then is the *core* of your embarrassments and I maintain that you ought either to have 50,000 more members, or 50 preachers and 50 wives less: but as the latter is impracticable, and to realise the former is a work of time; we must remain in *statu quo*, till the *decrease* of preachers and the *increase* of members come to a sort of par.[61]

This angry epistle finished with some downbeat comments on a 'mechanically produced' revival in the York circuit, the 'noise and nonsense' of which has increased the 'number of the lowest order, and driven many respectable people from our chapel. And numbers are all we have to boast of, for our money matters are little improved'. There could be no better delineation of the pecuniary advantages accruing to the Methodist system through the recruitment of the respectable at the expense of the disreputable.

If Bunting's correspondence, both incoming and outgoing, is littered with suggestions about how to make the connexion pay for itself, there is an equally luxuriant literature on the inexorable growth of a high concept of the pastoral office within Wesleyanism. Natural disposition, first-hand experience of the ranters, the lack of an available Methodist theology with which to fight the Calvinists and the threat to the Methodist itinerancy posed by Sidmouth, all persuaded Bunting of the need for a more educated and disciplined Methodist ministry. Indeed, his opinions were beginning to be formed at a surprisingly early stage in his ministry. When in London in 1804, for example, he informed a quarterly meeting that he would not submit himself to any evaluation of his ministry except by his 'peers', and while he was stationed in Manchester in 1807 he imitated the old Puritan tradition of the 'prophesyings' by gathering the preachers together to preach and discuss sermons.[62] Bunting was therefore a stout defender of the powers of the annual conference and of the legal hundred long before his own suggested change in the rules of composition allowed him access to both.[63] The growth of a high view of the pastoral office was resented equally by the metropolitan lay elite gathered around Allan and Butterworth, who regarded the Conference as a 'Court of the Star Chamber',[64] and those free spirits within the connexion who held fast to the doctrine of the priesthood of all believers. One such was Daniel Isaac who was censured by the Conference in 1816 for his book, *An Investigation of*

Ecclesiastical Claims, in which he repudiated the 'nonsense' that 'priests are a distinct body of men, specially designated by heaven to their holy employment, and solemnly set apart to it'. Rather, the best way of promoting vital religion and banishing error was to 'let the pulpit be open to all'.[65] In an almost prophetical preview of some of the issues which afflicted Bunting and Methodism in a more serious fashion over the Fly Sheets controversy in 1849, Isaac alleged that Conference, under Bunting's prodding, had convicted him without a trial on the spurious grounds that his book was a species of ecclesiastical Jacobinism which would call down the wrath of the government on the entire connexion. Isaac denied the allegation of Jacobinism by stating that he had waged an even more unrelenting war against the secret brotherhoods of the Durham miners than Bunting himself had fought against the Luddites.[66] It was clear, however, that the issue at stake was not about social and political radicalism, but about the nature of the Wesleyan ministry and the power of the pastoral office.[67] Bunting displayed in this case, as he was so singularly to demonstrate in other cases in the period 1820–50, a remarkable tenacity of purpose and an unwavering belief in the correctness of his own opinions. Whatever else one might say about him, he was certainly not a man to be trifled with.

By the time Bunting, at the remarkably early age of forty-one, accepted the signal honour of the Presidency of the gerontocratic Methodist Conference in 1820, both his principles and his influence throughout the connexion were already well in place. At a time when Methodism (just after Wesley's death) was almost without government, Bunting was the first preacher of stature to combine a clear vision of how the connexion should move forward with the administrative skills it so patently required. His correspondence reveals him to have been a perfectionist who liked to be in control, whether of his wife's frivolity or the connexion's alleged indiscipline. He was a remorseless editor of other people's work, a stern critic of other people's sermons and an unflinching opponent of other people's versions of the Wesleyan legacy. He also found it hard to forgive or forget his own mistakes. He was not an unfeeling man, as his reaction to his young daughter's death makes clear, but, over time, he learned to subject tender emotion to the disciplines of earnest religion and rigorous piety. Methodism was similarly subjected. As with many churchmen who grew up in the shadows of the French and Industrial Revolutions, European warfare and popular radicalism, Bunting worked out his ideas under cover from the most intense of spotlights. Once his opinions were fixed, they were not easily changed. He put his faith in a vision of Methodism as a federation of chapels, serviced by a well-instructed ministry and paid for by a pious and respectable laity. Connexional discipline and administrative efficiency were the means by which the vision was to be realized. In this way the old uniformity required by the post-Reformation Established Church was reimposed by a free church on its own voluntary adherents. The only option available for those with an alternative interpretation of the Wesleyan legacy was to fight both Bunting's vision and the structures set up for its accomplishment. The age of disunity was just around the corner.

6

THOMAS ALLAN AND METHODIST POLITICS, 1790–1840[1]

I wish that you would write a short history of all your proceedings in obtaining the New Toleration Act that it may be known to whose exertions the Methodists and Dissenters are indebted for so great an extent of their religious privileges. . . . It might be a history of the political opinions of the Methodists at the present time and of their attachment to Government, and might operate as a powerful example to their successors.[2]

Thomas Thompson, MP for Midhurst 1807–18 and a Methodist local preacher, made this suggestion to Thomas Allan, the London-based connexional solicitor, in August 1812. Allan was too discreet to attempt such a work and since historians often undervalue those who undervalue themselves, his role in the development of Methodist political opinions has been largely ignored. Described as a 'man forgotten by history' by the only historian who has not forgotten him,[3] Thomas Allan is revealed by his papers to have been the most important layman in the connexion in the critical years between 1800 and 1830.[4] Not only was he responsible for drafting trust deeds in a prolific period of Methodist chapel building, but he was expert at interpreting the complexities of post-Restoration ecclesiastical legislation as they affected the operation of the Methodist system. The Methodists had established a committee for guarding their privileges in 1803, but they needed someone schooled in the thought of Locke and Blackstone to tell them what those privileges actually were. Fortunately, Allan left behind an immense collection of private correspondence which sheds new light on the Methodist response to Lord Sidmouth's Bill in 1811, to the campaign for Catholic Emancipation from 1812 to 1829 and to the pressure from English popular radicalism, particularly in the volatile Peterloo years. In addition, there is valuable information on the tensions within Methodism, especially between preachers and laymen, as the movement became more denominationally self-conscious in the half century after Wesley's death.

The Conference appointed Allan as general solicitor for the connexion in 1803 and he was soon pressed into service to protect Methodist rights in the West Indies.[5] Seven years later, the dangers were nearer home and Allan wrote to Jabez Bunting asking the Conference to review four major areas of Methodist policy: the financing and administration of missions (only a third of the money given for this purpose was allocated to foreign missionaries), the selection and training of preachers, the spiritual instruction of Methodist children and the Methodist response to certain legislative proposals.

> Lord Sidmouth may possibly bring forward some motion before next conference which may have for its object the checking of the progress of itinerancy. The question then is supposing he should what must be the line of conduct of the Methodists? How are they to oppose Lord Sidmouth? – publicly or privately? By petition and to whom? Who are to be the active agents? The Committee of Privileges or who? If the Committee, what instructions are they to have and upon what principles are they to proceed? Are the Methodists to call themselves Churchmen or Dissenters or neither? Are they to unite with other sects who may petition and how far are they to co-operate? All these are serious questions.[6]

With the first major political conflict in sight, Allan was keen to conduct Methodist opposition on principles that accurately reflected the Wesleyans' distinctive position in English society. In this way 'conflict was forcing new denominational organisation into being'.[7]

In the summer of 1809 Lord Sidmouth was approached by the Bishops of Gloucester and Durham to consider changing the law with respect to the licensing of Protestant dissenting ministers. According to them, the legal requirements of the 1689 Act of Toleration were no longer adequate to deal with 'modern sectaries' who 'assembled in barns, in rooms of private houses, or in other buildings of the most improper kind, to hear the wild effusions of a mechanic or a ploughboy, perhaps not more than 15 years of age'.[8] What lurked behind the horror stories that reached Sidmouth was the feeling that the Church of England's manoeuvrability was hampered by the legislature at a time when dissenters were subject to few restrictions. Sidmouth and his Anglican supporters feared that the religious and political pillars of the state would both be undermined if the new ranters were not controlled. They realized, however, that little could be achieved without the support of the dissenters themselves, particularly the Methodists, whose system was based on an itinerant ministry and a plentiful supply of local preachers. In April 1811 Sidmouth opened negotiations with two leading Methodists, Thomas Coke, who always flattered those more important than himself, and Adam Clarke, who combined massive theological learning with immense political naivety. Sidmouth convinced them that it was in Methodism's best interest to support a measure designed to protect the respectable by eliminating the disreputable.[9] So it was with cautious optimism that Sidmouth presented his Bill to the House of Lords for its first reading on 9 May. The aim was to limit the supply of preaching certificates by insisting that every dissenting minister be attached to a specific congregation, and by stating that each preacher needed written recommendations from several 'substantial and reputable householders belonging to the said congregation'. If these conditions were met, then Justices of the Peace were legally obliged to issue a certificate. In introducing the Bill, Sidmouth stated that it was not his desire to 'cast any imputation upon the orders and classes of men', but there were persons claiming certificates 'who were cobblers, tailors, pig-drovers, and chimney-sweepers'.[10] This comment brought a bemused smile to Lord Holland's face and was seized upon by dissenters whose congregations consisted of such 'undesirables'.

Meanwhile, there were signs that Methodist laymen were mobilizing opposition to Sidmouth's proposals. Joseph Butterworth, a founder member of the Committee of Privileges and MP for Coventry 1812–18 and for Dover 1820–6, summoned Allan to an urgent meeting with himself, Adam Clarke and Walter Griffith to discuss the Bill.[11] As a result, a 'meeting of the general committee of the societies of the late Rev. John Wesley' was convened for 14 May. Although twelve resolutions were passed, there were three main reasons for the new Methodist hostility: Sidmouth's Bill would destroy the preaching pattern which Wesley established; many Methodists were simply unwilling to apply for licences under the epithet dissenter; and they feared they would be exposed to penalties under the Conventicle Act.[12] Armed with these resolutions, a deputation called on Sidmouth, but he refused to withdraw the Bill. Adam Clarke gave meagre consolation to Sidmouth for this Wesleyan change of heart by informing him that the real fire-power was coming from Methodist laymen, and by presenting him with Clarke's commentary on Genesis, which somehow illustrated 'the pure doctrines of the Church of England and the sound principles of the British constitution'.[13] Nothing could more clearly highlight the consequences of establishment pressure on the Wesleyan leadership in the Napoleonic period.

With Methodist policy more clearly defined, it was left to Allan to organize an effective opposition. On 15 May, Allan attended a meeting of dissenters at the London Tavern and, along with Butterworth and Benson, was elected to the committee responsible for whipping up dissenting opposition. Although the Methodists co-operated with dissenters, they cautiously preserved a separate identity and organizational structure. With the Committee of Privileges in continual session, Allan sent a copy of the Methodist resolutions to each member of the House of Lords, solicited the particular help of Lord Erskine[14] and sent messengers into the regions armed with petitions. By this stage, the localities needed little stimulation. John Ward, a Durham Methodist solicitor who felt that the Methodists had dragged their heels over this issue, promised the support of Lord Holland and six members of the House of Commons.[15] Jabez Bunting marshalled the Wesleyans in the Manchester and Liverpool districts. By noon on Tuesday, 21 May, the date of the second reading of Sidmouth's Bill, Allan was able to present Lord Erskine with 250 petitions containing over 30,000 signatures.

The debate in the House of Lords was something of an anticlimax, because the government and the Church had already deserted Sidmouth due to the intensity of opposition in the country. Still unwilling to retreat, Sidmouth's main tack was that the dissenters opposed his Bill because they did not understand it, an argument that did not impress Lord Holland, who stated that 'it was no light matter to tell that numerous class of persons, called Dissenters, that they were so stupid as not to understand acts of parliament that related to their own concerns'.[16] The Bill was lost without a division and Allan wrote appreciative letters to all the Whig peers who had spoken for the dissenting interest.[17]

The defeat of the Bill was not the end of the matter, because Allan soon discovered that justices at Quarter Sessions were behaving as if the Bill had become law. Allan compiled notes from all over the country of Quarter Sessions which refused to administer oaths in accordance with the Toleration Act.[18] Supporters of the Church in the localities were achieving in practice what had eluded Sidmouth in theory. Allan recognized that the administration of the law in English localities could not be changed overnight, so his main objective was to secure parliamentary legislation to give more protection to Methodist itinerants. With most preachers unable to cope with the legal technicalities of the English constitution, Allan was now at the peak of his influence within the connexion. At the beginning of 1812 he scribbled down a list of priorities: see Perceval, organize petitions and collections, be temperate in all correspondence, moderate the feelings of our members and excite their patriotism.[19] On 15 February, Allan requested a personal interview with Perceval about the state of the law on religious toleration, pointing out to him that

> if the law were to remain as it is now construed to be, the enforcing of the penalties of the Conventicle and other antiquated acts of a similar nature would deprive thousands of His Majesty's loyal subjects of their Property and of their personal liberty.[20]

Allan prepared notes for a one-hour lecture to Perceval on the nature of Methodism and its contribution to English society:

> 2. That Mr. Wesley *never intended* to form a *distinct sect* but merely to do good among the *existing denominations* of Christians but chiefly in the Church of England. Hence members of our Society consider

themselves as members of the Establishment and do not choose to rank with Dissenters. . . .

9. [On Methodism having no truck with seditious preaching.] We do not pretend to say that we could vouch for every individual but we expel the bad when found out, and our discipline is very strict. . . .

12. In times of scarcity and distress we may safely say that among colliers, miners and mechanics, Methodism has been the grand instrument of preserving subordination, and if governments were but acquainted with the happy effects of Methodism both in England and *Ireland* they would do their utmost to protect rather than discourage them. . . .

13. That we are not a political people, we simply wish to worship God and promote Christianity in the land by all means, and have been the steady friends of government. . . .

14. We conceive that the late conduct of the Magistrates is subversive of the principles of the Constitution as established at the Revolution.[21]

Allan's portrayal of Methodism as Anglican in sympathy, Protestant in character and disciplined in ecclesiastical organization, together with his assertions that Methodism was both the sustainer of a stable social order and the beneficiary of the religious liberality of the Glorious Revolution, shows how legal pressures forced Methodism into a conservative posture in order to obtain a liberal measure. With an appropriate mixture of sympathy and caution, Perceval urged the Methodists to wait for Ellenborough's judgement in a test case brought before the King's Bench. Allan then asked Perceval if the government would sponsor a relief measure should Ellenborough's decision go against the Methodists. Perceval dodged the question, but he assured Allan that the government had no desire to persecute religious societies friendly to the established order.[22]

At this stage, the Methodist solicitor tried to control Wesleyan action in the provinces so that he could continue in the role of honest broker in his dealings with government. On 24 February he wrote a letter, with the approval of the Committee of Privileges, to every circuit superintendent in the country, asking them to refrain from publishing or petitioning until authorized by the committee. This attempt by a metropolitan committee to establish connexional uniformity was new, and it was resented by some. In the midst of much rhetoric about the 'Jacobinical assertion of inalienable rights', John Ward told Allan that he would continue to do what he liked.[23] In April 1812 Perceval informed the Methodists that, after discussing the matter in the cabinet, he was prepared to support 'an application to Parliament for the purpose of affording relief'.[24] The case at King's Bench was still causing delay, but after Ellenborough presented his inconclusive judgement on 6 May, Allan drafted a suitable Toleration Bill.[25] At this crucial stage in the negotiations Perceval was assassinated, and Allan transferred his attention to Lord Liverpool, with whom he communicated at weekly intervals throughout June and July.[26] The result was the passage of a new Toleration Act on 29 July 1812. The Five Mile Act and the Conventicle Act were repealed,[27] magistrates were compelled to administer the oaths to those who asked to take them, and the law protected itself against abuse by stating that exemption from military and civic duties could only be claimed by ministers without any other calling but that of schoolmaster. The act was a personal triumph for Allan, who secured all his objectives without alienating any major section of English opinion, except the High Church die-hards. In the victory letter sent out by the Committee of Privileges, Allan thanked Liverpool and his cabinet, the Archbishop of Canterbury, Lord Holland and other Whig peers, Wilberforce and the Saints, the Protestant Society for the Protection of Religious Liberty (dissenters) and even the Quakers.[28] It seemed that the Methodists had never enjoyed such a respectable position in English society. However, there was another side to the story. The years 1811–12 saw an increase of tension between preachers and laymen, and between the metropolis and the localities. In addition, the perceptive could see that the Methodists, while posing as friends of the Church of England, had campaigned with the whole host of Protestant Dissent, and that their crusade for religious liberty was a cloak for self-interest. Representatives of radical opinion, including Cobbett, were not taken in.[29]

Nevertheless, the importance of the events of 1811–12 should not be underestimated, for the Toleration Act of 1812 marked an important watershed in the religious history of Britain some two decades before the more familiar changes of 1828–9. The Act established new principles as well as new practices. These were the inalienable right of every person to worship God according to conscience, the right of every person to hear and teach Christian truths without restraint from the civil magistrates or the licence of the crowd and the recognition that no one had the right to disturb the peace or escape from civic responsibilities under the pretence of teaching religion. Thus, despite pressure from Anglican bishops and Tory constitutionists, the English state was prepared to accommodate rivals to the Church of England in return for a more stable social order. Ironically, then, toleration was secured by political pragmatism and liberalism was the unintended beneficiary of religious enthusiasm.

Two things in particular stood out from the toleration debate. The political and religious establishment had neither the will nor the ability to squash the new Dissent, and the Methodists were forced to recognize that their preaching privileges depended upon their loyalty and good order in a period of radical ferment. This theme dominated the printed circulars and private discussions of the Committee of Privileges in the years 1812–19. This material is worth reproducing in some detail, not only for the support it gives to the traditional Halévy interpretation of Methodist history, but also because some of it is based upon a source which has not been used before and might conceivably never be used again.[30]

As soon as it became clear that Allan's Toleration Bill was secured, the Wesleyan conference of preachers sent out a circular to all members of Methodist societies. They were clearly worried about the effects of popular radicalism on the northern circuits:

> We, therefore, as faithful Ministers, cannot refrain from sounding a solemn alarm, lest any of our dear people should be drawn away by the dissimulation of evil-disposed men. We proclaim loudly and earnestly, 'Fear the Lord and the King: and meddle not with them that are given to change. Avoid them.'[31]

In 1817, the Committee of Privileges sent out a letter to meet the rising tide of radicalism after the Napoleonic Wars:

> It is with pleasure that the committee recognize the uniform attachment, shown by the Methodist societies at large, to the person of the monarch, and the constitution of the country; and they recollect how, at different critical and unquiet former periods, they have maintained a peaceable demeanour, and filled up the civil, social and religious duties of life, in the most exemplary manner. But in the present season of unparalleled distress they feel anxious to prevent every member of the Methodist society from being misled by the delusive arts of designing men; and to guard them in the most solemn manner against attending tumultuous assemblies; joining themselves by oath, or otherwise, to illegal political societies, and engaging in any projects, contrary to the duties of true Christians and loyal subjects.[32]

Naturally, not everyone obeyed the dictates of a metropolitan committee, and at a meeting in January 1818

> Mr Watson stated that much obloquy had been lately thrown upon our connexion respecting our political principles which it appeared necessary to repel. Agreed to write to the preachers who were at Derby, Belper, Cromford, Nottingham, Bury and Bolton last year to obtain from them accounts of the state of the societies in those places and of the conduct of the preachers relative to public affairs at the time of the late trouble which agitated the country. . . . [33]

The pressure from political radicalism was forcing the Wesleyan preachers to act as agents of social control, a task for which they received stimulation and support from the Committee of Privileges. The crucial year was 1819, when Peterloo forced political and religious establishments to take a more determined stand against working-class radicalism. Using expulsion as the ultimate weapon, Methodist circuit superintendents stood firm throughout 1819, despite radical-inspired rumours that they were in government pay. At Peterloo, Wesleyan conservatives were well served by 'the Manchester Methodist plutocracy',[34] who expelled working-class radicals with ruthless enthusiasm. However, the most revealing case of Methodist discipline in action took place across the Pennines in the North Shields circuit.

Shortly after Peterloo, William H. Stephenson, a teacher at Burton Colliery school and a Methodist local preacher, spoke out against the behaviour of the Manchester magistrates at a huge protest meeting in Newcastle. 'Most of the Travelling Preachers and respectable friends' in the area were offended by Stephenson's speech, and they urged his circuit superintendent, Robert Pilter, to strike him off the local preaching plan.[35] Unfortunately for Pilter, Stephenson refused to go quietly. He told his circuit superintendent that, since three-quarters of local Methodists were radical reformers, his expulsion would create havoc within the connexion. Pilter was sufficiently impressed by this threat to fix a district trial for Stephenson on 22 October, and, in the meantime, he wrote anxious letters to Jonathan Crowther, President of the Conference, and to Jabez Bunting. Crowther was unwilling to let politics become an issue of connexional conflict, especially since Kilhamites and ranters were prepared to welcome Wesleyan rejects. He recommended that Stephenson should be admonished, and warned about his future conduct. The subsequent trial was a model of those traditional English 'virtues' of freedom of speech, fairness and irresolution. The discussion of abstract politics was forbidden; the issue at stake was whether Stephenson was justified in attending and speaking at a radical meeting. The verdict went against the local preacher and he was asked to promise that he would never attend another public meeting. Stephenson refused on the grounds that a free-born Englishman could promise no such thing, and the meeting was adjourned until 5 November.

While the North Shields circuit agonized over their recalcitrant brother, the important decisions were being taken elsewhere, because the Stephenson case was taken directly to the Committee of Privileges in London by Jabez Bunting. Ironically, the committee met on the same day as Stephenson's first trial and it passed two resolutions:

> 1. That, under all the circumstances of the case, and considering the peculiar character of the Political Assembly lately held at Newcastle, this committee are of opinion, that it was highly improper that any Member of our Body should take any part in such a meeting, and much more so, that he should officiate as a Speaker; and that we think that any person who has thus acted should be immediately suspended from all public employment among us as a Local Preacher

or Class Leader, and should not even be allowed to be a Member of our Society, unless he promise to abstain from such conduct in future.

2. That it is the opinion of this committee that no persons who are enrolled as members of those dangerous Private Political Associations which are now prevalent in the Disturbed Districts of our Country, should be allowed to be Members of our Society, because, without adverting to the legal and political objections against such Associations it is, on Christian grounds, obviously improper for Members of a Religious Society to expose themselves to such scenes of temptation and turbulence.[36]

Although provoked into action by the Stephenson case, the Committee of Privileges received so much information about Methodist participation in radical meetings that it decided to issue a statement to all Wesleyan congregations. A subcommittee drafted the resolutions on 26 October and they were finally published on 12 November. Although this task was undertaken by Thomas Allan, he claimed in a letter to his son that 'the Resolutions are not mine. I approve of them as far as they go. I wanted something more terse and specific about reform which is the bewitching word'.[37] One can only speculate that since Bunting brought the matter before the committee, he was instrumental in preparing the final statement. Whoever was responsible, the first and most important resolution reiterated Allan's stance over Sidmouth's Bill:

1. That Christian Communities, who claim at the hands of the Civil Government the undisturbed and legalized enjoyment of their Religious Liberties, are bound to evince, by their loyalty, that they deserve the Privileges which they *demand*; because Rights and Duties are reciprocal, and the Government that affords us protection is entitled to our constitutional subjection and support.[38]

Robert Pilter was armed with the October resolutions of the Committee of Privileges when Stephenson was tried for the second time. Stephenson's colleagues relied upon his honour (no pledge was extracted) 'that he would not in future act against the declared opinion of his Brethren', and they voted seven to four against striking him off the local preaching plan. Pilter nervously and foolishly communicated the decision to Bunting, who took it straight back to the London committee. It was resolved

that Mr. Stephenson should be immediately suspended from the local Preacher's Plan, and from all official duties in the Methodist Connexion and also, that unless he unequivocally pledge himself to abstain from taking part in the public and private meetings of what are denominated the Radical Reformers, he be forthwith expelled from the Methodist Society.[39]

Stephenson was finally dislodged, not by his preaching colleagues in South Shields but by a metropolitan committee in which Bunting and Allan played leading roles. The decision had disastrous consequences for the Wesleyans in the Newcastle area, because fourteen Independent Methodist chapels were established within a year. But more than that, the Stephenson case illustrated the inner tensions within Methodism between London and the localities, between itinerant preachers and laymen, and between conservatives and reformers. The official Wesleyan statements of 1819 made it crystal clear to the working classes in the manufacturing districts that they could be politically active radicals or Methodists, but not both. Unsurprisingly, the serious decrease of Methodist membership in 1820 was not surpassed until the troubled year of 1851, and W. R. Ward has boldly stated 'that Peterloo had for ever severed official Methodism from urban revivalism'.[40]

The relationship between Methodism and political radicalism has provoked much controversy and considerable historical ingenuity,[41] but in the midst of all this the important points have not been made with sufficient clarity. Dickinson has suggested that the destruction of property in the Gordon Riots, the wave of patriotism resulting from the War of American Independence and the popular radicalism of the French Revolution stimulated a conservative ideological defence of the British Constitution. The basis of this defence was the belief that government was ordained by God and that constitutional liberty and Christian freedom were dependent on the law. Since the law guaranteed the protection of private property, conservative theorists could fuse the twin elements of liberty and property and sanction them with divine approval along with liberal helpings of prescription and pragmatism.[42] In contrast, the radicals constructed their ideas from the platform of natural rights, thereby posing a threat as much moral and religious as it was political and constitutional.

This is the point that emerges most clearly from the Methodist resolutions drafted by Thomas Allan in October 1819. Burke's footprints are everywhere:

4. It is the duty of the Methodist Societies to unite with their fellow-subjects of other denominations in every proper and lawful demonstration of attachment to our free Constitution, and of loyalty to our venerable Sovereign – in upholding, by every means in their power, the authority of the Laws by which we are governed – and in discountenancing and repressing all infidel and blasphemous publications, as well as all tumultuous, inflammatory, or seditious proceedings.

6. This committee expresses disapprobation of certain tumultuous assemblies, in which large masses of people have been irregularly collected, . . . of persons not resident in the places where such

meetings have been held, and calculated, both from the infidel principles, the wild and extravagant political theories, and the violent and inflammatory declamations, of those who have appeared as Leaders on such occasions, not to afford the opportunity of public deliberation, nor to effect any object of political utility, but to bring all governments into contempt, and to introduce universal discontent, insubordination, and anarchy.[43]

It is not so much the political objectives of the radicals that are rejected in Allan's resolution (in fact they are never mentioned), as their theory, theology, morality and methods. Radical ideology was regarded as by definition irreligious and immoral, that is why there could be no compromise.

Some historians have given the label Wesleyan Toryism to the views propagated by Allan and his colleagues on the Committee of Privileges in the Peterloo years.[44] In fact, these views were neither peculiarly Wesleyan nor specifically Tory. They were nothing more than a general affection for monarchy, loyalty and order, or, as John Walsh suggests, 'a manifestation of that political quietism and passive obedience which has frequently been a traditional mark of Christian political thinking since the days of the early Church'.[45] There is no evidence that Methodists were particularly interested in the complex political issues relating to king and cabinet, war policy, Irish affairs, economic strategy and party disagreements which exercised the minds of the professional politicians. Only when religious matters surfaced, as in 1811 over toleration, were the Methodists politically involved, and, ironically, they ran to the Whig peers. A general Wesleyan conservatism in the period 1790–1820 was only converted into Wesleyan Toryism in the period 1830–50 by the re-emergence of religion as a major element in party divisions for the first time since Anne's reign.[46] What made the politics of the Methodist leadership in the Peterloo years so corrosive was the degree of uniformity required, the zeal with which discipline was maintained and the way in which the Methodist system was itself cranked into operation by a clerical and metropolitan elite against the aspirations of quite substantial numbers of rank-and-file Methodists. Methodism, it seemed, had gone ecclesiastical.

Thomas Allan had taken his stand against political radicalism on the twin foundations of adherence to the British constitution and a conviction, formed by his negotiations with cabinet ministers in 1811–12, that Methodist preaching privileges depended on good behaviour. This regard for the Protestant constitution and religious liberty led Allan into the next phase of his political activity, for, if he was willing to exploit the spirit of the Act of Toleration on behalf of Protestant nonconformists, he was equally willing to ensure that Roman Catholics derived no benefits beyond mere toleration. Allan outlined the ideological basis of his opposition to Catholic

Emancipation in two pamphlets published in 1813; one was addressed to a Protestant dissenter and the other was a reply to Charles Butler's *Address to the Protestants of Great Britain and Ireland*.[47] Allan quoted Locke, Blackstone and Mansfield on toleration with approval, and drew a distinction between the right to enjoy religious freedom and the right to exercise political power:

> I therefore shall deny that the Roman Catholics, or any other class of men, have *any natural right to govern*. They, and all other men in a state of society, have a *natural right* to the free and peaceable enjoyment of their religion, and the full and free use of their mental and physical powers in the accumulation and alienation of property, whether in agricultural, commercial, mechanical, or professional pursuits, but to Govern, either supremely or subordinately, is not a natural right.[48]

Although, in public, Allan wrote in the manner of an eighteenth-century constitutional lawyer, in private he was concerned about the probable effect of Catholic Emancipation on the evangelical missionary crusade, especially in Ireland. In December 1812 Allan wrote to Butterworth about the possibility of soliciting dissenting help against Catholic Emancipation, but

> If nothing can be done I apprehend that we should have a meeting of our own Brethren and let them see how our Friends in Ireland are situated and how they are likely to fare when this wicked plot, contrived and supported by both wicked and infatuated men, shall have been fully executed. One consequence will be an end to Methodism in Ireland. Are not the Methodists in England to take care of this *privilege* of preaching the Gospel in Ireland?[49]

After careful consideration, the Committee of Privileges decided against coming forward 'as a body' to oppose Catholic Emancipation lest it should provoke retaliatory persecution in Ireland.[50]

With this avenue closed, Allan helped form the interdenominational Protestant Union in January 1813, for which he became chief publicist. For the next sixteen years his correspondence is riddled with draft resolutions, printed circulars and private letters on the subject of Catholic Emancipation, particularly in the crisis years of 1819, 1821 and 1825–9. During this period Allan did not pressurize the Committee of Privileges to take a connexional stand on the Catholic issue; rather he was content to operate through interdenominational agencies. The denouement came in 1829, and the role played by Wesleyan Methodism has exercised the minds of various historians. The basic problem to be resolved is why a notoriously anti-Catholic denomination did not take a more active part in the agitation against Catholic Emancipation.

As with all the controversial aspects of Methodist history, it seems, the debate was started by Halévy, who argued that the Wesleyans had no opportunity of making any official pronouncement on Catholic Emancipation because the Bill was rushed through parliament in the interval between two annual conferences.[51] This unlikely interpretation was well demolished by John Kent, who showed that the Wesleyans did not use the Conference for political purposes because they had at their disposal a smaller and more discreet body for political action, the Committee of Privileges.[52] In any case, why should the government fear the opposition of a dissenting body when it had already set out without the full support of the Established Church? In fact, Kent discovered that the Committee of Privileges did meet to consider Catholic Emancipation in 1829. His evidence came from two main sources, *A Memoir of the Reverend Joseph Entwistle*, by his son, and *Recollections of my own Life and Times*, by Thomas Jackson. Jackson stated that Adam Clarke joined with several other ministers and laymen to convene a meeting of the Committee of Privileges in mid-March 1829. Jabez Bunting, who was President of the Conference and a known supporter of Catholic Emancipation, was not informed of the meeting. This is Jackson's account of what happened:

> Dr Bunting, who was then stationed in Manchester, received intelligence of this meeting, and in the midst of its deliberations, unexpectedly appeared, asking for what purpose the Committee had been called together. On being informed, he said that the Committee had no authority to meet for any such purpose; and that, if it should pass any resolution in opposition to the Catholic claims, or propose to send any petition to Parliament against the Bill which was then pending, he would inform the Government that the Committee was acting without authority, and would enter his protest against its proceeding in the public papers.[53]

Kent concluded that this evidence was satisfactory because Jackson 'normally acted in concert with Jabez Bunting and therefore, there can be no doubt ... that Bunting prevented action against the Government virtually single-handed'.

This interpretation needs further modification in the light of the Bunting and Allan correspondence. Thomas Allan convened a meeting of the Committee of Privileges on 13 February 1829 because he feared that a Bill before parliament for the suppression of the Catholic Association might also affect Methodist societies in Ireland.[54] This was a familiar problem for the Methodist lawyer. In 1819 he obtained assurances from Lord Liverpool that the Seditious Meetings Bill would not affect properly constituted Methodist meetings.[55] On this occasion Peel was equally obliging, although he refused to change the Bill in case Catholic lawyers exploited the loopholes. Allan's vested interest in discriminating repression gives an insight into Methodism's vulnerability in British society. He did not fear government intentions so much as the possible interpretations of legislation by local magistrates.

Four weeks after Allan's meeting with Peel, the Committee of Privileges met again, this time to consider the issue of Catholic Emancipation itself. Two letters written by Allan to his son, one before and one after the meeting, are crucial to a proper understanding of what took place. On 9 March he wrote:

> From a note I received from Lord Farnham I called and had a chat with him and Lady F. who are exceedingly anxious that the Methodists should appear. It was impossible for me to make any promises till it shall be gravely considered for which purpose we are to have a meeting of the Committee of Privileges on Wednesday next. I feel it a very difficult question how to advise the Methodists to proceed as a Body. However I hope we shall be directed for the best. I have also had some conversation with my old friend glorious John Lord Eldon who received me very kindly. I wanted to know whether a Peer could demand an audience of His M. and present a petition. He will inform me.[56]

Ten days later he wrote:

> On the 11th inst the Committee of Privileges met, but on considering the Bill it did not appear to me to affect the Methodists more than other protestants and therefore *as a Body* it would hardly be proper for them to move, especially as there might be some who would object. Indeed I have always thought that they should not act *as a Body* unless they were likely to suffer as such. We therefore unanimously resolved that 'with respect to the Bill for the Relief of His Majesty's Rom. Cath. subjects now before the House of Commons the Committee of Privileges do not think it their duty to take any proceedings in their collective capacity; but every member of the Methodist Societies will of course pursue such steps in his individual capacity on this occasion as he may conscientiously think right.' At our meeting I did not observe one person present in favour of the Cath. claims but Dr. Bunting. The letters received were without variation against them and I have no doubt that the Methodists generally throughout the country are aiding in the general exertions.[57]

This account, which is supported by John Mason, the secretary to the committee, has not the same tone of pique as Jackson's version.[58] In accepting Jackson's account, Kent placed too much emphasis on his harmonious relations with Bunting, when in fact there were frequent petty quarrels between the two men when Jackson was editor of the *Wesleyan*

Methodist Magazine.[59] What happened in 1829 was that Bunting held firmly to a position that he had already outlined in a private letter – 'we *as a body* never have petitioned *separately*; nor should we now on a question so decidedly political in its aspect'.[60] This view was accepted by the meeting, not because of his threats or the weakness of a 'caught out' committee, but because it was demonstrably right. Of course, it nettled some that, on this occasion, Bunting's advocacy of the old Wesleyan 'no politics' rule perfectly suited his own political convictions, but old campaigners like Allan accepted the committee's decision without protest. In over twenty years of agitation against Catholic Emancipation, Allan had never used the official Wesleyan machinery. Nonetheless, the 'no politics' rule, which originated in the relatively temperate political climate of the eighteenth century, when Methodism was a relatively powerless collection of religious societies within the womb of the Church of England, was becoming increasingly difficult to operate. The Wesleyans had now to ask themselves three fundamental questions about any political issue before taking action. Did it affect Methodist privileges? Was it a religious or a political matter? To what extent should individual Methodists be allowed to express political opinions in public meetings? The answers given by the Wesleyan leadership were not always appreciated by the rest of the connexion. For example, on what grounds of consistency were Methodist radicals officially ejected in 1819 for appearing on political platforms, when whole hosts of Methodist preachers, eulogized in the House of Lords by Eldon, spoke at political meetings in 1829 without censure?[61] Operating a 'no politics' rule clearly conferred considerable political power on its operators.

For the Wesleyans, Sidmouth's Bill had been relatively straightforward, the campaign against political radicalism marginally less so; but Catholic Emancipation was a preview of many issues in the 1830s and 1840s when the boundaries between religion and politics were difficult to define. This was particularly true of the conflict between Church and Dissent over the right to supply elementary education to the urban proletariat in industrial England. Moreover, as religious politics became more complicated, men with strong convictions and unquenchable zeal for dusting down the rule books were able to emerge in a more powerful position. Bunting was such a man.

Meanwhile, Allan's political importance within the connexion declined in inverse proportion to the rise of a more professional, self-conscious and institutionalized ministry. The connexional solicitor resented this development for more important reasons than mere self-interest. Underlying his many arguments with the itinerant preachers was an ideological dispute about the nature of Methodism itself. The conflict began as far back as 1795 when Alexander Kilham wrote a pamphlet entitled *The Progress of Liberty amongst the People called Methodists. To which is added the Out-Lines of a Constitution.*[62] Kilham accused the preachers of various irregularities, mostly of a financial nature, and drafted a constitution 'to prevent any preacher from acting contrary to the interests of the society'. He wanted more lay participation in all aspects of Methodist government including the annual conference. Kilham's writings provoked a storm of opposition from the preachers. Amidst amazing scenes of Jacobinical scaremongering he was duly expelled from the connexion in July 1796 and one year later the Methodist New Connexion was born.[63] Allan wrote to Kilham in February 1796, a few days before his first trial by the Newcastle District Meeting:

> The intelligence which your letter conveys is to me truly astonishing. I saw your first pamphlet and that some of the Preachers should be exasperated at it I do not wonder, but that they should endeavour to expel you from the connection for it creates in me no little surprise. How can it be proved that there is any thing in it worthy of expulsion? . . . The Methodists I have long thought have been strangely duped by what are called *leading men*.[64]

In conclusion he stated that 'I cordially believe numbers of your remarks on a Constitution are very just', and if the plan was followed 'a Church Government Glorious would succeed'. Allan's politics were too conservative for him to risk anything on Kilham's behalf, but he was aware, at an early stage, that the potential power of the preachers within the connexion threatened his ideal of a responsible and enthusiastic laity devoted to the saving of souls. Allan received a rude reminder of Methodist discipline in action in 1808 when he was struck off the official Committee of Privileges' list on the basis of an unsupported allegation by a preacher that he was a Kilhamite.[65] Allan's legal training enabled him to reply with some well-chosen words about the propriety of such a judicial system.

Unsurprisingly, Allan's relations with the preachers were at their worst when he reached the peak of his influence within the connexion during the second decade of the nineteenth century. This was in spite of their joint campaign to secure Methodist privileges and control radicalism. The most persistent source of irritation was a legal suit that Allan contested on behalf of the Wesleyans. When the Methodist New Connexion was formed in 1797, the majority of the trustees of Hockley Chapel in Nottingham supported Kilham and obtained possession of the chapel. (Kilham's remains were interred there in 1798.) The Wesleyans contended that trust deeds did not allow the transfer of chapels in this way since the original connexion possessed the legal right regardless of majorities. While involved in this suit, Allan resigned as connexional solicitor in protest against the preachers' treatment of him.[66] The London preachers refused to accept his resignation because he had been appointed not by them but by Conference, and the affair blew over until its reappearance in 1814, when, in order to make good the Wesleyan claim to Hockley Chapel, Allan asked to see the manuscript Conference Journal. Thomas Blanshard, the connexional book steward, replied that

> the preachers present at the meeting reconsidered the matter of the custody of the Conference Journal and are still of the opinion that they can go no further than to produce it when their cause requires it either for your inspection or of that of any other person whom you direct.[67]

Allan was incensed by the implication that he was needlessly prying into forbidden areas, and he poured out his soul in a series of draft replies. Once again he threatened resignation and stated that 'this is not the first time I have thus been treated when acting for the Methodists as a Body. Indeed I can scarcely remember any public business for the Preachers as a Body where . . .'. Here the draft comes to a timely end. Allan wrote that underlying this history of conflict was the fact 'that many of the Preachers entertain and have expressed great jealousies that the lay members of the Society may acquire too much power'.[68] There is no record of how this dispute was finally settled, but the Wesleyans regained control of Hockley Chapel in 1817 and Allan retained his position on the Committee of Privileges.

Allan's view of Methodism was the old primitive ideal of an evangelistic laity taking out the gospel to the lower strata of English society. Of course, itinerant preachers were necessary, but all his life he fought against the growth of a high view of the pastoral office and of the powers exercised by the preachers in their collective capacity as the Wesleyan Conference. In 1830 he wrote to the President, George Morley, recommending that influential preachers within the connexion should once again engage in outdoor preaching.[69] Four years later he wrote several letters to his son about the proposed Methodist theological institution:

> I quite agree with you about the Methodist Academy. In conscience I could not support it. . . . They seem to expect a large number at Conference. I wish they may have peace amongst themselves. But unquiet spirits will always make disturbances. It is a sad thing that they cannot go on quietly pursuing the old plan of merely bringing souls to God.

> I quite agree with you about the Methodist College and I am rather glad that the North London Circuit quarterly meeting had a long debate about it and are against the scheme. I do think it would not be unfit for Methodism in itself but that it would occasion divisions and heartburnings amongst the Preachers themselves.[70]

Allan's pessimistic prophecy was amply fulfilled a few days later at the annual conference in London, when Bunting and Dr Warren clashed over

125

the proposed institution and Warren led yet another secession from Wesleyan Methodism.[71]

By 1840 Allan was convinced (rightly according to recent statistics) that a century of rapid Methodist expansion was drawing to an end.[72] He wrote to Edmund Grindrod, Superintendent of the London Circuit, that 'it has long been obvious that the lower classes generally speaking will not attend our chapels', and 'I have long contemplated with great concern the want of energy and zeal in some of our congregations'.[73] His remedies were to rub the noses of the eager young theological students in the dirt of the London slums, to procure small mission houses in areas of densest population and to get the local preachers involved in tract distribution and door-to-door visitation. To Allan this plan had all the hallmarks of primitive Methodism: evangelistic zeal, lay participation, concern for the lower classes and pragmatism. The fact that both Allan and Bunting in their different ways could claim to be authentic guardians of virginal Methodism shows the classical ambivalence of the Wesleyan tradition. The main fact to emerge from Allan's conflict with the preachers, however, is that, from a conservative and Wesleyan viewpoint, he was as opposed to the growth of ministerial pretensions as were the working-class radicals. For obvious reasons this has not received as much attention from Methodist historians as it should have done.[74]

Allan's final contribution to the evolution of official Methodist political opinions came in 1839 when Russell outlined the Whig proposals for national elementary education to the House of Commons. After declaring the obvious need for more education in the country he said that

> Government had been unable either to adopt a general plan of education, on which could be founded new schools . . . to which both clergymen and dissenters might subscribe, and had also been unable to give their adhesion to the system lately propounded, that the Church, and the Church alone, should conduct the education of the country.[75]

He proposed the creation of an educational board, composed of Privy Councillors and responsible to parliament, to distribute increased state grants according to local needs and to schools outside the two great national religious societies. The door was open for 'reputable' schools of all denominations, including the Roman Catholic Church, to receive state support. Allan's anti-Catholic prejudices were again raised and he urged the Methodist President, Thomas Jackson, to convene a meeting of the Committee of Privileges to oppose an educational system based essentially, in his view, on 'popery and infidelity'.[76] As was his custom, Allan was keen to establish the *principles* upon which the Wesleyans should resist the Whig proposals. He wrote to Bunting:

126

In addition to the objections you will state to the new scheme, I am satisfied we must gravely consider whether we must distinctly take the ground that we renounce all assistance from the government and insist upon our objection to the state being the regulator of the education of the population or disposing of the funds of the country in support of popery or the declared enemies of the authorized version and our conviction of the non-necessity of any general plan. . . . Now before tomorrow think of these things deeply, for considering your influence with the preachers much will depend upon your opinion and recommendation. I don't know whether I am mistaken but I seem to feel as if on points such as these there is not the same decided unanimity of feeling as existed when the battle was fought with Lord Sidmouth.[77]

Allan's anti-Catholicism and fear of government-inspired secularization forced him to employ a nonconformist argument, voluntaryism, to solidify Wesleyan opposition to a liberal measure. This same argument was pressed on Bunting by Edward Baines, editor of the *Leeds Mercury*, who later became the most influential advocate of voluntaryism in the debate about elementary education in England.[78] Ironically, the Whig proposals were opposed even more vehemently by Anglicans and Tories who thought that the Whig scheme was yet another dent in the Church's influence over national social policy. Early Victorian religion and politics were nothing if not engagingly pluralistic.

There was one further level of complexity, because Bunting, with customary political astuteness and crude self-interest, wanted something quite different from Allan. Realizing that Wesleyan finances were not up to educational voluntaryism, he wanted the system of state grants extended to the Methodists and other orthodox Protestants, but not to Unitarians or Roman Catholics.[79] Bunting desired part of the cake which the Church and dissenters were already eating but he had no desire to share it any further. This position was supported in parliament by Ashley,[80] but Edward Baines thought that 'Bishop Bunting' had been forced to resort to crude sectarianism in order to secure Methodist interests.[81] The charge was self-evidently true. Although the dissenters liked Allan's principles better than Bunting's politics, a close reading of the resolutions adopted by the 'United Committee of Wesleyan Methodists on the Proposed Plan of National Education' shows that Bunting's politics triumphed once again:

It [the government report of June 3] states that 'the Committee [of Privy Council] do not feel themselves precluded from making Grants in particular cases, which shall appear to them to call for the aid of Government, although the application may not come from either of the two mentioned Societies'. To this proposition, no objection would have been taken by this meeting, or by the religious community whose general principles and feelings it represents, if the extended powers which it confers had been duly limited and defined.[82]

The Wesleyans maintained this essentially sectarian position throughout the 1840s and they were eventually admitted to state aid in 1847, one year before the Roman Catholics secured the same terms.[83] Sectarianism hardly seemed worthwhile.

Apart from his contribution to Methodism and politics, Allan, as a good evangelical, was widely connected with philanthropic and missionary endeavours, at a time when evangelicalism reached the peak of its influence in English society. He was a committee member of the British and Foreign Bible Society when the infamous Apocrypha controversy split the evangelical world into sheep and goats, or rather the pragmatists and the dogmatists. From about 1819, the Bible Society distributed Bibles with the Apocrypha in European Catholic countries, in accordance with the old Pauline evangelistic strategy of being 'all things to all men'. In 1824, a group of Scottish Calvinists led by Robert and Alexander Haldane considered this policy was too pragmatic for their own high principles of scriptural canonicity. Allan's correspondence with the main protagonists in the conflict is a mine of information on evangelical attitudes at a crucial stage in their evolution.[84] Allan, like the Anglican evangelical Charles Simeon, argued for the old policy and resigned when this was not accepted. Celts, Calvinists and controversialists were leading a more conservative evangelicalism into the Victorian era.[85]

The most important part of Allan's massive correspondence, however, relates to his political activities on behalf of the Methodists. He achieved a powerful position within the connexion based on his legal and constitutional knowledge, when most Methodists were politically naive and legally under pressure from the state. The fact that they put up with his abrasive views on the Wesleyan internal polity shows how much they needed him. His task was not easy, because Methodism came of age at a time of profound social, political and ecclesiastical change. The complexity of the issues can be seen from his successive political stances. In 1811–12 he used the traditional friends of religious liberty, the aristocratic Whigs, to secure an enlarged toleration; from 1811 to 1819 he convinced governments of Methodism's conservatism and loyalty as distinct from the working-class radicals; from 1812 to 1829 he built up contacts with the traditional enemies of religious toleration, the ultra-Tory Protestant constitutionists, to keep out the Catholics; in 1839 he argued as a doctrinaire voluntaryist, an antecedent of Victorian liberalism, once again to keep out the Catholics. It is tempting to conclude from this that Methodism was becoming more conservative and more denominationally self-conscious as it secured an increasingly respectable niche in English society. This is largely the case, but Allan's real consistency lay in his evangelical desire to promote the Protestant gospel among the working classes in the early Industrial Revolution. Sidmouth wanted to control the Methodists; the radicals wanted a different sort of millennium; the Catholics wanted to renew the old competition; and Russell seemed to be advocating secularization and doctrinal indifferentism. Evangelical Protestantism was not short of enemies.

The Allan correspondence gives a picture of Methodism after Wesley's death that is rather like the role of a psychologically uncertain orphan. There was much speculation about what the dead father wanted for the child and there was no shortage of potential foster parents. In the first thirty years after Wesley's death this child needed a good lawyer, but even more it needed a strong father. This was the difference between Allan the layman and Bunting the ecclesiastic. Since our Freudian fascination for the powerful and machiavellian ecclesiastic is almost exhausted (we even have a history of Bunting's historians), perhaps this is an appropriate time to examine that other popularly distrusted professional, the lawyer.

7

GIDEON OUSELEY: RURAL REVIVALIST, 1791–1839

Gideon Ouseley was born in the year of John Wesley's second visit to County Galway, was 'converted' in the year of Wesley's death and died on the one hundredth anniversary of Wesley's introduction to field preaching. A Methodist rural revivalist could have no better pedigree. I first encountered him, not in a dream as many Methodist contemporaries seem to have done, but in the correspondence of Joseph Butterworth MP,[1] to whom Ouseley sent graphic details of the nature of Irish Catholicism for his controversial speeches against Roman Catholic Emancipation, and in the records of the Wesleyan Methodist Missionary Society, in which Ouseley stands out as the most flamboyant missionary of his generation.[2] In terms of published works, Ouseley's career can also be traced through his prolific anti-Catholic pamphleteering[3] and in the pages of William Arthur's unexceptional Victorian biography.[4] But by far the most revealing record of his life and work is to be found in the manuscripts collected by John Ouseley Bonsall, a Dublin businessman who hero-worshipped his missionary uncle.[5] The collection includes transcriptions of Ouseley's letters, reproductions of his journal – which Ouseley thought he had completely destroyed in 1814 after repeated rows with the regular Methodist preachers – and an unusual oral history dimension in the transcriptions of interviews conducted by Bonsall a few years before Ouseley's death. As a collection it is at once deeply personal in its disclosure of Ouseley's states of mind during religious conversion, illness and death, and of much wider historical significance in its evocation of half a century of religious conflict and social upheaval in Ireland. It is also revealing of Methodism itself in its period of transition from a network of voluntary societies serviced by itinerant evangelists to a settled, chapel-based, preacher-led denomination. But above all, the Ouseley collection is a record of the remarkable religious energy of its subject in proclaiming religious certainties to a generation made anxious by revolution in Europe and Catholic resurgence in Ireland.

Ouseley was born in Dunmore, County Galway, in 1762, the son of a freethinking, anticlerical father of minor gentry status and a pious mother who introduced him to the family collection of Anglican and Puritan literature. Of English ancestry, the Ouseley family was one of a declining group of substantial Protestant farmers who were surrounded by an overwhelmingly Catholic peasantry.[6] Despite his father's anticlericalism, Gideon was bound for a career in the Church of Ireland, and was tutored by the local Catholic priest who had been educated in Europe. Ouseley failed to win a place at Trinity College, married into a respectable Protestant family and acquired a farm which subsequently had to be surrendered, probably unnecessarily, after a law suit. (Butterworth later alleged that Ouseley approached legal difficulties like a Calvinist waiting for divine justice rather than as an Arminian working out his own salvation.)[7] Ouseley then entered a phase of dissolute living which was dramatically brought to an end by a drunken shooting accident in which he lost an eye and very nearly his life. With Young's gloomy *Night Thoughts* as his scarcely appropriate convalescent reading, Ouseley's close en-counter with death resulted in a lasting preoccupation with death and eternity. Ouseley's first experience of evangelical religion was in the meetings conducted in a local inn by a Methodist quartermaster attached to the Royal Irish Dragoons and stationed in Dunmore barracks.[8] Thus began a long and psychologically painful 'conversion' during which Ouseley encountered other Methodist itinerants and joined a Methodist society. The sense of inner struggle, anxiety and fear of death is well conveyed in his interview with Bonsall in which he described himself as 'harassed, perplexed, and hopeless'.[9] His 'conversion' when it came was one of those characteristic two-tier Methodist types in which justification preceded entire sanctification (forgiveness before cleansing) by several months. So intense was Ouseley's mental turmoil at this time that it became the emotional and conceptual foundation of much of his later preaching. Indeed, so frequently did Ouseley recall in tears 'that Sunday morning' when 'I got such a sight of hell' that the more sophisticated Dublin Methodist congregations came to dread the very sight of him.[10] Ouseley's 'conversion' in 1791, as with Wesley's in 1739, opened up the way for half a century of itinerant preaching characterized by unremitting zeal and energy. His ambition was to preach to every human settlement in Ireland in the language of the people, and it was not uncommon for him to travel 4,000 miles a year preaching twelve to fifteen times a week.[11] Ouseley's suspicion of ecclesiastical institutions and their clergy ensured that his early itinerant labours were undertaken as a freelance evangelist subject to no outside control whatsoever. But in 1799 he was invited by the Irish Methodist Conference to be part of a team of three Irish-speaking evangelists with a specific mission to the Irish Catholic poor in the wake of the Rebellion of the United Irishmen.[12] After the dark days of 1798 during which Irish Methodists regarded themselves as innocent victims of 'popish' disloyalty and violence,[13] Ouseley and his colleagues were sent on their way with the ringing endorsement of the Irish Wesleyan Conference. Many of the characteristic elements of the early nineteenth-century missionary crusade were evident in its annual address to the British Methodist Conference. There was the existence of an economically depressed, ecclesiastically exploited and morally corrupt people to whom the gospel must be taken as the only means of true enlightenment. There was a powerful feeling of divine favour inasmuch as 'His gracious providence' provided the opportunity. There was the appeal of the grand, heroic adventure to those who had 'entered upon one of the most arduous undertakings that had been attempted since the primitive times'.[14] Ouseley was thereby given a degree of Conference authority and financial support without ever being taken into full connexion as a regular preacher. Indeed, he refused to sign Wesley's Large Minutes as mere human compositions and jealously respected his right of independence and private judgement. In that respect Ouseley's career parallels both the American frontier preachers (Lorenzo Dow was a close friend)[15] and English revivalists, men and women, who proliferated in the quarter century after Wesley's death.[16]

It is difficult to recapture the sheer colourfulness, eccentricity and crackling energy of Ouseley's forty years as a missionary preacher in Ireland. He sang and preached, mostly in Irish, to large gatherings of people at county assizes, fairs, market days, funerals and wakes, in prisons and outside church services, to early morning gatherings of labourers and to travellers by the roadside. For almost half a century his life was a picaresque tale of daily adventures and narrow escapes, described by his distinguished brother, Sir Ralph Ouseley, as a futile assortment of wild-goose chases.[17] His preaching was unashamedly emotional and often produced disturbing scenes of physical and psychological excesses, but he had also an impish sense of humour and enjoyed a genial rapport with his audiences. If spiritually intense, he was also worldly-wise. He rang bells to announce his presence, stood in front of apothecaries' windows to deter missiles, used simple agrarian illustrations to engage his hearers and often began with distinctively Catholic emphases before giving them a concluding evangelical twist.[18] Educated Catholics thought this was devious, but Ouseley considered it to be a justifiable form of Arminian pragmatism. Above all Ouseley believed in *means* as well as ends and had a lifelong dislike of a passive and providential Calvinism.[19]

Although he was occasionally victim of both episcopal prosecutions and mobs encouraged by the Established and Catholic clergy, Ouseley was not unduly restricted from itinerant preaching.[20] But in order to obtain the minimum protection from the authorities Ouseley, with regret, had to take the oaths of allegiance and abjuration and register as a dissenting preacher. Even then the cry that there was no law for the Methodists was common, at least up until 1812 when the new Methodist-inspired Toleration Act afforded greater protection, in theory if not always in practice. Indeed, Butterworth explained in meticulous detail how Ouseley might benefit from the new Act if he took proper precautions:

> It is perhaps material for you to know that we had the word 'place' introduced into the Act, instead of 'Meeting House' or 'Chapel', on purpose to protect our congregations in the *Open Air*, as well as within doors; and wherever the priests are troublesome by all means get the consent in writing of some occupier of a field to hold meetings there. . . . I would do all this quietly, say nothing about it, but if any priest should disturb you after you have certified the place you can punish him.[21]

When not restricted by the law, mobs or other churchmen, Ouseley displayed all the skills of the natural outdoor orator in attracting and holding crowds. One-eyed, barrel-chested and with a liberal dose of native humour, Ouseley cut an extraordinary figure in the troubled landscape of post-rebellion Ireland. His early reports for Dr Coke, the director of the Irish mission, capture the flavour of dread and excitement.

> On Monday we came to Baillieborough. The market-people were assembled when we came into the street. We did not alight, but prepared to attack the devil's kingdom which still remained strong in this town. The Methodists wished us out of the street, when they saw the manner of our proceedings, riding on our horses, with our umbrellas over our heads, the day being wet, but a young girl was so alarmed that she feared the day of judgment was at hand.[22]

> We have preached two market-days and one Sabbath in the streets of Ballyshannon to vast congregations, who heard with the greatest attentions. We met with no opposition; the rich and learned seemed astonished, standing at a distance, and hearing us denounce the judgments of heaven against the crimes of a guilty nation.[23]

Ouseley's view of the Irish peasantry, who made up the bulk of his audiences, was that they adhered to a deeply pagan and superstitious form of religion upon which was grafted a veneer of Roman Catholicism that was itself superstitious and irrational. The Roman Catholic priests were, therefore, in his opinion, the beneficiaries of ignorance which they had a vested interest to maintain. Likewise, poor Protestants, because of the failings of the episcopal clergy, availed themselves of Catholicized quasi-magical practices to ward off death, demons, fairies and banshees.[24]

Predictably perhaps there was a tension in his mind about the validity of supernatural occurrences. He employed a remorseless Lockean empiricism to refute Romish miracles,[25] but was quite happy to accept Methodist dreams, visions, signs and exotic spiritual manifestations. Looked at another way this mixture of rationalism and romanticism was at the heart of Ouseley's personality, and indeed of much late eighteenth-century evangelicalism.[26] Ouseley's response to rural ignorance was to put his faith in itinerant preaching, Bible and tract distribution and elementary education. All three necessitated a strong commitment to the Irish language, predominantly but not exclusively as a vehicle for proselytism,[27] substantial support from the London-based evangelical societies and an attitude of passive acceptance from the Roman Catholic Church and its adherents. The first two were more easily secured than the last.

One reason for Catholic unease was the remarkable success of the Methodist Irish-speaking missionaries in the early years of the nineteenth century, particularly in southern and south-western Ulster where numbers in Methodist societies doubled in the period from 1799 to 1802. Growth on this scale was not matched until 1819 when Ouseley was once again at the centre of revivalistic excitement in Wicklow and Carlow.[28] It now seems probable that, notwithstanding Ouseley's intention to evangelize native Roman Catholics, his greatest successes were achieved in old English settlements and among displaced Protestant minorities from Britain and Europe. Despite his original intentions, therefore, Methodism's conversionist theology introduced an element of competition into the Irish religious scene which inevitably led to deteriorating relations with the Roman Catholic Church. To an unfortunate degree the ensuing conflict dominated the second half of Ouseley's life.

Ouseley's anti-Catholicism predated his evangelical conversion and was part of a wider anticlericalism. He drew a distinction between priests and educated Catholics, who were in a position to know better, and the ordinary people, whom he regarded as victims of priestly tyranny and insupportable financial exactions. He thought of the Roman Church as an imperialistic force reaching out into the British Isles, North America and the wider world; but Ireland was the battle front and the priests were his particular enemies. His experiences confirmed his prejudices. He alleged that priests incited crowds against him, burned his tracts, warned their flocks against hearing him, used public humiliation, whips and penances if they disobeyed, offered bribes to reclaim converts and threatened eternal damnation to the recalcitrant, and systematically eroded the material, educational and moral well-being of the Irish people.[29] To his surprise he got on perfectly well with some individual priests, but he had a particular dislike of those trained at Maynooth and stationed in Munster.[30]

Ouseley, it is clear, did not much like the Catholic Church, but his anti-Catholicism is rather more complicated than one might suppose. There are, for example, quite distinguishable phases in the development of Ouseley's anti-Catholic opinions. Between 1799 and 1807 Ouseley and his missionary colleagues experienced a number of unpleasant incidents at the hands of Irish priests, but these were generally shrugged off as one of the hazards, even blessings, of missionary endeavour. Three circumstances combined to produce a more hostile climate. The first was Dr Coke's request for accurate numbers of Roman Catholic converts, presumably to stimulate fund-raising for the Irish mission in England.[31] The published figures were sufficiently large to attract Catholic attention. Second, the reports of the Irish missionaries were reproduced in the connexional magazine and even taken direct to the secretive Committee of Privileges by Butterworth himself, with the result that both English and Irish Methodists began to ascribe a significance to the Irish mission quite disproportionate to its actual size and impact.[32] Third, after a period of acute opposition from priests, Ouseley wrote a series of letters to Dr Bellew, the Roman Catholic Bishop of Killala, detailing names, dates and places of anti-Methodist persecutions.[33] Bellew's response was that since the Methodist missionaries were neither ordained nor specifically legitimized by the civil authorities then they could scarcely expect protection from a Roman Catholic bishop. As a bishop of a church emerging from a century of penal laws, albeit loosely enforced, Bellew had no desire to clear the paths for itinerant zealots. After 1807, therefore, Ouseley was much more willing to engage in public controversies against Catholics. The thrust of his attacks also changed. Whereas earlier he had been more concerned with the social consequences of Catholic errors than with the errors themselves, after 1807 he unleashed a prolific pamphlet attack on Catholic dogma which was continued until his death.[34] The fact that Ouseley had time to write only when he was ill scarcely helped the tone of his works, which have been well described by his biographer as being full of 'home-thrusts, clever illustrations, and absurd dilemmas'.[35]

As is well known, the 1820s ushered in a more aggressive era of religious conflict in Ireland with the formation of the Catholic Association on one side and the intensification of Protestant proselytism on the other.[36] Apart from his undiminished commitment to preaching, Ouseley spent much of the decade publishing his own highly individualistic solution to Ireland's miseries. In a letter to the *Sligo Journal* in 1823, the substance of which was reproduced in letters to Butterworth and Wellington, he complained of the unacceptable financial pressures on the Irish Catholic poor.[37] With trade depressed and unemployment high they were nevertheless required to pay rents, tithes, church and county cess and, indirectly, the Presbyterian Regium Donum before they could even begin to meet the demands of their own church and clergy. His remedies were for more responsible landlordism, a more equitable and rational assessment of tithes, the state payment of Roman Catholic priests without requiring a veto or any other security[38] and an electoral register based on minimum educational standards to ensure that landlords would have to provide schools for their freeholders. Ouseley expected these proposals to loosen the bonds between Catholic priests and their flocks and to strengthen those between good landlords and their tenants. Agrarian grievances would thus disappear and the population would be delivered from Romish ignorance into truth, knowledge, equity, industry and prosperity, all of which, in Ouseley's mind, were indissolubly linked one with another. Indeed there is much populist Enlightenment rhetoric underpinning his more detailed proposals for social and ecclesiastical reform in Ireland.

Ouseley's views were unpopular even among his friends, for few evangelicals could accept that bad means – the state payment of Catholic clergy – could ever produce a good end. If Ouseley's political views were unpopular, his reputation as a second Saint Patrick in his zeal to convert pagan Ireland never stood higher. For the first quarter of a century of his itinerant labours he had been disliked by most of the Catholic clergy, the vast majority of episcopalian and Presbyterian clergy and by a powerful group of preachers within his own connexion. He had been an embarrassment to most Protestant landlords and had posed difficult problems for the civil magistrates. But by the late 1820s he was defended by the Protestant press in Ireland, patronized by the evangelical aristocracy, on agreeable terms with the most influential Protestant clergy and the recipient of more invitations from Britain and North America than he could ever hope to fulfil. As with Wesley before him, he found that the religious world, or at least a section of it, had a soft spot for ageing evangelists.

Ouseley toured the north of England in 1828 under the auspices of the Wesleyan Methodist Missionary Society (the invitation came from Jabez Bunting), and, as with his previous visit in 1818, he attracted large congregations and seemed to be particularly influential in reviving the faith and the anti-Catholicism of Irish Protestant migrants.[39] More generally, he was disappointed with the level of awareness about Ireland and the Catholic question in English cities only a year before the passage of the Catholic Emancipation Act. He informed Bonsall in April 1828 that 'the Protestants this side of the water are filled with apathy about popery, as if the case were *hopeless*, or that it is not worthy of notice. The latter is it'.[40] What surprised him even more, however, was the sheer weakness of Methodism in London. Ouseley had taken orders from Methodist missionary headquarters in London for a third of a century and was perplexed to find in 1836 that there were only around twenty Methodists among the 16,000 inhabitants of Wandsworth.[41] By the late 1830s Methodism was in fact stronger in the frontier zone of southern Ulster than it was in parts of the capital city of the Empire where it had originated a century before. Indeed it is a feature of the Ouseley papers that the evangelical grass always seemed to be greener somewhere else – in the east, on the North American frontier or wherever – as tales of missionary expansion were circulated to keep up morale and generate funds.[42]

Ouseley's own substantial contribution to mission came to an end in

1839. Right up to his death he still preached as often as he could and still urged the Methodist Missionary Society to send out more Irish-speaking evangelists to confront 'the religion of Rome' –

> some of the professed tenets of which are exquisite, pure, and apostolic, and essentially sound Protestantism; but its practical doctrines, framed by men of great parts, and by Councils, in order to uphold the glory of the Papacy, and support of its numerous clergy, are the very reverse, and are with all diligence passed on to the credulous for divine mysteries of faith. . . . Thus are the poor, unsuspecting people taught darkness for light, and are deceived and ruined. . . . Thus is our country filled with anarchy and untold mischiefs.[43]

Apart from his remarkable contribution to the establishment of Methodism in Ireland, Ouseley is of particular interest to the historian not only because his life is unusually well documented for such a humble figure, but also because of his highly individualistic style. Defying easy categorization, he is an interstitial character, operating in the crevices of Irish society in the half century after the French Revolution. As a result, his life is full of ambiguities, ironies and paradoxes. He was a member of an English family of small landowners who had exhibited military prowess, yet he was domiciled in a remote part of western Ireland among a diminishing handful of minor Protestant gentry surrounded by an overwhelmingly Catholic populace. Ouseley was the son of a pious mother and a freethinking, anticlerical father and both influences can be detected in him. He had access to English Reformation and Puritan classics, yet he was Irish-speaking and priest-educated. He was a defender of the Union between Britain and Ireland, of the Protestant landed interest and of the Church of Ireland, yet his sympathies were generally with the victims of such arrangements. But for his profound hatred of Roman Catholicism, Ouseley could easily have become a religious and political radical after the fashion of Joseph Rayner Stephens in England and Lorenzo Dow in the United States. Comparisons with the latter are particularly illuminating. Both were independent spirits with populist anticlerical convictions. Both were committed to vernacular preaching, both were captivating public performers, both had deep-seated aversions to traditional authority, both were avid publishers and both were associated with religious revivals wherever they went. Yet the striking difference between the two is that whereas Ouseley came to be patronized by the Irish Protestant gentry, Dow was a radical Jeffersonian who could begin a sermon by quoting Tom Paine and who 'sought the conversion of sinners at the same time as he railed at tyranny and priest-craft and the professions of law and medicine'.[44] Dow's advocacy of 'popular sovereignty and the responsibility of independent persons to throw off the shackles of ignorance and oppression' marked him out as a Jeffersonian republican of a particularly populist kind, whereas Ouseley's commitment to similar values led him into a lifelong campaign against priestcraft and the baleful influence of the Roman Catholic Church in Ireland. Ironically, the Irish Methodist elite, whose nerves had been set on edge by Dow's anti-establishment rhetoric in Ireland, used his republicanism as a convenient stick with which to beat Ouseley for his association with him. Ouseley's basic instincts were almost always populist, yet he spent his life trying to overturn the religion of the people and was rewarded with the approval of evangelical Anglo-Irish aristocrats such as Lord Farnham, the Earl of Roden and the Mountcashels who used landed influence and evangelical religion to help sustain their social status.[45] The politics of revivalism, in its different social and cultural settings, are engagingly unpredictable.

Ouseley's religious allegiances were similarly complicated. On the whole he disliked clergy and religious institutions, even of the Methodist variety. He was stoutly evangelical but intensely anti-Calvinist at a time when most Irish evangelicals were Calvinists. As a result he was never fully at home in the missionary projects of the so-called Second Reformation movement in Achill and Kingscourt, yet he was enthusiastic about the numbers of converts.[46] At the same time as his relations with the Irish Methodist elite deteriorated (to the extent that he was scarcely on speaking terms with any of the regular preachers in the last decade of his life) he became a *cause célèbre* in Britain and North America. He was a rugged individualist, a kind of religious gunfighter with his Bible in his hand and popery as the enemy. His portrait was published in the *Methodist Magazine* in 1828 and he received invitations from all over the world to preach to Irish Catholic migrants.[47] As with many such figures his reputation came to be admired more than the real person.

At the heart of Ouseley's personality and life's work was a sincere religious faith which was forged in the white heat of a traumatic and unforgettable religious conversion, and a genuine compassion for his country and his countrymen. Although persuaded that the root of Ireland's misery was religious, he was too close to the ground not to see that economic problems were just as serious. In fact much of his thinking was dominated by attempts to harmonize these apparent irreconcilables – hence the idea to pay Roman Catholic priests without preconditions. Unusually for a man of his evangelical intensity, he could see that human problems were not all caused by 'wilful wickedness', but could be the product of circumstances outside the individual's control. In a sense Ouseley too was a victim of circumstances beyond his control. He started his missionary campaign as an independent spirit, as critical of the Anglican ascendancy as he was of the Roman Catholic Church, but after half a century of turbulent Irish history and unremitting conflict between evangelical

Protestantism and a resurgent Irish Catholicism Ouseley joined the Orange Order and was warmly welcomed by the interests he had once challenged. Yet it would be to demean Ouseley's status as one of Ireland's most influential religious figures – and in however curious a way one of its best – in the post-rebellion era not to conclude that he helped initiate a new era of religious competition, the legacy of which still survives in modern Ulster.

PART III

THEMES: LAW, POLITICS AND GENDER

The themes chosen for this part are arguably the most important in the early history of Methodism and popular evangelicalism in the British Isles. My other reason for choosing them is that they each have been subjected to powerful single narrative interpretations which no longer offer convincing solutions to the problems they were designed to solve. It is only through an exploration of the ambiguities and paradoxes at the heart of Methodist expansion that one can begin to work towards a more realistic interpretation of what drove it on. Law, politics and gender are intriguing subjects in their own right, but they also serve to expose some of the essence of Methodism as a popular religious movement.

Methodism in England had its origins in a society governed, administered and regulated by legal processes. It was also a society overshadowed by the frightening religious and political instability of the seventeenth century. Religious movements outside the direct control of Church and State, whatever the assurances and guarantees proffered, were subject to close scrutiny. Methodism perplexed, annoyed and challenged traditional authority both at the centre and the localities. It was in, but not of the Established Church, and it exposed legal loopholes in post-Restoration ecclesiastical legislation. It was new, disruptive and socially divisive, and the authorities were not sure what to do about it. An investigation of the legal points at issue in the early decades of Methodist expansion reveals more clearly than any other possible approach the true significance of Methodism as a new form of popular religion in the English landscape. It was precisely because it sheltered under the umbrella of a relatively tolerant Church of England that Methodism was able to effect something approaching a religious revolution in English society. No religious movement did more to undermine a centuries-old pattern of parochial discipline and to open up the possibility of a more pluralistic society in which the right to hold, and, crucially, to propagate religious opinions, was protected by law. By this unlikely route religious enthusiasm contributed more to nineteenth-century liberalism than either its strongest supporters or severest critics are prepared to admit.

141

That this is not the only possible interpretation of Methodism's impact on English society is made clear by the historiographical snapshots offered in Chapter 9 on popular evangelicalism and political stability. The objective here is not only to introduce readers to the rich resources of Methodist historiography produced since the Second World War, but to suggest that the most dominant interpretive frameworks often lack a convincing grasp of the social and political milieu in which Methodist communities took root. Methodism and political radicalism are generally portrayed as polar opposites which the English working classes oscillated to and from, or as uncomfortable bedfellows which the Methodist pastorate sought to separate. There is, of course, evidence to support both propositions, but my contention is that neither form of analysis takes one very far into the social and political culture of the chapel communities themselves. Not only can Methodism be regarded as a species of ecclesiastical radicalism in its undermining of the control mechanisms of the Established Church, but many of the conflicts supposedly fought out *between* Methodists and radicals were often fought out *within* the Methodist polity itself. Moreover, the terms Methodism and, more particularly, radicalism are often used with astonishing looseness and anachronistic naivety. Both were broad churches, both changed over time and each intersected with the other in all sorts of different ways. By selecting for particular attention the antislavery agitation of the early nineteenth century and the urban radicalism of the Chartist years, I hope to show that processes of cultural brokerage may be more influential in shaping popular attitudes than either oscillation or repression.

A similar dissatisfaction with conventional interpretive frameworks is the starting-point of the last chapter on women and evangelical religion, though in this case the quality of work produced in the past decade is of a high order. My particular geographical concentration is on Ireland and in particular on its northernmost province of Ulster, but as the work on this subject has progressed faster and more creatively in North America than in Ireland, some of the analytical frameworks are borrowed from those carrying out research on Methodism in the USA. I have also been fortunate to have had the privilege of supervising an unusually talented group of North American and Irish historians of women and religion, who have done much, but sadly perhaps not enough, to peel back the layers of my ignorance. It is nevertheless clear to me that notwithstanding male rhetoric and prescriptions, the subject of evangelicalism and women will not yield up its dark secrets by means of the conventional narratives of separate spheres, economic marginalization and gender essentialism. Many women were devoted to evangelical religion and were used and abused by it, but necessity is indeed the mother of invention, and women were more often willing associates than unwilling victims of the religious causes they served. Whether one looks at language and symbol, or structures and organizations, the contribution of women to popular religion, as befits their majority status within it, was more powerful than one at first supposes. The purpose of Chapter 10 is to ask why women found evangelical religion so attractive and how it was they came to play such a major role in its experience, transmission and ideology. From the construction of domestic virtue to the expression of national identity, women were at the very heart of popular evangelicalism, and most of them knew it. No explication of the social and cultural mores of popular evangelicalism is even half complete without due attention to their stories.

8

METHODISM AND THE LAW IN ENGLISH SOCIETY, 1740–1820[1]

A set of people who stile themselves Methodists have infus'd their enthusiastick notions into the minds of vast numbers of the meaner sort of people in the Western part of this County, they are strenuously endeavouring to propagate themselves all over it: several have assembled frequently within this fortnight in the parish of Saint Ewe in which we live; and the Preacher they are so very fond of, is no better than a mean illiterate Tinner, and what is more surprising, but a boy nineteen years old. Doubtless your Lordship has heard much of these poor deluded creatures ... who for the most part are ignorant men, and have been notoriously wicked, but now under pretence of being both reform'd and inspired, they, and even women of the same stamp are adored Preachers: it is sufficient to say that many poor wretches have been drove to despair thro' their means, and multitudes of his Majesties subjects have been made useless in every station of life, by being persuaded, that unless they are Drones and Cowards they can not be saved.

As we are in the Commission of the Peace, we have endeavour'd to convince them of their errors by reason: which not having the least effect, we told them that we must put the Laws in force against them, to which they replied that they did not differ from the Church of England as by Law establish'd and therefore not guilty of any crime. ... They all affirm that they knew nothing of God or religion from any information receiv'd at Church, before they were instructed by these Preachers, which they say are become so by miracles.

(West Austell JPs to G. Lavington, Bishop of Exeter, 23 May 1747)[2]

Here is one of the earliest examples of a common legal dilemma which affected local benches of magistrates and church courts wherever Methodism took root in eighteenth-century England. The list of Methodist irregularities penned by the magistrates of West Austell (and other correspondents of Lavington from the West Country in 1747) is nevertheless particularly comprehensive.[3] By employing young, illiterate and female preachers and by dangerously dividing communities into the saved and the lost, the Methodists were allegedly responsible for undermining ecclesiastical discipline, social stability, communal harmony and public morality. The problem was what to do about it, because, in the absence of a clear lead from parliament, bishops or the high courts, local magistrates were uncertain about the state of the law in respect of voluntary religious societies. Seventeenth-century statutes provided some guidance, but they dealt, in the main, with separatist and seditious forms of Puritanism, Nonconformity and Roman Catholicism. Although the Methodists, as befits a new religious movement, were often accused of all three forms of religious deviance, they admitted to none of them, and were instructed by their leaders to hold meetings in accordance with the liturgies of the Church of England and to pay tithes without complaint.

How far Methodism should be allowed to shelter under the umbrella of the Church of England while developing its own style and structure, became one of the most controversial legal problems of the period between 1740 and 1820. For justices in the localities the key question was how to stop something which they instinctively believed to be misguided and dangerous, in a society which valued legal processes and which recognized a significant degree of religious toleration for all its Protestant trinitarian citizens. The issue was further complicated by legal ignorance in the localities, genuine confusion about the precise limits of toleration afforded by post-Restoration statutes, uncertainties about the respective responsibilities of church courts and quarter sessions in controlling religious deviance and, more prosaically, about who should bear the burden of legal costs.

These problems were not entirely new. In 'The English conventicle', his presidential address to the Ecclesiastical History Society, Professor Collinson drew attention to much legal confusion in seventeenth-century England about what constituted a conventicle.[4] Given the comprehensive nature of the Established Church, meetings of groups of more serious believers were always likely, but such gatherings were not originally separatist. In fact they were heavily based on sermons, repetitions and catechisms to guard against independent notions and esoteric experiences. Most Puritan conventicle members, as with later Methodists, were female, wished to be separated from evil, were pessimistic about the spirituality of the wider church, but were only reluctantly (and as a result of complex social and ecclesiastical pressures) pushed into a full-blown separatism with the resultant notions of a gathered church.

It was with Puritanism in mind and with Civil War memories to the forefront that Restoration lawyers and churchmen drew up the Conventicles Act. An Act with draconian penalties, which magistrates were understandably reluctant to enforce, was passed in 1664, expired in 1668, and renewed in a milder form in 1670 as 'An Act to prevent and suppress seditious conventicles.'[5] The purpose of the Act was to provide more speedy remedies against 'the growing and dangerous practices of seditious sectaries and other disloyal persons, who under pretence of tender consciences have or may at their meetings contrive insurrections'. One interpretation of this Act, therefore, and the one that Wesley held, was that for a conventicle to be unlawful it had to have a conspiratorial purpose.[6] From the Methodist viewpoint the real problem with the Conventicles Act was that it gave considerable powers of discretion to individual magistrates and empowered constables to use force to break into an alleged conventicle and, if necessary, to bring out the militia.[7] Unsurprisingly, therefore, in the eighteenth-century prosecutions against Methodists under the Conventicles Act were often accompanied by additional *or* counter prosecutions for assault and injury as was the case in Devon in 1751.[8]

The Toleration Act of 1689 did not, of course, repeal the Conventicles or Five Mile Acts; it simply exempted 'their majesties' Protestant subjects, dissenting from the Church of England, from the penalties of certain laws' subject to the fulfilment of clearly stipulated conditions.[9] It also required the formal registration of preachers and meeting-places by a bishop or archdeacon, or at the quarter sessions. Both the Conventicles Act and the Toleration Act were drafted in response to the kind of Protestant Dissent that emerged in the seventeenth century. Some aspects of this legislation, most notably who was entitled to become a preacher and what exactly was a conventicle, were defined so imprecisely as to create ambiguities when a new kind of associational religion emerged in the 1740s.

Wesley realized perfectly well that early Methodism teetered on the brink of legal irregularities, but he also had respect for English law and for ecclesiastical discipline. Accordingly he had interviews in 1738 with Edmund Gibson, Bishop of London from 1720 to 1748, author of *Codex Juris Ecclesiastici Anglicani* (1713) and a leading authority on ecclesiastical law.[10] Wesley asked directly if Methodist societies were conventicles. Initially Gibson was evasive because of his unwillingness to jeopardize the early eighteenth-century Anglican societies in London and because the Methodist system was new and undeveloped. Six years later Gibson published his opinions in *Observations upon the Conduct and Behaviour of a certain Sect usually distinguished by the Name of Methodists*.[11] Gibson stated that Methodists were in defiance of the government of the country by posing as Anglicans while behaving as dissenters. Methodist claims to be free from penal legislation without fulfilling the stipulations of the Toleration Act was, in the bishop's opinion, merely a legal manifestation of Methodist antinomianism. Even if Methodists should avail themselves of the relief afforded by the Toleration Act, Gibson believed that field preaching remained illegal since it was legislated against in 1670 and not exempted in 1689. Quite apart from such civil offences, Gibson alleged that the Methodists were guilty of a range of serious ecclesiastical malpractices. Itinerant preaching undermined the territorial cure of souls, voluntary societies weakened church discipline and Methodist teaching devalued ethics by encouraging extremism, exclusiveness and religious experience.

Wesley's response was, at least on the surface, quite straightforward and formed the basis of his societies' legal defence before magistrates.[12] Methodists were not dissenters, therefore the Toleration Act was irrelevant to them. The Conventicles Act was designed to 'provide remedies against sedition'. Methodists were not seditious, quite the reverse. Field preaching was legal in theory and safe in practice because it was conducted in daylight to known crowds which were much smaller than both Methodists and Anglicans alleged. If ordination was properly understood to be for a gospel ministry, not to a specific territorial location, then itinerant preaching was not an offence against the Church. Such principles were easier to defend in learned debate than they were in English localities, especially during periods of foreign warfare and domestic instability when tolerance of Methodists could not be guaranteed. As time passed, therefore, Wesley had to accept the inconveniences of Methodism's uncertain legal position, and from at least 1748 (though more commonly from the late 1750s) Methodist preachers and owners of meeting-places applied for certificates under the Toleration Act to guard against intimidation.[13] Wesley refused to accept, however, that registration amounted to separation from the Church; rather it was a device to protect life and property from the licence of the crowd.

Uncertainty within Methodism about its legal status was reflected in the courts themselves. In the case of Rex v. Moreley, a Kent JP named Monypenny acted against local Methodists under the Conventicles Act in 1760 and inadvertently exposed jurisdictional disagreements between King's Bench and quarter sessions over the implementation of the Toleration Act.[14] Six years later in Rex v. Justices of Derbyshire, which came to King's Bench on a writ of mandamus, Lord Mansfield judged that the magistrates were wrong in refusing to register a Methodist meeting-house, but that they retained the right to decide if the meeting-house qualified for relief under the Toleration Act.[15] Thus what was given in one hand by registration could be removed by the JPs exercising discretionary power. In this way jurisdictional disputes and fine distinctions added to the difficulties of both Methodists and magistrates in applying old laws to new conditions.[16] In such circumstances, toleration of Methodists in English localities depended more upon the urgency of the social situation than on the application of widely accepted principles. This was unsatisfactory for all concerned, but it was not intolerable, at least until the revolutionary pressures of the period 1790–1820 when the law could no longer cope with the strains placed upon it. By then the need for new statutes had become imperative.

Whatever the complexities of the law with regard to preachers and conventicles, the great majority of cases relating to Methodism which came before the law in the localities had to do with infringements of public order, assault, riot and damage to property. Opponents of the Methodists alleged that they disturbed the peace by breaking known laws, while Methodists in turn claimed they were victims of mobs unrestrained by those responsible for maintaining civil liberties. Why then were Methodists so frequently the victims of mobs in both Britain and Ireland between 1740 and 1770?

John Walsh's seminal essay on the subject drew attention to the importance of social superiors in conferring legitimacy on anti-Methodist mobs.[17] Clergy and gentry, farmers and merchants, even magistrates and constables encouraged the belief that, since there was 'no law for the Methodists', mobs were virtually indemnified against prosecution, costs and damages. The reasons for such opposition are legion. Early Methodists were looked upon as 'disturbers of the world', the new Levellers, and were thus victims of remarkably resilient Civil War memories. 'Cromwell like you did first pretend', went the *Methodist and the Mimick*, 'religion was his only end; but soon the mask away did fling, pull'd down the Church and killed the King'.[18] More realistically, perhaps, Methodists appeared to undermine traditional authority by criticizing the vices of social superiors and the worldliness of the parish clergy. In particular, itinerant, lay and female preachers crossed traditional boundaries of hierarchy, law, sex, age, wealth, education and religious vocation. All this appeared to be beyond control because Methodism's nationwide organization cut across the parish, county and diocesan boundaries upon which English local government and the administration of the law depended. To make matters worse, Methodism often took strongest root in marginal areas, scattered settlements and new industrial environments where the traditional social cement was weakest.[19] Unsurprisingly, then, anti-Methodist rioting was seen from one perspective as an instrument of social control, and mobs were often led by the clergy, local government officers and men in livery.[20] Wesley's description of it was 'the clamour either of the great vulgar or the small'.[21]

It would be wrong to conclude, however, that anti-Methodist disturbances were merely the result of influence from above, for that would not of itself explain why Methodists ran into legal difficulties in the localities. If the problem had been merely the inadequate interpretation and enforcement of the law in the localities then a writ of *certiorari* could have solved the problem. The use of such writs was common throughout the early modern period as a means of overcoming local prejudices, yet at the same time it was realized that, in practice, the discretionary and flexible interpretation of justice in communities was the mainstay of order. In other words, the informal nature of much of the administration of justice, even in the eighteenth century, meant that local attitudes did not stand alongside or outside 'the law'; rather, they were among its primary constituents. In short, Methodists ran into legal difficulties in English localities in the 1740s and 1750s because they were sufficiently unpopular with sufficient numbers of people to make them vulnerable. The mechanism by which vulnerability was translated into active hostility, with all its legal consequences, was good old-fashioned rumour mongering. There was no shortage of material.

Early Methodism was frequently viewed as a religious cloak for sexual orgies.[22] Methodist love-feasts, holy kisses, spiritual trances and private meetings at night were easily misunderstood, but there were also allegations of pre-nuptial fornication, bastardy, debauching of maids (even against Wesley himself)[23] and of sexually active preachers on the move. Only a fraction of such allegations yielded enough evidence for prosecutions in church courts or quarter sessions, but the rumours were sufficiently persistent to create a receptive climate of anti-Methodist opinion in small communities. One sworn affidavit can stand for all:

> That at some Meeting he hath known & been present when woman [sic] have been taken from the Rooms where they met & carried them into Bedchambers & thrown upon Beds where they have lain in fits or swoons, & the preacher has cried at the same time that they should let them alone for the Spirit was entring them. And that he hath known several of them leave their Work & labour by which they & their Family where [sic] to be supported to attend the runnagate preachers, & that in the Yard many of them have drawn Workmen from their Labour to preach to them to the great Hindrance of the King's Works. That he hath frequently himself contributed to their Collection but knows not how the Money is disposed of.[24]

As well as allegations of appropriating money for undeclared and scurrilous purposes, rumours abounded of Methodists inducing madness and displays of paranormal behaviour, of practising witchcraft and cunning arts, of maliciously circulating prophecies of misfortune and of inducing miscarriages and serious illnesses.[25] Most rumours, as seems to be the case with new religious movements, concentrated on four main areas: exclusivity and community fragmentation, hypocrisy and sexual irregularities, maladministration of money and widespread corruption, and the erosion of traditional values by introducing new and more rigorous standards of behaviour. For while Methodism was viewed from one perspective as a succession of highly charged sexual encounters, it was more realistically feared as a recrudescence of old puritanism against a consensual and convivial village culture. Some of Lavington's correspondents from the West Country in the late 1740s found it difficult to separate fact from fiction in the maze of contradictory rumours in circulation, but the more astute observers drew attention to early manifestations of Methodism's puritanical discipline, especially in its sabbatarianism and criticisms of drunkenness, card-playing, wrestling, village festivities and popular sports.[26] Pretending to be better than other people and driving a wedge between the 'saved' and the 'lost' were criticisms of Methodism that survived in rural communities at least until the end of the nineteenth century.[27] Similarly, there were frequent allegations of Methodism splitting families, as women and children were thought to be more susceptible to emotional religion than were adult men.[28]

Methodism was thus perceived to be new, disruptive and divisive, whether in families, villages, parishes or the state. As a result, apart from the customary element of hooliganism, most anti-Methodist rioters saw themselves as acting in defence of traditional values and community solidarity.[29] Most riots, with some unfortunate exceptions, were more concerned with ritual humiliation and intimidation than with serious violence against persons and property. Wesley's response to such violence, which he abhorred, is best followed through two well-documented and contemporaneous case-studies, one in Lancashire and the other in Cork.

In Colne in east Lancashire the Rev. George White, after preaching and printing against the Methodists, raised a mob to drive them out of the parish. There followed a number of anti-Methodist disturbances culminating at Barrowford in August 1748.[30] A mob under the leadership of one Richard Bocock, a deputy constable, and escorted by a drummer to attract attention, seized Wesley, Grimshaw of Haworth and some others. They were brought before James Hargraves, a surveyor of the king's highway, and were subjected to a good deal of petty humiliation and drunken abuse.[31] Hargraves alleged that Wesley had infringed the Conventicles Act and disturbed the peace, and asked him for a pledge never to return to the area. Wesley supplied the familiar answer that since he was not a dissenter he could not be convicted under the Conventicles Act, and suggested that, notwithstanding the legal point at issue, he was still entitled to protection from mobs on the king's highway. Wesley in turn asked Hargraves for a pledge to restrain mobs within his jurisdiction or risk legal proceedings against him, and later informed him that he had sought advice from Sir Dudley Ryder, the Attorney-General and a family friend, and from William Granville, a Gray's Inn barrister and 'serious' Christian. This and other cases affecting Methodists came before the quarter sessions in Preston, but Wesley, as was his custom in such cases, short-circuited local prejudices by taking it to King's Bench on a writ of *certiorari*. Such cases were expensive (Wesley estimated between thirty and forty pounds); there was therefore a premium on success to help defray the legal costs. The plea rolls of King's Bench show that Hargraves was dismissed as surveyor of the king's highway in the township of Colne.[32] Wesley later boasted that he won all the cases he took to King's Bench, but Frank Baker records at least one expensive failure.[33] Wesley's strategy, then, was to use eminent contacts and legal processes to overcome local prejudices, and to eradicate mob action by establishing that there was 'law for the Methodists'.[34] As case-law built up, he used it to warn future protagonists. In general terms, then, Wesley had confidence in English law and its interpretation by metropolitan courts, but he had little faith in local justice.

Wesley's strategy for coping with anti-Methodist rioting is more easily discerned than the 'cognitive structure' and specific motives of the rioters themselves.[35] It has become clear, for example, that riots launched in the name of one cause often concealed hidden motives or alternative agendas.[36] E. P. Thompson has warned against assuming 'automatic' responses of communities, when a whole range of contingent circumstances and local relations were involved. This certainly seems to have been the case in Colne where Anglican pastoral supervision had been for some time in the hands of Roman Catholic apostates, including the Rev. George White who clearly took the lead in instituting anti-Methodist forays. White was a mercurial figure. He combined razor-sharp polemical skills, acquired in the disputation classes at the English College in Douai, with immense pastoral ineffectiveness. He was described as a man

> neither devoid of parts or of literature, but childishly ignorant of common life, and shamefully inattentive to his duty, which he frequently abandoned for weeks together to such accidental assistance as the parish could procure. On one occasion he is said to have read the funeral service more than twenty times in a single night over the dead bodies which had been interred in his absence.[37]

The anti-Methodist riots in Colne, as in other parts of the country, can only be interpreted properly in the light of more information about the social, religious and political fault-lines of particular communities when Methodism was first introduced into the locality.

The most prolonged and serious anti-Methodist rioting in the late 1740s took place not in England, but in Ireland, when Methodism was first introduced into the cities of Dublin and Cork. The riots in Cork were particularly protracted.[38] The rioters were led by Nicolas Butler, a ballad singer and mock preacher, who was allegedly in the pay of the corporation and the clergy, and who forged an alliance between the two most notorious Cork gangs, the Blackpool and Fair Lane mobs. There was virtually no restraining authority: the mayor and sheriffs refused to take action, the bishop and the clergy were publicly opposed to the Methodists, the assize courts sided repeatedly with the rioters, and the local gentry and merchants wanted an end to Methodism. Lavington's confidante reported back faithfully:

The assize ended yesterday.... The Judges order'd that all the Methodist preachers, or what we call swadlers, to be indicted, the bills to be found as presented as vagabonds which was done. Williams this day lenight attempted to preach as usual. The Mob quickly took him off his stage and narrowly escaped, the Heads of their Society waited on the Judges, paid several lawyers, but received the above for their satisfaction. We expect they will not be of any long continuance with us. Hundreds of familys are destroy'd by them, Women leaving their Husbands, others Mad.... Our Mayor, Sheriffs and the whole grand jury was with me. The Judges warrants are out searching for the preachers, but they hide in dark corners.[39]

Wesley was genuinely perplexed to find his societies the victims of both ascendancy hostility and 'popish' mobs:

Upon the whole one question readily occurs, whether, setting aside both Christianity and common humanity, it be prudent thus to encourage a popish mob to tear Protestants in pieces. And such Protestants as are essentially and remarkably attached to the present government! Nay, and on that very account peculiarly odious both to Papists and Jacobites.[40]

Seeing no hope of legal redress in Cork itself, Wesley suggested to his brother Charles that they should seek help from Stanhope (the Lord Lieutenant), the Duke of Cumberland (the Captain-General of British land forces) and the Archbishop of Armagh. Similar action was taken by the Countess of Huntingdon and some wealthy Dublin Huguenots. Ultimately, the demise of Butler, and more effective action from the military, brought the Cork riots to an end, but the alleged activities of 'popish' mobs confirmed Wesley's deep-seated fear of Catholic illiberality and his lack of confidence in Irish law.[41]

As in Colne, the interpretation of anti-Methodist rioting in Cork needs to be earthed in its local setting, but the evidence is inconclusive. The most judicious contemporary assessment came from the author of the Cork Baptist Church Book, who was at once impressed by Methodist zeal and disturbed by its vulgarity.

From their first appearance the novelty of preaching in the fields, their seeming zeal and disinterestedness gained them a multitude of hearers. What gave them countenance at first and warded off resentment of the Protestants was that they constantly declared they were not come to form any new party among Christians, that they only desired to win souls to Christ. The multitudes of all ranks of people that resorted to the fields to hear them gave rage to the magistrates and 'tis not improbable but the mob were countenanced in disturbing their assemblies, 'tis certain that such kind of assemblies are subject to tumults and therefore, tho' our government is the most indulgent in the world to everything that has the appearance of religion, yet the laws do not protect such wild promiscuous assemblies. Besides there was some reason to think that the working people were interrupted from their labour and while out of pretense of religion they ran after such preachers their families at home were left destitute.[42]

In addition to this version of Puritan sobriety, the author, in a formidable list of charges, accused the Methodists of empire building, money grabbing, family splitting, heiress hunting and 'sheep' stealing. The rub of the matter was that in a country where the Protestant ascendancy depended upon a variegated mixture of landed and clerical influence, penal laws and military control, the demotic appeal of Methodism threatened the very social stability upon which other interests relied. The established order in Cork delivered Methodism into the hands of popular ruffians because their own position was less at risk from short, sharp bursts of popular disorder than from a new form of associational religion, which not only threatened the old Protestant denominational order, but also portended a new kind of religious competition between Protestants and Roman Catholics. Methodism was simply more dangerous and more disruptive than it was worth, and with the authorities sending clear signals of where their sympathies lay, the path was clear for the urban 'meaner sorts' to extract their ritual humiliation.

In the period 1740–70, therefore, in both England and Ireland, Wesley could do no more than appeal to those in authority to apply the laws they professed to live by. In that respect he used his knowledge of the law and his social contacts from his Oxford days to seek protection for popular pietists from ruffians of all social ranks. After 1770, as Methodism became less feared, less persecuted and less novel, mob attacks largely petered out, and Wesley's use of the law for self-defence was made almost redundant.[43]

This comparatively restricted chronology of disturbances in the localities was not matched by a similar reduction in pressure on the Methodists from the Church of England and from the state. In fact, just as the growth and establishment of Methodism made it less feared as a novel and disruptive force, it paradoxically made Methodism more feared as a serious competitor to the Established Church. Nevertheless, with Convocation not sitting, and with administrations reluctant to diminish religious toleration, there was comparatively little, in legal terms at least, that the Church of England could do about Methodism. Moreover, in the period 1740–90 Methodist numbers were small, geographically dispersed and not always resented by the resident clergy. Visitation returns even show some confusion about whether Methodists should be recorded as dissenters or not. Even Lavington, that most inquisitorial and, at times, prurient of bishops, acknowledged limits beyond which it was not wise to go. Nevertheless, those Anglicans who wished to act against the Methodists had a number of possible options open to them. By closing their pulpits to Methodist preachers, and by legitimizing the actions of the mob, the Anglican clergy could force Methodists on to a collision course with the law in the localities. The sheer bulk of anti-Methodist literature produced by Anglicans shows no lack of ideological support for such actions. More specifically, clergy and churchwardens could take advantage of Methodism's ambiguous status under the Toleration Act by initiating prosecutions against Methodist conventicles.[44] Occasionally the diocesan authorities refused to register Methodist meeting-houses, but this does not seem to have been widely practised and was generally discouraged by the bishops themselves.[45] There are cases too of clergymen refusing to admit Methodists to parish communion (often under pressure from their flocks), but most bishops advised them to avoid total exclusion in favour of sound instruction to reclaim the wayward.[46]

The most common forum for legal action against the Methodists was the church courts. The morals of early Methodists were under particularly close scrutiny, and there are also cases of penalties, including excommunication, against unlicensed lay preachers.[47] One of the most intriguing of the early actions against Methodism took place in York in 1755–6. The case began with a presentment made against William Williamson, a vicar choral of the Minster and incumbent of a city parish within the capitular jurisdiction, at the visitation held by the dean and chapter in 1755.[48] His accuser was Joseph Boyes, curate of Saint Samson's in York, who alleged that Williamson frequented a Methodist conventicle in his (Boyes's) parish, 'thereby not only setting a bad example to the said Joseph Boyes's parishioners, but to the city in general and giving occasion to libertines to raise objections against the Established Church'. In defence, Williamson brought an action against his accuser for wrongful presentment which was decided in his favour in the dean and chapter's court, but Boyes then appealed (with local clerical support) to the archiepiscopal court.

This long-running and expensive case not only highlights the complicated overlapping jurisdictions of visitation and permanent courts within the Church of England, but is also a mine of information about the nature of Anglican opposition to early Methodism as Boyes and his legal advisers dragged up every possible offence. Williamson was thus accused of breaking the ninth and seventy-third canons of the Church, the Tudor Acts of Uniformity, the Restoration statutes against Nonconformity and his own ordination vows. More colourfully, he was accused of resorting to 'the night revels of the Methodist meeting' which was

a place of bad fame and Reputation and the practices therein are said to be profane and superstitious, great numbers of persons of both sexes being frequently assembled there at very unreasonable hours in the night, the doors for the most part being locked, barred and bolted, in such private assemblies none being admitted without tickets with Popish pictures and devices upon them as of the Virgin Mary, a Crucifix, or a Lamb, porters being usually placed at the door of the meeting house to hinder admittance to and to thrust such persons back as are not known to be of their sect, which has given great umbrage and offence to the sober and well meaning part of the parishioners.[49]

Although nerves may have been set on edge by the outbreak of the Seven Year's War, it is ironic that an evangelical Anglican of Methodist sympathies should be victim of vague allegations of sexual licence and crypto-Catholicism.[50] Williamson nevertheless won the case, illustrating that church courts were far from crude instruments of Anglican intolerance.

Of more lasting consequence for the history of Methodism was the dispute surrounding a Calvinistic Methodist chapel in Clerkenwell in the years 1777–80.[51] As curate of the parish of St James Clerkenwell, William Sellon claimed the right of preaching in the chapel, the right of nominating its chaplains and the right to the money accruing from its sittings. When these claims were refused, Sellon began a suit in the consistorial court of the Bishop of London against two preachers – who happened to be associated with the Countess of Huntingdon – for irregularly preaching in a place not episcopally consecrated and contrary to the wishes of the curate of the parish. Verdicts were duly obtained, and the chapel closed. Lady Huntingdon then became its proprietor, renamed it Spa Fields Chapel and claimed that the preachers were her own private chaplains. Sellon instituted further proceedings to stop visits from other preachers. The lawsuits were expensive, and Lady Huntingdon was advised that the law was against her. Accordingly, she was forced to take shelter under the Toleration Act and register her chapels as dissenting meeting-houses. With more property at stake by the 1780s there was also a more general registration of Wesleyan Methodist meeting-houses which had earlier been rather haphazard (see Appendix, p. 161).[52] Legal inconveniences thus hastened the pace of Methodist separation from the Church of England, even if Wesley still refused to accept the dissenting logic of registration. Early associational Methodism could withstand legal pressures, albeit at the expense of mob violence, but chapel-based Methodism required firmer legal protection for its property.

A less quantifiable but ultimately more insidious consequence of Methodist growth for the Church of England was the part played by Methodism in further eroding the capacity of the Established Church either to require or to persuade the population to attend church services.

Two clerical comments from different parts of the country in the late 1780s illustrate what was going on:

> My Lord we still have near 20 persons amongst us, [illi]terate, who absent themselves from their parish church, [and go] at a distance every Sunday for what they call ['rea]l ministers' who, they say, alone preach Christ; and they generally find their favorite at a meeting-house in Woking. Upon being advised to do an act of real Christian charity by presenting to the bishop of the diocese every clergyman whom they may find not preaching the Gospel, that so the propagation of error may be prevented, they reply that 'the bishops of the present day are not proper judges; they themselves not being taught of God'. These persons find a mystical meaning in every passage they hear. . . . These persons deny themselves to be sectaries, for they say all the creeds, all the liturgy [and the] articles of the Church of England, though not perhaps all the words, and very few of them cant.[53]

> Our village for several Sundays past has been infected with a Sect of Impudent, New Fangled, rambling Teachers, called Methodists; Sorry I am to inform you, that Mr Samuel Lawton, One of your Principle [sic] tenants should harbour 'em in his Barn, and protect 'em from the Populace. It causes the public houses to be crowded with Drunken People all the day; it draws the Parishioners from their respective Parish Churches, set apart for, and dedicated to God's honour and worship, and therefore destructive of Christianity. By giving this Inconsiderate, unthinking man a line would for ever oblige, Sir.[54]

The exercise of private judgement in matters religious, the breakdown of parochial boundaries and discipline, the erosion of deference and the availability of new alternatives all combined to make it more difficult for the clergy to prescribe attendance at the parish church. The fact that Methodists could claim to be adherents to the creeds and liturgies of the Established Church made it more, not less, difficult for the Church to take effective action. Moreover, the demotic attraction *and* repulsion of these 'impudent, New Fangled, rambling Teachers' in local communities produced a social ambience antithetical to the maintenance of clerical control. Whether by offering a religious alternative for the more zealous, or, alternatively, by supplying identifiable targets for the mirth of alehouse culture, Methodism further eroded the persuasive power of the Established Church at the same time as its lack of powers of coercion became ever more manifest. Methodism thus played an important part in a much broader process of religious change in eighteenth-century England, as a centuries-old pattern of enforced ecclesiastical discipline and uniformity on a parish basis slowly gave way to a concept of religion as a voluntary commitment by free individuals in a pluralistic society. By the end of the eighteenth century, it seemed that the Church was powerless to stop this process. Moreover, it soon became clear that the state could do no better.

The rapid growth of Methodist and other kinds of itinerant preaching in the 1790s created the same unease among church people as the growth of corresponding societies occasioned among politicians.[55] They were seen as fruit of the same tree. As a result, more episcopal and clerical abuse was heaped upon the Methodists in the 1790s than in any decade since the 1740s. Pretyman-Tomline, Bishop of Lincoln and Pitt's old tutor, played an important role. Information from visitation returns and from the remarkable rise in meeting-house registrations (see Appendix, p. 161)[56] persuaded the bishop to commission a report on the state of religion in a hundred parishes of his diocese. The report told a sorry tale of Anglican weakness in the face of the gradual secularization of rural society and competition from predominantly Methodist itinerant preaching.[57] Three kinds of Methodists were distinguished: those who professed membership of the Church of England and attended the sacraments within the Church; those respectable Methodists who had moved outside the Established Church and administered their own sacraments; and those wild men and women of popular religion, the ranters, whose ignorance, superstition and anti-establishment rhetoric made them the bishop's prime targets.

From the late 1790s until the introduction of Sidmouth's Bill against itinerant preaching in 1811, conservative ecclesiastics urged the government to tighten up the law on the issue of preaching certificates, which in itself represents a shift in opinion from concern about conventicles to the need for control over those servicing them.[58] Politicians were on the whole reluctant to diminish religious toleration after a century of gradual relief, and preferred instead to urge dissenting denominations to impose their own controls. Such a policy came under fresh strain in 1811 when a House of Lords report appeared to show that the Church of England was on the verge of becoming a minority religious establishment. Although meeting-house registrations are a notoriously unreliable guide to the actual strength of Dissent in relation to the Church of England, the fact that meeting-houses outnumbered Anglican churches and chapels on a ratio of 7:5 left no one in any doubt that something amounting to a revolution in English religious practice had taken place in the quarter century after the French Revolution. Unsurprisingly, the number of dissenting registrations was particularly large in the northern dioceses of York and Chester, and in the Methodist strongholds represented by the dioceses of Lincoln and Exeter.[59] Moreover, there was widespread recognition that itinerant preaching and the Methodist class system had driven a coach and horses through the existing laws.

Although Sidmouth's Bill against itinerant preaching was, owing to lack of support, withdrawn without a division, there was a conservative reaction in the localities as quarter sessions all over the country refused to administer the oaths to Methodist preachers. Licences were refused because claimants were not ministers of a separate congregation, were thought to be deliberately avoiding military service and parochial duties or were held to be completely unsuitable for spiritual leadership.[60] As Ellenborough stated in King's Bench:

> neither the dissenters themselves, nor the legislative, could have meant to exempt from disabilities, or extend clerical privileges to every fanatic, enthusiast, who, without learning or sense, or the approbation of many of their own body, should pretend to have a call from heaven to instruct mankind.[61]

Ellenborough even appealed to the high ministerial qualifications demanded by the Presbyterians during the Protectorate as a rebuke to modern enthusiasts. Ellenborough's opinions proved to be as antiquated as his historical parallels, for a new Toleration Act was passed in 1812 giving the sort of rights to dissenting preachers he thought unimaginable only a year before.

After eighty years of legal uncertainty and episodic persecution, Methodism, which had frightened local justices in the 1740s and again in the 1790s, was instrumental in extending the frontiers of religious toleration in nineteenth-century England. Liberalism was thus the unintended beneficiary of religious enthusiasm. There is yet a further irony. Whereas in the mid-eighteenth century the Methodists were at the receiving end of religious, civil and community intolerance, in the generation overshadowed by the French Revolution the Methodist leadership showed itself to be equally intolerant of radicals, revivalists and female preachers within its own ranks.[62] Men like Kilham, Bourne and Stephens found themselves at the receiving end of Methodist 'justice', which to them compared unfavourably with the civil rights enjoyed by free-born Englishmen in the wider society. The case of Alexander Kilham is particularly instructive.[63]

Kilham was the most vocal radical within the Wesleyan connexion in the 1790s. His antipathy to the Church of England and his vigorous advocacy of Methodist sacraments outside the confines of the Established Church (effectively a blueprint for formal separation), made him a formidable opponent of anything resembling hierarchical church government within Methodism itself. Over the issue of sacraments, he opposed the compromise position adopted in the Plan of Pacification of 1795 because it gave too little power to the people, and too much to the Methodist 'House of Lords', the chapel trustees, and to the 'House of Popes', the Methodist Conference.[64] In similar vein, Kilham made a string of serious allegations about the private machinations and financial corruption of the Methodist ministerial aristocracy.[65] What Kilham wanted was more power for the laity in all aspects of connexional government and more financial accountability to the connexion from the leading preachers. Kilham therefore struck raw nerves of anticlericalism and anti-corruption among the more politicized artisans of industrial England. But with Methodism under increasing pressure from the government to control popular radicalism within its own ranks, Kilham found himself in an increasingly weak position and he was duly expelled from the connexion at the annual conference in 1796. In what was virtually a mirror-image of the claims made by Wilkites twenty years earlier, Kilham alleged that his trial infringed the sacred legal rights of Englishmen.[66] He was not given a list of the charges, he had no advocate, he was not tried by known laws, and he was not judged by a jury of the people. He stated that he would have expected this kind of treatment from absolute monarchs and the papal hierarchy, but not from the deliberative assembly of a Protestant voluntary religious association in the freest country in Europe. What Kilham had discovered, of course, was that the administration of law within Methodism was based even more on the need to protect established interests than was the case in the wider society. The poachers were now the gamekeepers.

Moreover, unlike Wesley in his dealings with eighteenth-century magistrates, radicals within the connexion soon discovered that within Methodism the higher the court the rougher was the justice meted out to them. Thus, Methodists who spent much time and money in the eighteenth century trying to find relief under the law, found themselves facing a series of crippling secessions in the nineteenth century which turned ultimately on the unacceptable application of connexional laws.[67]

Another significant change over the period is that the alarm of the 1790s expressed itself far more clearly at governmental level and within the Anglican episcopate than in local riots. Riots there were, but not that many, considering the vehemence of pamphlet attacks and the unprecedented level of official pressure. Revealingly, perhaps, some anti-Methodist disturbances in the 1790s were directed against the preachers and their financial exactions in a period of high food prices.[68] In any case, by the turn of the century those with a penchant for rioting were able to find far more potent targets than Methodist societies.[69] Representatives of the old order in Church and State were still alarmed by popular pietists, but their power of initiating direct action by 1800 was not what it had been fifty years earlier. Methodism's legal problems also changed, from the need to secure the basic rights of freedom of assembly and protection from mob violence in the eighteenth century to the desire for fair and equal treatment in a more pluralistic society in the nineteenth. The former gave early Methodists a unity of purpose which the latter could never match.

APPENDIX
CERTIFICATES FOR METHODIST MEETING-HOUSES FILED IN THE LINCOLN DIOCESAN REGISTRY (480 PARISHES), 1770–1813[a,b,c]

Year	Number
1770–4	7
1775–9	40
1780–4	6
1785–9	29
1790–4	85
1795–9	103
1800–4	91
1805–9	117
1810–13	113

Notes

a Only two specifically Methodist certificates are filed before 1770 (both in 1759), but it is clear that some Methodists applied under the common epithet 'Independents' to avoid complicated disputes both within their own community and with the authorities.

b The table does not represent a complete record of Methodist registrations since there was a smaller number of contemporaneous registrations at the quarter sessions of magistrates.

c Registration certificates are, of course, a notoriously unreliable guide to the actual numerical strength of Nonconformity, but they were a prime source for Anglican assessments of Nonconformist development. In that respect perceptions can be as important as realities.

9

POPULAR EVANGELICALISM, REFORM AND POLITICAL STABILITY IN ENGLAND, c. 1780–1850

The generation overshadowed by the French Revolution was the most important generation in the modern history not only of English religion, but of most of the Christian world. For the Revolution altered forever the terms on which religious establishments, the chief device on which the nations of the West had relied for christianising the people, must work.[1]

This generation also witnessed the unprecedented growth of evangelical religion in the British Isles and North America which had the unintended effect of refashioning the old denominational orders in both places.[2] Indeed, so dramatic was the impact of popular evangelicalism on the shaping of British society that historians have tried to make appropriate connections between its growth and other major social, political and cultural changes which took place at the same time.[3] These have often filtered down into standard evangelical interpretations of the past rehearsed in countless sermons and popular histories. As every evangelical schoolboy/girl knows Methodism saved England from revolution; the Clapham Sect, with William Wilberforce to the fore, secured the end of the slave trade and of colonial slavery; evangelical sobriety cleaned up a dissolute nation and contributed the work discipline and moral earnestness which lay at the heart of England's 'greatness' in the Victorian period; and evangelicalism supplied the religious zeal which fought back the secularizing dynamics of the eighteenth-century Enlightenment and secured the central place of religion in British society until at least the First World War. Historians, of course, take great pleasure in spoiling good stories and the precise role of evangelical religion in each of these areas has been the subject of constant revision and modification as historical techniques have become ever more sophisticated. In general this has resulted in less attention being paid to the heroic careers of evangelical leaders and rather more to the relationship between evangelicalism and other profound structural and cultural changes in early industrial Britain.[4]

162

Nowhere has this tendency been more marked than in the rapidly changing historiography of the anti-slavery agitation.

The importance of this movement should not be underestimated. More people signed petitions against slavery in the fifty years after 1785 than for any other single issue in British politics, including the extension of the suffrage or the reform of parliament.[5] Indeed the style and techniques of the anti-slavery agitation, from mass petitioning to the extraction of pledges from parliamentary candidates, served as models for subsequent religio-political crusades mounted by evangelical nonconformists in the nineteenth century.[6] Historians are in general agreement that the remarkable growth of evangelicalism and the simultaneous growth of mass abolitionist sentiments in British society must be linked in some way, but the questions are how and how much?

The traditional evangelical interpretation, dating back to Thomas Clarkson's first narrative of the abolitionist movement in 1808, is based on the activities of an influential group of evangelical parliamentarians and philanthropists who overcame the vested interests of the powerful West Indian lobby and secured a great humanitarian victory.[7] More refined interpretations emphasizing the central role of evangelical religion in the abolition of slavery have still not lost their influence despite the arguments of those who prefer to locate abolitionist success within the economic framework of free market capitalism or within the political framework of advancing liberalism.[8] For example, perhaps the most distinguished historian of British abolitionism, Roger Anstey, laid great emphasis on the conjunction of the Enlightenment and the evangelical concern for liberty, benevolence and happiness. Evangelical theology, with its dynamic emphasis on providence, redemption and Christian freedom, could, with equal legitimacy, be directed against the spiritual bondage of sin and the physical bondage of slavery. 'In the very warp and woof of Evangelical faith', he wrote,

> slavery, of all social evils, stood particularly condemned, and because slavery and freedom represented the externalisation of the polar opposites of the Evangelicals' inmost spiritual experience, they were impelled to act in the cause of abolition with a zeal and a perseverance which other men could rarely match.[9]

In an even more vigorous attempt to emphasize the moral and religious components of the anti-slavery agitation, as opposed to the political and economic, it has been suggested that 'the "vitality" of the Anti-Slavery Movement and its ultimate success can be viewed in the perspective of its evangelical dynamic'.[10] For the evangelical critics of slavery, the sins of a guilty nation could only be expiated, and the wrath of an angry God could only be averted, by the dedicated and unremitting actions of the faithful.

Explaining the success of the anti-slavery agitation in terms of its 'evangelical dynamic' is not without its problems however. Not only were many evangelicals not abolitionists, including the majority of those who lived in the southern states of the USA, but it is clear that the mass mobilization of anti-slavery sentiment in Britain extended far beyond the evangelical constituency. It was also viewed with some unease by some of the more politically conservative evangelicals who feared popular disorder almost as much as they hated slavery. Wilberforce was uneasy about mass petitioning in the late 1780s and even as late as 1833 Jabez Bunting wrote that

> I decidedly think that the holy cause of Anti-Slavery has already been disgraced and prejudiced in some quarters by the system of 'agitation', after the fashion of Irish Papists and Repealers, which has been employed to promote it. The wrath of man worketh not the righteousness of God.[11]

Extensive research on the mobilization of public opinion against slavery, including the ubiquitous petitions, has confirmed the importance of popular evangelicalism to the anti-slavery agitation, but it has also shown that evangelicalism, of itself, did not create mass mobilization; rather abolitionism proliferated in the same ideological and political context which was also favourable to evangelical Nonconformity.[12] In short, abolitionism attracted the support not only of the evangelical middle classes who had an economic as well as a religious interest in abolition, but also appealed to the urban artisans as part of a wider political protest against paternalism and dependency during the early Industrial Revolution. Both abolitionism and popular evangelicalism thrived in the kinds of urban communities that emerged in the early stages of industrial growth and they shared some similar characteristics. Both were attacked for undermining traditional authority in Church and State in the period of the French Revolution; both were based on voluntary associations and made extensive use of touring lecturers (itinerant preachers) and popular print (religious tracts); both led to enlarged spheres of action for women and sometimes children; and both were capable of appealing to different social strata and of creating communities in which moral/religious values were treated seriously. But evangelicalism also had something distinctive to bring to the anti-slavery movement. The dramatic expansion of overseas missions in the first third of the nineteenth century helped narrow the geographical and psychological gap between social realities in Britain and the colonies which some have argued was an essential precondition of a genuinely popular mobilization against slavery. Problems of mission, including the ignorance of slaves and the preaching restrictions imposed by planters, began to occupy more space in religious periodicals in the 1820s. Tales of imprisoned missionaries and of persecuted slave converts added emotional intensity to the annual meetings of the missionary societies. Richard Watson told the anniversary gathering of the Wesleyan Missionary Society in 1830 that overseas missions had increased

> our sympathies with the external circumstances of the oppressed and miserable of all lands. It is impossible for men to care for the souls of others without caring for their bodies also. . . . We cannot care for the salvation of the negro, without caring for his emancipation from bondage.[13]

Although the most important early impulses of anti-slavery sentiment in Britain are to be located within the ranks of the Anglican evangelicals of Clapham, the Quakers and some of Wesley's followers, it was not until the 1820s that the anti-slavery movement enjoyed the mass support of an increasingly powerful evangelical Nonconformity. The fact that this support was enlarged still further by a radical libertarian strand of politics among the British working classes made the anti-slavery movement a force to be reckoned with by the early 1830s. In that sense the abolition of slavery in British colonies was neither an economic necessity whose time had come nor a disinterested political gesture from an established political elite, but was, to a considerable extent, a victory for new religious and political forces unleashed both by evangelical enthusiasm and by the structural changes in British society in the period of the Industrial Revolution.

The relationship between those structural changes – on a much wider canvass than mere anti-slavery sentiment – and the rise and influence of evangelical religion, is one of the most bitterly contested and largely unresolved debates in modern British history. To a remarkable extent the great French historian, Elie Halévy, set an agenda at the beginning of the twentieth century, which, for good and for ill, has cast a powerful intellectual spell over the subsequent writing of the history of popular evangelicalism. According to Halévy, early industrial England, by comparison with its European neighbours, possessed an unusual and potentially volatile degree of political, economic and religious freedom. In Europe's most advanced capitalist country dynamic forces of anarchy and social revolution were moderated and redirected by a remarkable resurgence of puritanism in the shape of the evangelical revival. Methodism was thus the antidote to the revolutionary Jacobinism that undermined the *ancien régime* in France, and 'the free organisation of the sects was the foundation of social order in England'.[14]

Halévy believed that evangelicalism, for all its popular idiosyncrasies and bourgeois hypocrisy, was the chief engine in the creation of a free and ordered society based on widely accepted notions of 'voluntary obedience'. Paradoxical though it may seem, therefore, the freest country in Europe was saved from the frightening consequences of anarchic libertarianism by the fact that its national Established Church 'left the sects outside her borders entire liberty of organization, full power to form a host of little states within the state'. Evangelicalism thus spawned a host of new religious associations, from Methodist societies to pan-evangelical charities, and worked for the reformation of society and its morals, not primarily by legal coercion, but by the power of voluntary effort and religious enthusiasm. In this way English freedoms were secured by the proliferation of communities of grace.

There is now general agreement among historians that Halévy exaggerated both the fragility of England's *ancien régime* and the power of evangelicalism to save it from its inner contradictions. There are nevertheless two things at least worth saving from Halévy's set of hypotheses. The first is the importance of evangelical religion in forging a rough harmony of values between the pragmatic and moralistic middle classes and the skilled and respectable sections of the English working classes who were notorious in Europe for their solid virtue and capacity for organization. The second is Halévy's emphasis on the relative tolerance of the Church of England and the capacity of Methodist groups to separate from the Established Church and from one another in a reasonably ordered and disciplined fashion. But the key here is not so much the libertarian sentiments of the Methodists, nor indeed their lofty principles, as any student of the bitter rivalries associated with such splits will testify, as the profound influence of legal frameworks in helping both to articulate religious grievances and to manage their potentially disruptive consequences.[15] What Halévy ascribed to the sole influence of evangelicalism, therefore, may, at least in part, be attributable to earlier traditions of constitutional and legal chauvinism among all sections of the English population. If popular evangelicalism did indeed stabilize early industrial society, part of the reason may be that it was able to exploit and to benefit from structures and values that were already in place.[16]

The important issues raised by Halévy have not gone away. Since the Second World War a number of significant attempts have been made to construct alternative narratives of the role of popular evangelicalism in the age of the French and Industrial Revolutions. Although different in their presuppositions, scope and methods, many of these accounts contain at least some shared conclusions. My intention is to select one influential work from each decade since 1945 to illustrate not only the range of interpretations, but also to highlight the avenues of enquiry worth pursuing in the future.

Although Robert Wearmouth's *Methodism and the Working-Class Movements of England 1800–1850* was first published in 1937, it was reprinted immediately after the war and represents a century-old tradition of Methodist scholarship on the relationship between popular evangelicalism and working-class political movements. The secret of Methodist success was located in the opportunities it afforded laymen to assume important positions of responsibility within the Methodist polity. Some

20,000 local preachers, 50,000 class leaders and still more trustees, stewards, exhorters, prayer leaders and Sunday school teachers all learned the disciplines of leadership which were then applied to a variety of working-class causes from trade unionism to Chartism.[17] As with personnel, so with structures. Methodism's

> connexionalism, its large-scale finance and enterprise, its division into districts, circuits, and societies, its propaganda methods of itinerant preaching and Sunday open-air meetings, its society class and weekly penny subscription were all copied at some stage or another by the political reformers.[18]

In this way Methodism operated as 'a kind of Radicalism in the religious world, while Radicalism acted as a kind of Methodism in the political sphere'.[19] Methodism could thus bask in plaudits both from the right (for inculcating the discipline that saved Britain from revolution) and from the left (for nurturing the leadership skills of political reformers and trade unionists). According to Wearmouth, Methodism also pioneered a powerful fusion of individualism and collectivism. 'Methodism developed a highly successful type of religious collectivism', but before 'the majority of Methodist recruits could be used in a collective capacity they had to learn discipline, self-control, and even self-sacrifice'.[20] In the light of the subsequent historiography of Methodism, Wearmouth's real achievement was to draw attention away from the Wesleyan Conference and itinerant preachers and to place more emphasis on the Methodist lay leadership of all the connexions in the localities. He also intuitively grasped (as a Durham coalminer himself) that there was no necessary incongruity between Methodist and radical objectives in the first half of the nineteenth century. It is nevertheless a pity that some fifty years later we still do not have an authoritative treatment of the lay leadership of Methodism in the period of the Industrial Revolution.

A more conceptually fertile, if inevitably more speculative, analysis of evangelicalism in British society at the turn of the eighteenth–nineteenth century came from the pen of Victor Kiernan in the first issue of *Past and Present* in 1952 in which he suggested that

> two conceptions of religion were living in England side by side, and the French Revolution compelled a choice between them. One was of religion as the formulary of an established society, its statement of faith in itself; the other as a catastrophic conversion of the individual, a miraculous shaking off of secret burdens. One was fixed on this world, the other on the next.[21]

Since the Established Church was too frightened by the collapse of the Catholic Church in France and was 'too worm-eaten with patronage and pluralism' to meet the new challenges, Kiernan states that it was left to the evangelicals to forge the kind of changes in English society which led first of all to a greater emphasis on the individual and then eventually to a peculiarly English variety of liberalism. Evangelicalism thus brought together the

> developing sections of the middle classes, gave them an independent outlook, relieved their fears of the more elemental forms of mass unrest, showed how a respectable working-class could be led by a respectable middle-class. In fact it prepared the ground for 19th century English Liberalism.

For Kiernan, incipient class conflict was kept at bay by 'the mystical cable of theology' and religious revivalism combined a 'censure on the powers that be, including the absentee prelates and selfish aristocrats of 1800' with a 'dissuasive of popular rebellion'. Kiernan's Marxist analysis did not allow much scope for a sympathetic assessment of Methodism, but his realization that the French and Industrial Revolutions marked a point of no return for the Church of England, together with his conviction that evangelicalism could be properly understood only as an integrated part of other social, cultural and political processes, helped shape subsequent interpretations.

An even more pungent Marxist interpretation of Methodism, perhaps the most influential ever written, was published a decade after Kiernan's pioneering article by E. P. Thompson in his book *The Making of the English Working Class* (1963). Part of Thompson's remarkable influence on Methodist historiography stems from the imaginative power of his language. It is the colour, the passion, the eloquence, the rhetorical overstatement, the metaphoric and symbolic affluence, and the foreshortening of argument in the interests of coherence and force that make his work on popular religion so gripping. Thompson's phrases, some of which were borrowed from others, have livened up many a tired page of undergraduate prose: 'psychic masturbation', the 'chiliasm of despair', 'religious terrorism' (borrowed from Lecky), the 'promiscuous opportunism' of Methodist theology, the 'working paroxysms of the artisan', the 'box-like, blackening chapels' of the industrial districts, the 'Sabbath orgasms of feeling' and the 'valley of humiliation of the poor' all testify to the poetical brilliance of Thompson's writing. But there is more to it than that. At the heart of Thompson's interpretation of Methodism there is both a powerful historical method and a theoretical coherence which are not easily disturbed by mere empirical challenges. The clue to understanding both is to be found in Thompson's last book on William Blake and the Moral Law.[22] In playfully declaring himself to be a fellow member of Blake's obscure sect of 'Muggletonian Marxists' (in the sense of an intellectual tradition, not, of course, a historical reality), Thompson was not only aligning himself with the radical antinomian tradition of popular Dissent stretching from the Puritan fringes of the English Civil Wars to the metropolitan sects of the late eighteenth century, but was also, both consciously and unconsciously, associating himself with a particular historical method. The method is made explicit in the old Muggletonian rhyme, 'Since by contraries all things are made clear, without contraries nothing can appear', which, according to Thompson, was the 'dialectic which came to influence Blake's whole stance – his historical, moral and utopian thought'.[23]

Thompson's Methodism is built on the dialectic of 'the two contrarieties'. As with a solenoid empowered by electrical current, both the compelling energy of the Methodist movement and of Thompson's historical reconstruction of it may be attributed to the dynamic tensions of oscillation. Sometimes this is explicit, as in Thompson's explanation of the social processes of religious revivalism and political radicalism: 'we may suppose something like an oscillation, with religious revivalism at the negative, and radical politics (tinged with revolutionary millenarialism) at the positive pole'.[24] But more often the method is so seamless or, to stick with the original metaphor, the solenoid spins so fast that it scarcely seems to be moving at all. Thompson is at his most persuasive in those memorable passages where he wrestles with the 'many tensions at the heart of Wesleyanism'. There are contrarieties everywhere: in the spiritual egalitarianism of the Methodist message and its authoritarian ecclesiastical structure; in the religion of the heart and its repression of spontaneity; in a religion allegedly founded on love which 'feared love's effective expression, either as sexual love or in any social form which might irritate relations with Authority'; in the libertarianism of grace which was sabotaged by works-righteousness driven on by the fear of backsliding; in the 'moral civil war' that was waged between the chapel and the pub, the wicked and the redeemed, the lost and the saved; and in the tension between the kingdom without and the kingdom within, between the kingdom here and now and the kingdom hereafter. Such tensions, Thompson freely admits, could be creative and energizing, but it is the main burden of his argument that the reverse was more typically the case. Ultimately Thompson conceived of Methodism as a 'disorganization of human life' in which spontaneity was sacrificed to discipline, joy to sin and guilt, and goodness and love to the glorification of pain: 'to labour and to sorrow was to find pleasure, and masochism was "Love"'.[25] The energy of the solenoid, it seemed, served only to empower a generation of 'religious invalids' who found themselves in their weakness 'violently recast into submissive industrial workers'. Hermaphroditic, mulish and mindless, Methodism subverted the noble intellectual traditions of radical Dissent.

Thompson's preoccupation with ideas of oscillation and displacement of energy did not allow him to see much that was admirable in the

169

Methodist tradition, nor did it permit him to explore its complexities. He exaggerated the power of Bunting's Conference to the neglect of local preachers in English localities; he paid only lip-service to the idea that rural Methodism could represent a radical challenge to Anglican paternalism; he assumed too easily that English workers were 'victims' of Methodist indoctrination when most were willing participants in a voluntary association which offered them tangible benefits; he overestimated the work-discipline, political submissiveness and sexual repression of his male Methodists and he dealt not at all with the female majority; he failed to answer the question *why* such large numbers should find his unattractive Methodism so attractive and answered instead the more angry question of how *could* they submit to such 'religious terrorism'? Yet more detailed criticisms could be offered from page to page of his chapter on the transforming power of the cross, and yet no one has offered such a compelling account of the Methodist *experience* in the early Industrial Revolution. But his is more the compelling power of the disappointed prophet than of the meticulous historian. That is why it remains such an immensely enjoyable read and such a dangerous piece of social history.

Thompson's refusal to accept that Methodism, apart from its irregular fringes, could operate as a radical force in early industrial society was challenged a decade later in W. R. Ward's *Religion and Society in England 1790–1850* (1972) which still remains the best-researched and most complex portrait of urban Methodism in the north of England. Indeed, so complex is the argument and so dense is the compression of evidence and ideas that Ward's book has not the influence of less worthy and more accessible accounts of the Methodist experience. What makes it so complex is Ward's conviction that the great awakening of the eighteenth century was both an international event transcending national boundaries and a religious movement deeply embedded in the social, political and economic peculiarities of specific regions.[26] The English version operated within a state too weak to put down Dissent or to overhaul the national Established Church, and came to fruition in a period when the Church of England's pastoral mission was hampered by increased clerical wealth and unprecedented clerical representation on benches of magistrates.[27] In the atmosphere of crisis generated by the French Revolution, prolonged warfare, demographic expansion and extraordinarily rapid social change the old denominational order, which had been in place since the late seventeenth century, was simply blown apart by a great outpouring of undenominational evangelical religion. Ward writes that

> R. W. Dale later charged the evangelicals of this period with being insufficiently political; part of their defence must be that they were threatened with the loss of their basic rights of prayer and preaching. With those potent weapons, they proceeded to the ruin of the Church

as a national establishment, with all the political consequences that entailed.[28]

The strength of Ward's argument, and the reason why it is so difficult to synthesize, is the way in which he brings together what are often kept apart, the social tensions generated by class conflict and the religious tensions generated by denominational conflict. As English society experienced crisis after crisis, especially in the 1790s, 'the swelling tide of anti-establishment sentiment in popular religion' not only eroded the control mechanisms of the Established Church, but also forced a heightened denominational consciousness among newer groups like the Methodists whose leadership now had to learn to control the very forces from which they had benefited. Ward shows how in industrial towns across the north internal battles raged within Methodism over lay participation in church government, styles of evangelism, control over the burgeoning Sunday schools, the financial support of a new clerical class and the extent of denominational control over the political affiliations of the membership. As the growing corpus of local studies has made clear, the precise resolutions of these tensions varied from place to place and from time to time, but what is not any longer in doubt is the way in which the internal squabbles within Methodism both reflected and articulated much wider social tensions in English society in the first quarter of the nineteenth century.[29] The Methodist polity was not only a training ground for talent, as Wearmouth has it, or an instrument of social control, as Thompson has it, but was also a lightning conductor for conflicts endemic in early industrial England. It is Ward's considerable achievement to have shown more clearly than anyone else exactly how the stresses and strains of a new industrial society acted on the old denominational order of pre-industrial England.

Thompson the Marxist and Ward the ranter clearly come at their subject from very different starting-points, but they do share similar convictions about the parlous state of the Church of England in the Age of Revolution and a measure of contempt for the way in which Jabez Bunting and his supporters sought to impose connexional discipline in the most undisciplined of times. Ward's account of the expulsion of Methodist radicals in the wake of Peterloo and his insightful treatment of the way in which the financial resources of connexion were harnessed in support of a higher doctrine of the pastoral office within Wesleyanism are stepping stones to his general conclusion that although Methodism proved to be a sufficiently popular movement by 1820 to undermine the old order in Church and State, it was, by 1850, in no position to be the bearer of an alternative national faith. By then English religion had settled into a pattern which offered little long-term prospect of a successful resistance to the cold winds of secularization and the growing power of the state.[30]

Subsequent local studies of Methodism in the north of England have largely borne out Ward's principal arguments and have shown in greater detail the ways in which changes in the socio-economic structures of local communities were reflected in internal unrest within Wesleyan Methodism. They have also shown that the ubiquitous Sunday schools, as much as anything, represented the popular culture of Methodism and made them such important prizes for the contending parties in connexional disputes. Conversely, there is evidence to suggest that Ward may have exaggerated both the degree of undenominational religious zeal in the earlier period and the extent of denominational competition and hostility in the later period.[31] Pan-evangelical co-operation for the task of Christianizing the non-churchgoing population often survived the more publicized and more heated political disagreements over tithes, church rates and national education. Moreover, the tentacles of Buntingism did not extend to every nook and cranny of every circuit any more than all itinerants came to be regarded as centralizing agents of connexional control. Most itinerant preachers continued to be welcomed by their circuits; had it been otherwise the entire Methodist structure would have experienced even more severe difficulties than those with which we are already familiar. In short, Methodism in the age of Bunting, as was the case in previous generations, was a much more variegated species than one might suppose from an over-concentration on connexional politics to the exclusion of local peculiarities. Ward was himself well aware that 'in a period in which change and conflict are of major importance, factors promoting change and conflict, views capable of generating policy, receive more attention than factors of stability which have been in any case too much the stock-in-trade of writers in the history and sociology of religion'.[32] Ward's reward for eschewing the blandness of history based essentially on underlying continuities was the creation of a series of vivid sketches of provincial Methodism in the Age of Revolution which will remain the benchmark for some time to come.

My own contribution to the subject of Methodism and politics published a decade after Ward's study was an attempt to trace both the official political attitudes of the connexional leadership and the unofficial politics of dissentients who refused to come into line.[33] Both were investigated against a backcloth of anxiety and revolution which often set the parameters for the controllers and the controlled. I attempted to show in a more systematic, if no more convincing, fashion than Ward that the Methodist polity was itself an intense theatre of conflict which mirrored, sometimes uncannily, the political and constitutional issues at stake between 1780 and 1850. As such, particular attention was given to the legal and political attitudes brought into Methodism from its surrounding constituency as well as to the more familiar attempts to impose connexional control from the centre. Even in politics, the relationship between Methodism and its surrounding culture is best explored through processes of cultural brokerage than through mere imposition alone. Hence the conflicts fought out among trustees, preachers and people over the sacraments in the 1790s were often interpreted as the clashing forces of property, clericalism and democracy in which the legal rights of the free-born Englishman were vigorously asserted against established interests. Similarly, in the period 1800 to 1820 pressures from the government to control itinerant preaching combined with pressures from below (in the shape of popular revivalism, political radicalism and working-class educational aspirations) to force the connexional leaders of Wesleyanism into a vigorous conservative counter-attack. They were helped on their way by a surprisingly luxuriant anti-Catholicism, reinforced but not created by Methodist experiences in Ireland, and by a residual affection for the acceptable face of religious establishments. Central to my approach, as with Ward's, was a conviction that although class conflict helped shape many of Methodism's internal cleavages, class alone was not the only, nor always the most important, framework for understanding the relationship between Methodism and politics in the early Industrial Revolution. Nor was it simply a matter of accepting the old Thompsonian oscillation between religious enthusiasm and radical politics, for religious enthusiasm (both consciously and unconsciously) was often the engine of radical change and nineteenth-century radicalism was not as secular in its aspirations as socialist historians have tried to suggest. My aim was rather to show how Methodism contributed to the increased religious pluralism of the British state and then had to cope with the political consequences of its own success, both in relation to the increasingly bitter conflicts between Church and Dissent and to the conflicts between those who wanted to uphold the status quo (both inside and outside the connexion) and those who wanted to change it in one direction or another. The picture thus presented was unashamedly complex, ambiguous, multifaceted and unamenable to a single narrative description beyond the recognition that both in politics and religion Britain was an immeasurably more variegated and pluralistic nation in 1850 than it had been in 1780. Methodism not only contributed more than any other movement to that process, but also helped make the transition more ordered and more peaceful than otherwise might have been the case. Those raised on a diet of Halévy and Thompson found this conclusion too timid, while those more in touch with real Methodism in the localities, as opposed to the theoretical constructions of its interpreters, found the situation to be even more complex than I had supposed.

The final resting place in this decade by decade survey of scholarship between popular evangelicalism and politics is Alan Gilbert's essay on 'Religion and political stability in early industrial England'.[34] Gilbert's argument is that evangelical Nonconformity did indeed make a major contribution to England's political stability, not because of the effectiveness of official Wesleyanism in subduing connexional radicals, but because Methodism as a religious movement deviating from the Established Church acted as a 'political "safety valve" for the pressures of early industrial politics'.[35] Gilbert states that the 'rank-and-file proclivity towards moderate radicalism offered an effective alternative for many in the society who may otherwise have gravitated towards extremism'.[36] There is much that is admirable about Gilbert's interpretation and the epithet 'moderate radicalism' is sure to appear in many an undergraduate essay as a convenient solution to an old conundrum. The way in which Methodism as a religious movement is presented as a radical challenge to the Established Church and not as an opiate substitute for a genuine political radicalism, an interpretation shared by Ward, Obelkevich and myself, is itself an indication that the conventional Marxist attempts to prove otherwise have not been persuasive.[37] Gilbert supports his argument that popular evangelicalism made a decisive difference to the political stability of early industrial England with five main propositions: Methodism was a truly national movement; popular evangelicalism was sufficiently strong within the key social groups (urban artisans) to be a major influence on popular politics; the Methodist movement as a whole paid little attention to the more extremist anti-radicalism of the Wesleyan leadership; Methodists were sufficiently imbued with radical notions to make them a potentially disaffected people; and the disciplines of Methodism exercised a moderating influence on the political behaviour of its adherents. The fact that Gilbert's earlier work was so distinguished for its pioneering work on religious statistics makes one more ready to accept his statement that 'the historian ought perhaps to think in terms of something approaching 20 per cent of the most politicized section of the adult lower orders being associated with chapel communities'.[38] Equally convincing is his suggestion (echoing Wearmouth) that Methodism imposed self-discipline and restraint even on the political radicals within its sphere of influence and may have plucked off many potential leaders for more extreme radical causes.

There are nonetheless aspects of Gilbert's treatment which are not so persuasive. The impression is given that the real reason for the numerical success of popular evangelicalism is that it was a 'a political "safety valve" for the pressures of early industrial politics'. This interpretation is simply a more refined version of Thompson's displacement of energy model which failed so conspicuously to get at the heart and centre of Methodism's attraction as a 'religious' movement. The use of metaphors like 'a safety valve', whether intentional or not, create the impression that popular religion is simply a displacement of something rather more important and more essential, and therefore removes the need for the historian to encounter it on something like its own terms. Similarly, Gilbert does not spend much time defining his use of the terms radicalism or 'moderate radicalism'. From the examples chosen for illustrative purposes he appears to be using a conventionally eclectic definition of radicalism to include Luddism, political reformism and general anti-government sentiment. In contrast, moderate radicalism is defined as the expression of 'more or less legitimate opposition to a reactionary regime'.[39] The problem with these definitions is that they explain at once too much and too little. The assumption upon which they are constructed is that religious adherence and popular radicalism lie at opposite ends of the spectrum and that what Methodism succeeded in doing was to bring them together in a more moderate synthesis. What is lacking here, it seems to me, is a convincing grasp of the social and political milieu of chapel communities in the crucial period 1790–1850, and a sense of the eclectic prejudices and enthusiasms that shaped local religious and political conflicts. The issues that aroused the most intense passions were not always to do with class conflict, parliamentary reform and the extension of the suffrage. Whenever chapel communities roused themselves to political action in this period they were as much concerned with protecting itinerant preaching, abolishing slavery, resisting Catholic Emancipation, eroding Anglican privileges, establishing elementary education, fighting for control of the Sunday schools, campaigning for a greater measure of ecclesiastical democracy and reforming public morals, as they were with the 'radical' demands of working-class political leaders, many of whom treated the religious enthusiasm of the evangelicals with the utmost contempt. Moreover, even within the chapel communities themselves, conflicts over who controlled the preachers, the conduct of revivals and the style of worship occasioned as much heat as the more familiar political problems investigated by historians. Many of these issues were of course overlaid by elements of class and cultural conflict, but the precise relationship between them is deserving of more sensitive treatment than is permitted in some studies devoted more to the history of the Halévy thesis as an historical hypothesis than to the history of evangelicalism as a popular religious movement. The danger of this approach is that the religious motivation, enthusiasm and objectives of the faithful are conveniently set aside in order to move on to the 'big' questions of assessing the cultural and political impact of apparently monochrome religious movements. It is not clear to me, however, that the second stage of this analysis can be accomplished with any degree of conviction without some appreciation of the religious convictions of the participants and the way in which those convictions shaped and were shaped by the surrounding environment.[40] There is still a need for sensitive local studies in which the religion of the people is located firmly within the economic and social structure of their communities to understand more clearly how religious deviance intersected with other frameworks, including attitudes towards law and authority, work and poverty, paternalism and protest, family and fertility, time and leisure, and faith

175

and morality. Only then will the relationship between religious deviance and popular politics move beyond the single narrative approach to uncover the mentalities of chapel communities in the early Industrial Revolution.[41]

Good recent examples of what can be achieved include the work of Smith and Winstanley on Oldham and its surroundings. Smith offers a convincing interpretation of how religious life became more pluralistic without leading to the capitulation of the Established Church, which, after the failure of Church and King mobs in the 1790s, showed a capacity to reform itself and to tolerate its rivals. But religion was also an agent of reform as 'almost all the churches provided a natural home for local radicals in their associational culture of rational recreation and self-improvement'.[42] This analysis is taken further in Michael Winstanley's work on Oldham radicalism and the origins of popular liberalism in the period 1830–52.[43] By rejecting the primacy of frameworks based on social class and economic structure alone, he is able not only to show a continuity of radical objectives based on 'retrenchment, tax reform, democratic accountability and local self-government', but is also able to demonstrate that there was a symbiotic relationship, not a polar oscillation, between militant Nonconformity and political radicalism. Campaigns for 'the removal of restrictions on Dissenters, the abolition of slavery in the colonies, the ending of fiscal and political privileges of the established church, factory reform, repeal of the Poor Law Amendment Act', temperance and teetotalism, and the preservation of unsectarian Sunday schools, all reflected a preoccupation with moral and religious reform which was not antithetical to radical objectives, but rather informed them. Even Oldham's 'Chartism continued to reflect the characteristics of the improving dissenting culture of the 1830s' in its teetotalism, moral improvement, class meetings and religious symbolism, and in its repudiation of the time-wasting frivolities of popular celebrations.

The point in dealing with this at some length is to show that the relationship between popular evangelicalism and political radicalism throughout the period 1790–1850 is best regarded not as a 'safety valve' or as 'moderate radicalism' (which implies the same political content expressed in a more socially acceptable way), but as a symbiotic relationship stemming from Methodism's part religious and part social challenge to Anglican paternalism and aristocratic government. The residual influence of Thompson's oscillation theories and of Hobsbawm's ideas on the concurrent expansion of an essentially separated Methodism and radicalism, have supplied the dominant intellectual framework even for those historians who disagree with them.[44] Moreover, it is vital to see not only that religious deviance and political radicalism could inform one another, but also that the same contentious issues could be fought out as vigorously *within* the Methodist polity as they were *between* Methodism

176

and other established interests. For example, Winstanley's conclusion that concern over taxes and political accountability provide the key to understanding popular politics throughout the nineteenth century, could, with equal validity, be applied to the Methodist system itself. There is, for example, considerably more material in Methodist correspondence between 1790 and 1830 relating to Methodist financial exactions and to questions of local control and accountability (whether over preachers, Sunday schools, revival methods, missionary strategy and policy formation) as there is on the much more widely reported conflicts over Luddism, political reformism and Chartism. It is not that the Methodists were an unpolitical people, as their leaders were so fond of telling government (though, of course, many were), nor that their connexion could not be disturbed from top to bottom during times of severe economic depression and political excitement, but that their politics, in the main, did not conform to the sterile and unhistorical categories assigned to them by later generations of historians often with little feel or sympathy for the religion and culture of chapel communities.[45]

This selective survey of some six decades of scholarship on Methodism and popular politics in the Age of Revolution has of necessity emphasized the complexities and ambiguities at the heart of a religious movement which has consistently defied tidy historical explanations. But Gilbert is quite right to urge that the complexity of the early history of evangelicalism should not preclude serious attempts to advance a coherent interpretation of its social and political influence on the nation. The starting-point, however, has to be a proper grasp of the sheer variety of the eighteenth-century evangelical revival, in terms of geography, theology, denomination and social class. Even within one of its most powerful traditions, that of Methodism, John Wesley's famed empiricism (perhaps the most important of all the defining non-theological elements of evangelicalism) threw up different patterns in different places at different times. The varied sources of Wesley's inspiration and the

> very varied contexts into which Methodism found its way are crucial to the understanding of the man and his movement; for they intensified as nothing else could have done the empiricism which he absorbed from the Enlightenment. Single-model accounts of Methodism ... ignore the breadth of its origins and the breadth of the problems it encountered.[46]

Comparative studies of Methodist growth rates in different parts of the North Atlantic world in the early nineteenth century (see Chapter 1) nevertheless suggest that, however diverse the Methodist experience may have been from region to region and from country to country, Methodism generally made its fastest gains in expanding societies where traditional patterns of religious and social control were under the most serious threat. This was true of England, where a fatal combination of major structural and demographic changes, on the one hand, and the profound impact of the French Revolution, on the other, seriously eroded the capacity of the Established Church to retain its role as the chief instrument for Christianizing the poor. English society being what it was, therefore, the crisis of authority at the end of the eighteenth century occurred more dramatically in the organization of religion than in the organization of the state. From this perspective it is possible to view the remarkable growth of Methodism, Sunday schools and county associations for promoting itinerant evangelism as radical religious challenges to the paternalistic Anglican establishment. As against traditional Marxist interpretations of the social impact of popular religion, therefore, evangelicalism in early industrial England may be more appropriately interpreted as a religious expression of radicalism than as an opiate substitute for it. Largely undenominational religious associations eroded the religious control of the Established Church, not by the political means which the Church had always feared, but through the cottage prayer meetings and itinerant preaching of an increasingly mobilized laity.

Whether one looks at the anti-slavery agitation or the growth of religious pluralism and its relationship to the Halévy thesis, popular evangelicalism made a powerful contribution to the erosion of old privileges in Church and State and facilitated adaptation to an increasingly liberal and capitalist society. Some of these reforming enthusiasms were self-conscious and purposefully planned for, others were shared symbiotically with other great reforming forces in early nineteenth-century society, and still others were essentially unexpected by-products of its own remarkable growth. A dynamic and socially diverse movement cannot be reduced to a single cohesive theory about religion and the evolution of the British state without diminishing the complexity of human motivation on the one hand and the sheer variety of popular evangelicalism (including its rural expressions) on the other. The manifold processes of cultural brokerage between popular evangelicalism and the communities in which it took root offer more satisfying possibilities than the search for a single narrative, which is, by definition, unnecessarily reductionist.

10

WOMEN AND EVANGELICAL RELIGION IN IRELAND, 1750–1900

The conventional analytical frameworks for understanding the roles of women in the eighteenth and nineteenth centuries are not wearing well, nor were they ever likely to. Separate spheres, public and private habitations, the cult of domesticity, economic marginalization and gender essentialism have all been found to explain too much, too little or nothing at all.[1] Often manufactured on the basis of the thinnest of prescriptive literature or on the back of inadequate conceptions of the social functioning of early modern societies, gender narratives were constructed in tandem with other conceptual frameworks for understanding the rise of industrial society. Unfortunately, the predominantly Marxian analysis of early industrial capitalism, which for so long had been in the ascendancy, was itself showing signs of wear and tear at precisely the time it was pressed into service most assiduously to explain the experiences of women. The public/private dichotomy has proved equally problematic, for, as Amanda Vickery has stated,

> in a historian's hands, a public role can mean access to anything from politics, public office, formal employment, opinion, print, clubs, assembly, company, the neighbourhood, the streets, or simply the world outside the front door. However, we should take care to discover whether our interpretation of public and private marries with that of the historical actors themselves.[2]

Complaints about the inadequacy of standard conceptual frameworks should nevertheless not be pressed too far, because through them the subject was opened up in a far more sophisticated way than was possible under either the old tokenism or its early feminist replacements. The challenge now is not to take refuge in an impenetrable cocoon of complexity, but to generate new concepts and categories 'with more sensitivity to women's own manuscripts' and to the cultural particularities of time and place.[3]

The study of evangelical religion adds its own complexities to the reconstruction of the lives of women, not only because it has played such

179

an important role in helping to form the culture of middle-class female domesticity,[4] which until now has dominated the debate, but also because as a religious movement evangelicalism transcended national boundaries, social classes, religious denominations and psychological stereotypes.[5] Moreover, religion, for both men and women, was at once a profoundly private affair and a means of connecting with other spheres of life in which meaning was constructed and expressed. The aim of this chapter is to explore the ambiguities inherent in women's experiences of evangelical religion primarily in Ireland in the eighteenth and nineteenth centuries and to attempt to make connections between religion and other important cultural frameworks including national identity, social class, domestic values and moral reform. The picture that emerges is not easily encapsulated by the prevalent narratives described earlier, but resembles rather a series of concentric circles which have the capacity to expand and retract according to circumstances. Women were able to exploit the sheer pragmatism of evangelical religion (in its zeal to harness every resource, including women, for its redemptive mission) as they moved from more confined to more expansive circles of influence without ever being able to redraw the boundaries altogether. Sometimes they were forced to move back again into more restricted circles by the repressive power of some aspects of male-defined evangelical spirituality.

On a superficial level, at least, the story is easily told. In the eighteenth century the religious energies of evangelicalism operated as a sort of pincer movement from above and below. Aristocratic women of evangelical sensibility were able to use their money and social influence to promote the cause of serious religion from above at the same time as new religious movements, especially Methodism, opened up more dramatic possibilities from below.[6] It has for long been suggested that Methodism attracted a disproportionately female following wherever it took root in the British Isles and North America in the eighteenth and nineteenth centuries, but only recently has this suggestion been subjected to rigorous statistical scrutiny.[7] In an admirably extensive survey of membership lists, Clive Field has shown a female mean of 57.7 per cent in a combined sample of some 80,361 members.[8] Although this percentage varied considerably from one circuit to another, it was remarkably consistent over time and from region to region. The statistical mean for Wales, Scotland and Ireland, for example, was identical to that for the east-central counties of England, and the variation from one region to another operated within a relatively tight band from 55.7 to 60.8 per cent. Moreover, Field's figures, at least for the period before 1830, offer no support for the speculative generalization that urbanization was accompanied by an inexorable feminization of religion.[9] That this happened in the long run is not much in doubt, but in the early stages of industrialization and urbanization, the proportion of female church attenders and class members in towns, as with other

180

cultural barometers, was more likely to reflect the pattern of the surrounding rural constituency than obey the tidy logic of subsequent theoretical constructions. Field's conclusion is therefore that 'Methodism was rather more female in its composition than the adult population as a whole where, at the census of 1821, the statistic was 52.3 per cent for those aged fifteen and above',[10] but the disparity between the proportion of women within Methodism and the wider population, though significant, is not as overwhelming as is sometimes implied. In terms of marital status the proportion of 'single' Methodist members (24.6 per cent) was significantly smaller than in the adult population as a whole (29.3 per cent in 1851), but *within* Methodism the proportion of single and widowed women was conspicuously higher than the proportion of single and widowed men. Unfortunately, Methodist class membership lists are constructed in such a way as to leave few clues about the extent of the practice of intermarriage within the boundaries of the religious community. The likelihood is that it was extensive, but not as uniform as the pattern within the Irish Quaker and Moravian communities. There is as yet no satisfactory data available for Methodist fertility rates, but it would be interesting to know if Albion Urdank's discovery of a link between evangelical Nonconformity and much higher than average birth rates in Gloucestershire is capable of a wider application to other nonconformists in other places.[11] At stake here is not only a link between high birth rates and the economic prosperity associated with dissenting religion, but also a possible link between fecundity and the cultural securities and sense of optimism for the future supplied by chapel culture.

With so much raw data still unknown about the distribution, marriage patterns and fertility rates of women within popular evangelicalism in Ireland, it is wise to proceed with steady caution to more interpretative and conceptual frameworks, but the effort has to be made, and the resources for such an analysis are incomparably better now than they were a decade ago when the first faltering steps were taken. Most historians agree that the evangelical revival offers a vivid illustration of 'Thirsk's Law' at work.[12] In the breakup of old patterns and in the early stages of the forging of new ones, women were able to achieve a temporary position of influence in the early stages of the evangelical revival which was not sustained into the nineteenth century when male ministers, trustees and administrators reimposed a substantial measure of control. By that stage, however, a vast array of voluntary religious associations had opened up new opportunities for female endeavour which supplemented and refined, but did not threaten, the authority of men. This was an important and largely uncontested qualification, for while the boundaries within which women's influence was permitted were stretched for essentially pragmatic purposes, they were neither redrawn nor discarded.

Predictably, it was not in the well-established denominations but in the new versions of popular, pietistic Protestantism which emerged throughout seventeenth- and eighteenth-century Europe that women's contribution became more visible. Although exhibiting considerable organizational and theological diversity, religious communities such as Quakers, Moravians and Methodists had some common attributes which both attracted and utilized female adherents. In their forms of worship, for example, there was more emphasis on emotion and experience than on tradition and formality. Moreover, with greater reliance placed on inner truth than on received dogma, the role of a mediatorial clergy was undermined as that of the laity was simultaneously enhanced. New organizational structures and, in the early stages at least, the lack of suitable meeting-places outside the home, also encouraged a degree of flexibility which gave women easier access to a range of religious functions. Various interpretations have been offered to explain the importance of women in such movements. While eighteenth- and nineteenth-century commentators shared the underlying assumptions of Max Weber's statement that women were especially receptive to 'religious movements with orgiastic, emotional or hysterical aspects to them', recent studies have draw attention to more tangible considerations.[13] Some have suggested that women were attracted into the new sects by the wider scope of activity offered to them by the concept of spiritual equality, while others have shown how the moral values of the new religious movements, including temperance, frugality, fidelity and self-improvement, had a daily relevance to women who were concerned for the physical and moral welfare of their families.[14] Moreover, the search for motivation must also distinguish between characteristics based on wider cultural patterns and those specific to gender. For example, although accepted notions of what constituted 'natural' female behaviour helped to perpetuate ideal stereotypes, the characteristics upon which they were built, including zealous expressions of piety, excessive spirituality and emotional responses to evangelical sermons, were common to both men and women in this period. In addition, women are no more a cohesive social entity than men and a shared gender does not in itself produce a common experience. Criteria such as social status, age and personal circumstances shape religious behaviour as they do other areas of life.

At all levels of society, women, either individually or as part of a wider network, played an important part in establishing links between religious groups and the communities in which they were situated. In the early days of a new religious movement, for example, success or failure was often determined by specifically practical considerations, and this was an area in which respectable, pious and independent women were especially useful. Itinerant preachers needed an introduction into the community and a place to rest and hold meetings on their long and arduous circuits. Methodist sources in Ireland, as with contemporaneous accounts of

Methodist growth in the American colonies, abound with examples of the support given and initiatives taken by women in introducing Methodism into the towns and villages of Ireland. Mrs Alice Dawes, an evangelical widow and the principal supporter of Methodism in Belturbet, received the preachers and fitted up a room for their accommodation; the first preaching place in Armagh was rented by Mrs Russell, Mrs Isabella Maxwell and Mrs Jane Justice in 1762, and there are many examples of women inviting preachers to make use of their homes.[15] Such women gave moral support and encouragement as well as practical aid to preachers. They also served as links between rural societies and the Methodist central leadership. Some corresponded with Wesley, for example, to comment and advise on individual preachers. In 1769, Mrs Bennis' request to Conference for the appointment of an itinerant preacher to Limerick was noted by Crookshank as 'the earliest instance on record of the voice of the people being heard in connection with a preaching appointment'.[16]

Methodism's concern to draw in those on the periphery of society, the sick, the aged and the distressed, gave official recognition to traditional female ties and endowed them with a more tangible moral authority. Piety and respectability were more important attributes for sick visitors and class leaders than wealth, property or social status. The dynamics of female classes, which seemed more durable than their male counterparts, elicited comment from many visiting itinerants and kept the impetus going when the initial enthusiasm had died down. Female prayer meetings were also noted as peculiarly successful examples of piety and devotion. Indeed the loyalty of Methodist women to their all-female classes suggest that 'they not only conjured up a sense of female solidarity, but to some it also offered a respite from their husbands' direct control'.[17]

It was in the Methodist classes that women really 'transcended the stereotypical roles' of 'listeners to become active participants', but it was as preachers and exhorters that their contribution proved most controversial. Since the great majority of early Methodist itinerant and local preachers were not ordained, there was no official ban or prohibitive qualifications to deter female enthusiasts. Wesley's own position shifted over time from outright opposition to cautious acceptance within some clearly prescribed limits. He told Sarah Crosby that Methodists, unlike Quakers, had not abandoned biblical injunctions against female preaching, but that it was appropriate, under certain conditions, to admit exceptions.[18] Women were not to itinerate or unnecessarily or provocatively to usurp the place of men. He advised Alice Cambridge, when dealing with critics, to

> Give them all honour and obey them in all things, as far as conscience permits. But it will not permit you to be silent when God commands you to speak; yet I would have you give as little offence as possible;

and therefore I would advise you not to speak at any place where a preacher is speaking near you at the same time, lest you should draw away his hearers. Also avoid the first appearance of pride or magnifying yourself.[19]

Women were therefore regarded as instruments of divine providence to meet exceptional circumstances, an interpretation confirmed by their popularity. Blind and emotional, Margaret Davidson drew large crowds with the 'fervour and fluency of her witness',[20] and Alice Cambridge attracted numbers 'amounting to eight or ten thousand persons' on a tour of Ulster at the beginning of the nineteenth century.[21] However, early acceptance, or at least tolerance, soon gave way to caution and then condemnation, as female preachers fell victim to the same tide of connexional reaction as swept over ranters, radicals and revivalists in the first two decades of the nineteenth century. The Conference of 1802 decreed it 'contrary both to scripture and to prudence that women should preach or should exhort in public'.[22] Female preaching did not end immediately within the Wesleyan connexion in Ireland, or indeed in England where it also fell victim to Conference disapproval in 1803. In Ireland women who felt the call to preach were left with few alternatives, but in England women were able to shuffle over into Primitive Methodism and then into independent revivalism where the torch could still glow brightly, but without the necessary institutional structures it could not easily be passed on to successors.[23] Female preaching may have been an affront to institutional decency, but, ultimately, women could get only so far by subverting or bypassing religious institutions. In the long term they needed access to denominational power more than the denomination, under Buntingite manacles, appeared to need them. Later in the century, the growing evidence of denominational failure in the face of apathy and infidelity led to a modest reassertion of the old evangelical pragmatism in the shape of denominationally controlled training hostels for female domestic missionaries.[24] But these were the small crumbs on offer from the table of male control, not part of the loaf which tantalizingly had seemed to be on offer at the beginning of the century.

In Ireland, it is plain that those preachers who most ardently supported their female counterparts were themselves 'enthusiasts' who were frequently out of favour with an increasingly conservative Dublin leadership.[25] Those women who did continue the practice increasingly confined their activities to their own sex. Thus, while Alice Cambridge had addressed mixed congregations in the late eighteenth century, including a regiment of soldiers together with their wives and children, by the 1830s male followers of Anne Lutton were reduced to dressing in women's clothing in a vain attempt to hear her preach.[26]

Women's preaching should thus be seen as exceptional and transitional, rather than officially sanctioned and accepted. Even at the peak of their influence, women preachers, as with their later nineteenth-century overseas missionary counterparts, were seen as supporters in places not adequately serviced by men alone, and were never accepted as regular preachers to settled circuits. Even when female preaching was common, women never succeeded in altering, or even attempted to alter, the conventional relationships between men and women within religious communities. For, while their opponents reviled them for casting off the virtues of their sex, their supporters were equally careful always to refer to them in terms of their womanhood. Thus they were portrayed as either exemplifying or denying their 'nature'. Anne Preston, her supporters said, lived a 'life of feeling';[27] Alice Cambridge was neat, plain and greatly opposed to evil-speaking.[28] When speaking of Anne Lutton, the Victorian Methodist historian C. H. Crookshank felt it necessary to explain how such a woman, 'of respectable parents and trained in fear of the Lord', overcame her 'natural' female reticence:

> Called of God to proclaim to her fellow countrywomen the love of Christ, had she consulted her own feelings merely, her natural diffidence, deep humility and dislike to prominence would have presented an insurmountable barrier. But, believing that the Lord commanded, she dare not disobey and He crowned her labours with abundant blessing.[29]

The 'essential' nature of woman was thus accepted by both sides as determining the extent and nature of her activities. Modesty and humility precluded any prominent public role and the predominance of emotion over reason was regarded as a further limitation of the value of her contribution. Gideon Ouseley, although a known supporter of female preaching, remarked of a young female preacher that while she was good at recounting her own experience and blessings, 'her knowledge was not equal to her zeal and some of her remarks were confused and incoherent'.[30] Ironically, more sedate Methodist men regarded Ouseley in exactly the same light.

The practice of female preaching, exhorting and witnessing was never as widespread in Ireland as it was in England and North America, nor was it ever the bearer of a radical and dissonant spirituality. Although there were considerable *regional* variations in the incidence of female preaching in the North Atlantic world (stronger in the north of England and in the northern states of the USA, and virtually non-existent in parts of the south of England and in the southern states), the *chronological* pattern was remarkably similar from place to place. Women enjoyed a more extensive public role in the early period of Methodist revivalistic expansion between 1790 and 1820 than they were able to sustain into the second quarter of the nineteenth century. There also seems to be a difference in tone between the more unconventional women described by Deborah Valenze in early industrial England and the more conservative white preachers identified by Cathy Brekus in the USA.[31] Although both groups of women, in the very act of public preaching, were expressing a degree of social protest against economic change and social dislocation, some of the English women were of a lower social status and were less likely to be on good terms with the mainstream Methodist denominations than their American counterparts. There is not much evidence to suggest that the female preachers in either country grafted a radical political message on to their radical challenge to traditional ecclesiastical practices. It may be one of the ironies of history that Methodist women in the later nineteenth century were less ecclesiastically radical, but more politically self-conscious than their pioneering predecessors.

It is difficult to compare the situation in Ireland with the rest of the North Atlantic world because the raw data does not as yet exist. Such impressionistic evidence as there is seems to indicate that Ireland, like the southern states of the USA, was both too divided and too conservative in its social mores to facilitate a vigorous tradition of female preaching. The debate ought not merely to reside in preaching alone, however, because the public performances of women, whether as preachers or exhorters, were but the tip of the iceberg of Methodism's oral culture. Methodist classes opened up the way for women to express their feelings and opinions to one another outside the confines of normal domestic discourse. These communal soul-barings offered a system of mutual support for women which strengthened their sense of solidarity as they battled against the sins and values of the wider world. But Methodist women, as parallel studies in the USA have shown, were also part of a religious movement in which Methodist men displayed more emotion and used a more 'feminine' vocabulary than was common among their contemporaries.

> Over and over again, with almost ritual intonation, we hear the language of tender and uncontrollable emotionalism – the language of women's nature and behaviour. Preachers and believers felt and wept, trembled and groaned; persons melted and softened and sank into God; hearts were 'tendered' and filled and comforted. The power of God evidenced itself in the 'quickening amongst the members', like the first stirring of life in the womb, and the passive voice dominates. . . . Here was a religious language that women could instantly embrace.[32]

The paradigm of separate spheres cannot explain this complex set of interactions. Although men largely retained control of public preaching and classes were separated by gender, cultural exchange nevertheless occurred in all sorts of ways, from language to ministry and from private discussions about religious progress to the raucous public celebrations of the love-feasts. If part of Methodism's success as a popular religious movement, according to Edward Thompson, was owing to its ability to bridge the cultural gap between elite and popular culture, a similar bridge, employing some of the same materials, was in operation between the sexes.[33]

The existence of such a bridge in the social landscape of eighteenth-century Ireland attracted controversy as much as it did traffic. Conventional interpretations of women's inherent weakness and emotional vulnerability also contributed to the growth of opposition to Methodism. Those hostile to the influence of itinerant preachers pointed derisively to the enthusiastic female response to their ministry by alleging that they were engaged in a deliberate process of spiritual and physical exploitation. Since it was almost always the woman of the house who first made contact with itinerants and, consequently, she who most often introduced the rest of the family to meetings, this was not simply an academic point. One orthodox minister was scathing about the 'opportunism' of itinerant Methodist preachers: 'Having a form of Godliness, they work on the minds of the unsteady and wavering and of all who are given to change, they creep into houses; they lead captive silly women.'[34] The mob violence which so often accompanied early Methodist activities was frequently related to their success among the women of a family or community. In Fermanagh in 1768 the Henderson family, with a large mob in tow, besieged the Methodist Armstrongs for two days to starve out two preachers who had converted their daughter.[35] There are many such examples of evangelical preachers taking advantage of feminine weakness, and inevitably this was not always confined to mere persuasion. The private minutes of the Methodist Conference in Ireland and the private correspondence of Bishop Lavington from the south-west of England suggest that relations between some itinerants and their female followers reached a degree of intimacy deemed 'unnatural' and unacceptable.[36] The connection between sexual and religious excitement was frequently made by contemporaries and there is no doubt that some revivalist preachers were charismatic, romantic figures whose rhetorical appeals for submission provoked a less than orthodox response. The emotional nature of conversions, particularly during periods of revival, and the privacy and exclusiveness of class and band meetings, added to local suspicions. Dramatic conversion experiences, the intensity of religious ardour and the repentant sinner's subsequent change of lifestyle, all of which could be interpreted as 'unnatural', also led to charges of madness, while the success of zealous preachers left them open to accusations of witchcraft.[37] Other tensions between the lives of the 'revived' and the families and communities in which they lived were exacerbated by the decree of the Methodist Conference that parents were forbidden to encourage children to marry 'unawakened persons'.[38] In cases where loyalty to family and sect were not in conflict such regulations enhanced the cohesiveness of the community of faith, but the reverse was frequently the case. Examples of domestic discord abound, especially in the early stages of Methodist penetration into Irish localities.

Many of the discordant themes associated with early Methodist revivalism in Ireland surfaced again in an extraordinary way during the great Ulster revival of 1859. As the flood-tide of religious excitement burst the banks of traditional Victorian reserve, women, especially young working-class women, were associated with a remarkable range of 'religious' experiences from visions, clairvoyance and prophecy to hysteria, stigmata and physical prostrations.[39] As the learned Presbyterian clergy scratched their heads in search of convincing explanations for such spiritual mayhem, women and even children achieved temporary positions of power as direct mediators of divine blessing. While it would be a mistake to replace the inadequate chiliastic theories of such behaviour (with their selective emphases on social and economic dislocation) with too much female purposefulness (women seizing religious power for self-fulfilment), it is undoubtedly the case that for a brief period in the middle of the century conventional patterns of female behaviour were set to one side. It would be difficult to substantiate the case, however, that such a transaction led to any permanent change in the relationship between the sexes, except in the sense that many clergymen became even more unwilling to accommodate themselves to the inconveniences of unrestricted religious enthusiasm.

A 'safer', and in the long run a more influential window of opportunity for women, was made available by the intensification and diversification of evangelical activities in the nineteenth century. Through the network of voluntary societies and organizations which clustered around the religious denominations, many women were given an opportunity to engage in social and administrative work in their communities. The domestic sphere widened to take in Sunday schools, foreign and domestic evangelistic missions, and temperance, educational, Bible and tract societies. The ubiquitous reports of these societies indicate the areas in which it was felt women could be particularly successful – teaching, sponsorship, promotion and persuasion. Sunday school teaching rapidly became an acceptable expression of female religious devotion. It was a leadership role which offered an important outlet for piety as well as a position within the community, but one which could also be regarded as an extension of the traditional domestic duties of guidance and teaching. A handbook for Sunday school teachers announced

A woman's information influences the present comfort and future state of her family; if her house be well-ordered, the husband forsakes the ale-house and where there would have been want there is plenty. It is the mother who instructs the children, to her they look up for all they want and in general as she is, so are they.[40]

There was clearly a disproportionate number of women working in this area and schools for female teachers were operational from the early nineteenth century. Through evangelicalism, persuasion became a way of life for thousands of women in nineteenth-century Ireland. The Hibernian Bible Society noted that working-class men were much more open to persuasion from lady visitors when it came to buying Bibles,[41] and its impressive distribution statistics owed much to the efforts of these voluntary labourers. The 1830 report of Religious Tract and Bible Society noted the success of the Ladies' Association in promoting the circulation of tracts and books and in establishing libraries.[42] Similarly, the Ladies Society of the London Hibernian Society was by 1830 running 190 schools with some 8,000 scholars, and the Ladies Auxiliary to the Irish Society employed a small army of Scripture readers.[43] Into this mixture of spiritual and practical work women brought their traditional domestic skills and applied them in a wider field. Their efforts did not go unappreciated, especially by those voluntary societies which struggled against the rigidity of ecclesiastical hierarchies. The records of the Church Missionary Society, for example, reveal the way in which women's auxiliaries were used to establish a base in Ireland, getting around the barriers imposed by the church on male-dominated societies which were regarded, especially in Anglican circles, as a threat to clerical authority.[44] Ladies' auxiliaries also helped establish the ubiquitous penny-a-week subscription as the main resource of the evangelical religious societies. It was in the area of finance, in fact, that women proved themselves to be indispensable assets. By helping to unleash the 'power of the purse' in a systematic and regular fashion, women were at the very heart of a remarkable Victorian industry of religious and moral campaigns in Britain and in Ireland. Aside from their direct, individual donations, the collectors of penny-a-week subscriptions were invariably either women or clergymen and they also acted as treasurers to local branches and as organizers of the more traditional fund-raising events such as bazaars and the sale of 'fancy work'.

Specifically female philanthropic societies, both evangelical and non-evangelical, also flourished in the mid-nineteenth century, and this type of involvement, while still largely secondary and supportive in nature, and still within the traditional arena of charity and benevolence, was important in offering an outlet to women's industry and talent outside the home and family circle. Women gave their time, commitment and local knowledge to the furtherance of these causes, and the result was a growing professionalism and a considerable broadening of physical and spiritual horizons. Closer involvement in charitable work, of whatever kind, certainly gave the upper and middle classes an opportunity to confront the realities of poverty and neglect, and opened up direct contact with everyday social problems from which they had been largely protected. Ultimately this led to a social extension of their perception of Christian duty. Pious platitudes may often have been served up with the soup or administered with dressings, but there is at least some evidence of individuals going beyond the narrow constraints of proselytism. Societies such as the Belfast Ladies Relief Association may have been mainly concerned to 'imbue the minds of scholars with the truth and spirit of the gospel', but the industrial schools they set up, supplied by women teachers and superintendents, offered other more concrete benefits to famine-stricken communities.[45] The evangelical industry of charity in the Victorian period was, in the main, neither fuelled by repressed social guilt nor motivated by any desire to restructure the social order. It was essentially an expression of Christian duty and piety by women who thought that society could be transformed by voluntary zeal and the daily disciplines of compassion. For the women engaged in it, philanthropy expanded their horizons, alleviated their boredom, increased their status, nurtured their professionalism and introduced them to leadership roles that would otherwise not have come their way. In her recent book on women and philanthropy in Ireland in the nineteenth century, Maria Luddy makes a useful distinction between largely benevolent and largely reformist philanthropic organizations. The former were more likely to be run entirely by women, but within a carefully restricted sphere of action, while the latter more often brought women into contact with men and the world of public and political action. The sturdy minority of female suffragists in nineteenth-century Ireland, such as Isabella Tod, were more likely to have been nurtured within the reformist than the benevolent tradition of female philanthropy.[46] Conversely, it was in the latter societies that women were most likely to encounter the many petty restrictions of having to operate within organizations run by men. Some made the transition from religious philanthropy to political activism as a natural expression of their social education, but most accepted the reality of male control over political and economic power at the same time as they dealt 'small blow after small blow to the idea of male supremacy' in the field of moral and social reform.[47]

The areas in which female zeal and male control came into their most direct interface within evangelicalism were temperance campaigns and foreign missions, for women were *needed* by men to wage a joint war against the intemperate at home and the infidel abroad; and they knew it. The resultant construction of Christian womanhood in the prescriptive literature of evangelical Protestantism is riddled with paradoxes:

Domestic ideology and the superior piety of women were used to demonstrate the crucial influence of women in the home as the

190

preservers of a sober nation. Yet, the various weaknesses of women made them susceptible to the ravages of 'drink' and their descent into evil put the family, and by extension all of civilization, at risk. Temperance activities afforded middle-class Ulster Protestant women an avenue in which they could expand their range of work, yet they themselves expressed concerns that their work for the temperance cause do nothing to render them less womanly.[48]

Women were both morally powerful and morally weak. They were required to exercise moral influence over their husbands, but were not to attempt to control them. They were to be responsible for the moral education of their children, but were also expected to be the broken-hearted mothers of intemperate sons. Women were, of course, expected to remain temperate themselves, but were *more* subject to moral condemnation than their husbands and sons if they failed. Protestant women, as trophies of a 'superior' religious civilization, were expected to be more sober than their Roman Catholic counterparts, the drunken 'Biddies' of many a Protestant tract. Pious women were to be mobilized by the Protestant clergy and the lay leaders of the evangelical voluntary societies for an unremitting war against intemperance, but they were not to mistake mobilization for civic empowerment. Women were to be foot soldiers not generals and their weapons were those of moral persuasion not political pressure. Their conduct in the campaign was as important as the result of the campaign itself, for the 'mannish' woman was as much feared by Irish evangelicals as the drunkards within their own sex. The latter disfigured the streets and slowed down the wheels of industry, but the former had to be encountered in their own cherished citadels of home and church.

The conventional interpretation that English and Irish female temperance crusades were less politically aggressive, and therefore less emancipatory, than their American equivalents is broadly correct. Brożyna has shown how the shock tactics advocated by visiting Americans were carefully repudiated by both evangelical men and women in Ulster who preferred the 'quiet, unobtrusive' approach to the 'startling or sensational' tactics of their bolder North American sisters.[49] There is nevertheless some evidence from the pages of the *Irish Temperance League Journal* at the end of the nineteenth century and from the records of the Ulster Women's Christian Temperance Union in the early twentieth century that through temperance campaigns women were inexorably introduced to wider public issues relating to child welfare, municipal reform and policing. The world of 'drink', as the evangelicals themselves well understood, was no more confined to the separate spheres of public and private than the lives of the women who fought so unremittingly against it, but Ulster evangelical women, in the main, trusted more to the moral persuasion of womanly virtue than to the political agitation for anti-drink legislation.

In the field of foreign missions, women were at first confined to supportive committees and auxiliaries and to fund-raising for male missionaries whose reports were generally designed to appeal to a maternal nature. However, the Zenana Mission, founded by the Presbyterian Church in 1873, promised women a more central and challenging role. Under its full title, The Female Association for Promoting Christianity among the Women of the East sent out female missionaries.[50] As well as offering traditional medical, educational and child-care facilities, this mission had a particular concern for the Zenana, that is, the part of the Indian household set aside for women, and to which men, including evangelical missionaries, had no access. While the setting up of the female mission was therefore essential to fulfil missionary objectives, it also gave local women the opportunity to consider the position of their eastern counterparts and to experience a different culture. Although the actual number of female missionaries leaving Ireland for Calcutta was small, home-based branches were kept well informed. By its second year the mission had 124 congregational auxiliaries in Ireland with over 6,000 members.[51] The idea of women missionaries became more acceptable as the century progressed; in 1887, the queen's Golden Jubilee year, it was reported that there were about 500 female missionaries in India attached to a variety of denominational societies. The majority of these were native teachers and Bible women taught by Europeans, but a door had been opened through which many women would pass in the following decades. The new venture required courage and assertiveness, and undoubtedly brought fulfilment. It was stressed, however, that their teaching of the gospel was secondary to the primary medical and educational functions of women missionaries, and thus they remained firmly within traditional female boundaries.

The annual reports of the Zenana Mission offer an intriguing glimpse into the respective roles of the sexes in late Victorian religion. The first report confirmed that the mission had an all-female general committee, female secretaries and treasurer, and a committee of ministers available for consultation.[52] However, at the annual general meeting, all the speeches were made by men, and the images which the women held of themselves were often a pure reflection of those held by their male counterparts. 'We are born to serve the world', was the rallying cry offered by one Zenana missionary. Although these particular women had to undertake arduous training, in a new language, in kindergarten methods and in medicine, and although their letters are suggestive of the difficult adjustment to the climate, food and culture in the places in which they found themselves, the language in which their experiences were couched reaffirmed their perception of women's subordinate role and their willing acceptance of male perceptions of their worth. The importance of language, imagery and symbolism in perpetuating conventional gender roles should not be overlooked. A male speaker at the Zenana annual general meeting stated that

> There is something about female piety that singularly adapts it to missionary enterprise. . . . Everyone knows that the graces which shone with perfect lustre in the character of Christ were mainly the feminine virtues. Submission, love, tenderness, self-sacrifice, devotement, sympathy, are characteristic features of the piety of women; and when joined with gifts, knowledge, and grace they make a model missionary. Without preaching, without descending to the lecture-room, or the arena of controversy, the Christian woman may go about doing good and to an extent that a seraph would envy.[53]

Behind the sturdy minority of women who went overseas stood an army of female supporters at home who had their Christian graces nourished by a remarkably ubiquitous prescriptive literature in which the cult of domesticity was broadened from Irish hearths to embrace the whole world. The alleged spiritual and social equality of Ulster Protestant women was repeatedly contrasted with the thraldom of their 'heathen' sisters in the East. Such propaganda carried the double advantage of cementing a Protestant identity in Ulster and of persuading Ulster women that both their religion and their men had always promoted their highest good. Nearer home, reports from home missions to the Roman Catholics of Ireland contrasted Protestant knowledge and freedom with the destitution, drunkenness and superstition of Roman Catholic women.[54] The cause of foreign and domestic missions both reinforced female Protestant identity and offered seemingly unlimited opportunities for women to take control of support at home and experience dazzling new opportunities abroad where the threat to traditional gender roles was rendered less important by distance.

It is the continuing emphasis on traditional feminine virtues by the men who ran the evangelical voluntary organizations, and for whom the 'essential' nature of men and women predetermined religious as well as social roles, which most clearly emerges from a reading of the sources. The controversial nature of many religious meetings, with their emphasis on action and resolution, reinforced these perceptions. In contrast to the heated political debates of men, it was suggested that 'the religion of a woman ought to be an impassioned weakness, and that sweet spirit which was typified by the dove should spread its wings upon her'.[55] The *Belfast People's Magazine* also stressed the moral superiority of women, and the duties incumbent upon them:

> Let all females be persuaded, that God did not intend them, by any means, for mere servile purposes, but designed them to be truly helpmates to men; and, therefore, let them with a religious regard to

the end of their creation, study by every winning grace, by every angel virtue, to lead those with whom they may be connected to happiness both here and hereafter.[56]

Women's power to influence men – for good or evil – was clearly recognized, but any evaluation of their worth placed them in a complementary and submissive relation, for 'upon the virtues of women much of that of man depended, and the religious habits of the sex could not fail to exercise a salutary influence'.[57] Similarly, while evangelicals encouraged the participation of women in many areas, it was clear that their moral authority was to be used not to erode traditional boundaries, but as an instrument in the regeneration of the family (at which most evangelical prescriptive literature was directed) and then of the wider society. Women supplied much of the money (as collectors), the administrative expertise and the social skills necessary to maintain the popular status of evangelical societies, but men retained their official status and continued to exercise authority and determine policy. Traditional arrangements and traditional values were not only retained, but upheld by evangelical theology and its predominantly male application to the realm of family life and social ethics. On the whole, women accepted, even welcomed, the cultural role conferred upon them by men in the evangelical strongholds of Victorian and Edwardian Ulster. They also selected aspects of Christ's personality with which to identify and unquestioningly drew upon the prevalent cult of evangelical domesticity, which after all offered tangible benefits when set alongside the domestic circumstances of women exposed to rougher and more irreligious households.

Women's contribution to popular Protestantism in this period is not easily reduced to facile categories. They certainly provided ammunition for critics, particularly in the early stages of evangelical enthusiasm, but as evangelicalism took on an aura of respectability, with congregations becoming more settled and the dignity of the pastoral office replacing the excitement of the circuit horse-rider, women became less controversial but more central to evangelicalism's social creed. Inevitably, the limits of women's actions were circumscribed by men, and the much vaunted importance of female example in terms of piety, humility and service was widely disseminated through family and social structures. But in these traditional areas women were not simply victims but willing participants in a campaign of moral reformation. It is, however, in the relation between popular Protestantism and home life that their presence was most significant. In a faith which relied strongly on idealized notions of domesticity, this should not be underestimated. It was not only that women enabled evangelists to establish a foothold in the family and the community, but that their activities ensured that religious values penetrated all aspects of everyday life in a way that institutionalized religion could not. Women's civilizing influence was evident too in the combination of holy charity and biblical education so common in the nineteenth century. The social events over which they presided – bazaars, teas, sales and Sunday school celebrations – tied the church or chapel closer to the community and established links which remain central to Ulster Protestant culture.

The mechanisms through which this process took place show how an idealized construction of womanhood was a central component to the competing nationalisms of late nineteenth-century Ireland. Although the idealized domestic piety laid out for both Catholic and Protestant women contained almost exactly the same elements, each demonized the other's women. In the eyes of Protestants, confessionals and convents subverted family ties and degraded women. In the eyes of Catholics, Protestant women were agents of the imperial and modernizing forces that were everywhere sapping the cultural integrity and piety of Catholic Ireland. Protestants thought that Catholic women were particularly prone to drunkenness and sluttishness, while Catholics thought that Protestant women lacked religious feeling and spiritual devotion. Even their respective demonologies, however, had a revealing structural difference:

> Ulster evangelical Protestants wrote with dread of the spread of 'Romanism' and its 'unnatural' doctrines concerning women and the family, yet their writings were primarily a criticism of what they believed Catholics did to their own members, how it supposedly denigrated domesticity amongst its own. Catholic censure of Protestant anti-family activities, was, however, based on criticism of what Protestants were accused of doing to Catholics.[58]

For Protestants, the Roman Catholic religion was itself the pernicious force, while for Catholics, it was not so much Protestantism itself as the political, cultural and social power it had over them that was most resented. In this way the competing forces of British Protestant unionism and Irish Catholic nationalism confronted each other not only at the hustings, but also in their respective family units and in their rival constructions of female piety. To the outsider, Protestant and Catholic constructions of female piety appear as 'small differences' within an overwhelmingly male, religious and bourgeois framework, but to the inhabitants of late nineteenth-century Ireland they were as far apart as heaven was from hell. Each tradition guarded their idealized pictures of their women and families with intense loyalty, for while external threats to cultural homogeneity were bitterly resented, it was the enemy within that was potentially the most dangerous. What after all was worth defending in a culture which showed signs of crumbling from within its own homes and families? Ulster's evangelical Protestants guarded their civilization not only by their vigorous political campaigns against Home Rule, but also by their constructions of female piety and family virtue. The religious foundations of much philanthropic effort in nineteenth-century Ireland were both 'a cohesive and divisive force' in Irish society. They contributed much to the trans-denominational piety of Irish life, but they also set up competing Protestant and Catholic philanthropic institutions which bound their women more into the broader structures of clerically dominated churches than into a united sisterhood. The great religious divide separated women as comprehensively as it separated their husbands and sons.[59]

This chapter was introduced with the suggestion that the most powerful narratives constructed by historians and sociologists to make sense of the experiences of women in the British Isles in the eighteenth and nineteenth centuries have proved inadequate for the task. What is offered here is not a convenient alternative, but rather a selection of the range of frameworks which need to be considered. Evangelical religion provides a particularly intriguing context within which to investigate the roles of women, because its missionary and moral pragmatism both offered new opportunities for women and reinforced their subjection to male authority with the sternest of theological arguments. It was a movement based on preaching and persuasion, and women excelled at both. It was a movement grounded in domestic piety and moral restraint, and women were vital to its success in both spheres. As it developed over time evangelicalism came to be associated with cultural power and national values, and women, both consciously and unconsciously, became vital ingredients in the construction of communal and national identities. As these patterns unfolded some women benefited from them while others suffered; some co-operated while others resisted; some sought further extensions of influence while others retreated into the home; some resented the power of men while others submitted to it as unto the Lord; some were transparent and accommodationist while others were discreet and subversive; some were angry and frustrated while others were patient and calculating; some made important breakthroughs in the early excitement of change while others had to watch the gains clawed back by fearful and unimaginative men; some were victims of powerful social and economic forces while others were vigorous historical agents in their own right.

Recent research into photographic representations of Irish women (arguably the most precise, immediate and accurate of images) shows how sensitive the historian needs to be in this area. Patriarchal assumptions, commercial realities, folksy sentimentality, deliberate deception, civic posturing and blazing revelation all emerge with the prints from the darkrooms into the light.[60] If even the instantaneous opening and closing of a lens can reveal such layers of complexity, historical reconstructions of women's experience should aim for nothing less.

CONCLUSION

Evangelical religion in general, and its Methodist species in particular, were powerful shapers of religious cultures in Britain and Ireland in the eighteenth and nineteenth centuries. As this collection of studies has shown, there is scarcely a framework of life, from law to gender and from politics to domestic piety, that was not deeply affected by religious enthusiasm of one kind or another. Fundamental to my approach has been the assumption that there is no 'best way' into these questions, but that in each area popular evangelicalism threw up its own paradoxes and ambiguities in all the aspects of life it affected. It thrived on sectarian competition, yet expanded the boundaries of religious toleration, in England if not in Ireland. It opened up new opportunities for women and constructed ideologies to keep them in their place. Its sturdy individualism and private piety made it an unlikely vehicle of political reform, yet the political history of the British Isles cannot be understood without reference to it. It nurtured radicals, ranters and prophetesses, and brought forth ecclesiastical bureaucrats to control them. It repressed and emancipated, perverted and purified; it was acquisitive and benevolent, insubordinate and loyal, industrious and emotional. It yields up its secrets discreetly and unexpectedly. It can be no more brought to life by the celebratory instincts of its stoutest defenders than by the savage attacks, often nurtured by private and public resentments, of its severest critics; but as is the way with history, both traditions have added some lustre to the debates.

My own approach has to do with the structural divisions of this book. Most of the important questions about Methodism are closely bound up with explanations for its growth and decline. For explanations to be convincing they must operate at two levels: comparisons from country to country and from region to region across the North Atlantic world, and intensive local studies to catch the flavour of particularity and to test the validity of much grander constructions. Explanations based on growth alone, however, as Edward Thompson observed a generation ago, do not take one very far into the nature of evangelical experience or into the manifold processes by which individuals and their communities had their lives altered by the religion of the cottage and the chapel. Methodist histories which ignore Methodist people are not worth the paper they are written on. The great social processes of liberal capitalism and religious pluralism are not distinct from the people who forged them.

But Methodism also needs to be treated thematically as well as individually and communally. The themes of law, politics and gender, though they have helped to penetrate to the heart of what was distinctive about Methodism, are by no means exhaustive. More needs to be said about the language of Methodism (in a far more sophisticated way than Thompson's hymns), its traditions of spirituality (African-American, female, bourgeois and so on) and its precise relationship with the rhythms of work, ritual and festival.

If there is a single connecting argument in what has gone before it is founded on the conviction that single-narrative approaches to the writing of Methodist history have done more harm than good. The beguiling certainties they induce are miles away from the wild eclecticism of much of the popular enthusiasm they purport to represent. In saying this, one is not capitulating to some kind of post-modernist despair about the impossibility of finding coherence in the mess of the past, but the reverse. It is only when complexity has been laid bare that the precise patterns of cultural brokerage between Methodism and its surrounding environment can begin to be understood.

NOTES

1 'MOTIVES, METHODS AND MARGINS': A COMPARATIVE STUDY OF METHODIST EXPANSION IN THE NORTH ATLANTIC WORLD, C. 1770–1850

I should like to record my thanks to Nathan Hatch and Bill Faupel, who organized the conference on Methodism and the Shaping of American Culture 1760–1860 at Asbury in October 1994 at which an earlier version of this paper was presented. I am also grateful to Mark Noll, who supplied a characteristically excellent comment on my paper; to Richard Carwardine, George Rawlyk, John Wigger and others who took part in the discussions; to Bill Kostlevy who gave generously of his time to introduce me to the rich literature on American Methodism; and to Hugh McLeod, Reg Ward and John Walsh who have helped me make comparisons I would otherwise not have noticed. While their generous contributions have improved the final result, all remaining flaws, sadly, are my responsibility alone.

1 E. P. Thompson, *The Making of the English Working Class* (rev. edn), Harmondsworth, 1968. Some of Thompson's essays also contain material of interest to historians of Methodism: 'The moral economy of the English crowd in the eighteenth century', *Past and Present*, no. 50, 1971, pp. 76–136; 'Anthropology and the discipline of historical context', *Midland History*, 1, no. 3, 1972, pp. 41–55; 'Patrician society: plebeian culture', *Journal of Social History*, 7, no. 4, 1974, pp. 382–405; and 'Eighteenth-century English society: class struggle without class?', *Social History*, 3, 1978, pp. 133–65. For an example of the influence of Thompson's work on North American scholars see G. W. Olsen (ed.), *Religion and Revolution in Early-Industrial England: The Halévy Thesis and its Critics*, Lanham, Md., 1990; and A. Dawley, 'E. P. Thompson and the peculiarities of the Americans', *Radical History Review*, 19, 1978–9, pp. 33–59.

2 Thompson dealt with the early critics of his treatment of Methodism in the Postscript to the Penguin edition of *The Making of the English Working Class*. These included R. Currie and R. M. Hartwell, 'The making of the English working class?', *Economic History Review*, 2nd series, 18, no. 2, 1965.

3 Thompson, *Making*, p. 918.

4 *Ibid.*, pp. 402–11.

5 *Ibid.*, p. 920.

6 *Ibid.*, pp. 397–8.

7 *Ibid.*, p. 398, n. 1.

8 *Ibid.*, p. 404.

9 *Ibid.*, pp. 411–40.

10 S. Desan, 'Crowds, community and ritual in the work of E. P. Thompson and Natalie Davis', in L. Hunt (ed.), *The New Cultural History*, Berkeley, 1989, pp. 47–71.

11 John Walsh made a plea for more serious treatment of rural Methodism in his contribution to J. Obelkevich, L. Roper and R. Samuel (eds), *Disciplines of Faith: Studies in Religion, Politics and Patriarchy*, London, 1987.

12 This argument is worked out most clearly in W. R. Ward, *The Protestant Evangelical Awakening*, Cambridge, 1992, but Ward's earlier articles on the origins of religious revival still retain their value. These have been collected in one volume entitled *Faith and Faction*, London, 1993. The most important are 'Orthodoxy, enlightenment and religious revival' and 'Power and piety: the origins of religious revival in the early eighteenth century'.

13 W. R. Ward, 'Pastoral office and the general priesthood in the Great Awakening', *Studies in Church History*, 26, 1989, pp. 303–27.

14 See, for example, J. Walsh, 'Methodism at the end of the eighteenth century', in R. Davies and G. Rupp (eds), *A History of the Methodist Church in Great Britain*, London, 1965, vol. 1, pp. 277–315.

15 W. R. Ward, *Religion and Society in England 1790–1850*, London, 1972. The main themes are expressed in a shorter and more accessible form in 'Revival and class conflict in early nineteenth-century Britain', in *idem, Faith and Faction*, pp. 285–98.

16 See D. M. Valenze, *Prophetic Sons and Daughters. Female Preaching and Popular Religion in Industrial England*, Princeton, 1985; and D. W. Lovegrove, *Established Church, Sectarian People: Itinerancy and the Transformation of English Dissent, 1780–1830*, Cambridge, 1988.

17 J. Obelkevich, *Religion and Rural Society: South Lindsey, 1825–1875*, Oxford, 1976.

18 N. Scotland, *Methodism and the Revolt of the Field*, Gloucester, 1981. See also R. Moore, *Pit-Men, Preachers and Politics: The Effects of Methodism in a Durham Mining Community*, Cambridge, 1974.

19 For rather different interpretations of Methodism's contribution or otherwise to England's *'ancien régime'* see J. C. D. Clark, *English Society 1688–1832*, Cambridge, 1985, pp. 235–47; and D. N. Hempton, 'John Wesley and England's "Ancien Regime"', in Stuart Mews (ed.), *Modern Religious Rebels*, London, 1993, pp. 36–55.

20 W. R. Ward, 'The Evangelical Revival in eighteenth-century Britain', in S. W. Gilley and W. J. Sheils (eds), *A History of Religion in Britain*, Oxford, 1994, pp. 252–72.

21 A. D. Gilbert, 'Religion and political stability in early industrial England', in P. K. O'Brien and R. Quinault (eds), *The Industrial Revolution and British Society*, Cambridge, 1993, p. 89; and *idem*, 'Methodism, Dissent and political stability in early industrial England', *Journal of Religious History*, 10, no. 4, 1979, pp. 281–99.

22 D. Hempton, 'Methodism and the law, 1740–1820', *Bulletin of the John Rylands University Library of Manchester*, 70, no. 3, 1988, pp. 93–107.

23 All the major surviving collections of Methodist correspondence from the period 1790–1820 and the private minutes of the Committee of Privileges after 1803 testify to the efforts made to keep Methodists loyal to the established order. See D. Hempton, *Methodism and Politics in British Society 1750–1850*, London, 1984, pp. 55–115.

24 R. Currie, A. Gilbert and L. Horsley, *Churches and Churchgoers: Patterns of Church Growth in the British Isles since 1700*, Oxford, 1977, pp. 40–2.

25 T. Bartlett, *The Fall and the Rise of the Irish Nation: The Catholic Question 1690–1830*, Dublin, 1992.

26 See the revealing graph of Methodist membership growth rates in Currie, *et al.*, *Churches and Churchgoers*, p. 41. The best interpretation of Methodism in the troubled districts of the north of England in these years remains Ward, *Religion and Society*. See also E. P. Stigant, 'Wesleyan Methodism and working-class radicalism in the North, 1792–1821', *Northern History*, 6, 1971, pp. 98–116.

27 D. M. Thompson, *Nonconformity in the Nineteenth Century*, London, 1972, pp. 147–55. See also, B. I. Coleman, *The Church of England in the Mid-Nineteenth Century*, London, 1980; and J. D. Gay, *The Geography of Religion in England*, London, 1971.

28 M. A. Noll, *A History of Christianity in the United States and Canada*, Grand Rapids, Mich., 1992, p. 153.

29 J. C. Deming and M. S. Hamilton, 'Methodist revivalism in France, Canada and the United States', in G. A. Rawlyk and M. A. Noll (eds), *Amazing Grace: Evangelicalism in Australia, Britain, Canada and the United States*, Montreal and Kingston, Ontario, 1993, pp. 124–53.

30 N. O. Hatch, *The Democratization of American Christianity*, New Haven, 1989.

31 Noll, *A History of Christianity*, p. 153.

32 Hatch, *Democratization of American Christianity*, p. 9.

33 *Ibid.*, p. 227.

34 W. W. Sweet, *Religion in the Development of American Culture 1765–1840*, New York, 1952, p. 150. See also *idem*, *Methodism in American History*, Nashville, 1953. For an assessment of Sweet's strengths and weaknesses see K. E. Rowe, 'Counting the converts: progress reports as church history', in R. E. Richey and K. E. Rowe (eds), *Rethinking Methodist History: A Bicentennial Historical Consultation*, Nashville, 1985, pp. 11–17.

35 The comment is taken from a review by J. H. Laski of R. F. Wearmouth, *Methodism and the Working-Class Movements of England 1800–1850*, London, 1937, in *New Statesman and Nation*. Wearmouth was a prolific writer on all aspects of the impact of Methodism on the English working classes. See *idem*, *Methodism and the Common People of the Eighteenth Century*, London, 1945; *Some Working-Class Movements of the Nineteenth Century*, London, 1948; *Methodism and the Struggle of the Working Classes*, Leicester, 1954; *The Social and Political Influence of Methodism in the Twentieth Century*, London, 1957; and *Methodism and the Trade Unions*, London, 1959.

36 C. D. Johnson, *Islands of Holiness: Rural Religion in Upstate New York 1790–1860*, Ithaca, NY, 1989; Obelkevich, *Religion and Rural Society*. See also J. Rule, 'Methodism, popular beliefs and village culture in Cornwall, 1800–50', in R. D. Storch (ed.), *Popular Culture and Custom in Nineteenth-Century England*, London, 1982, pp. 48–70. For a bibliography of other local studies of British Methodism, particularly in an urban setting, see R. Davies, A. R. George and G. Rupp (eds), *A History of the Methodist Church in Great Britain*, London, 1988, vol. 4, pp. 744–5.

37 T. Entwistle, *Memoir of the Reverend Joseph Entwistle*, London, 1867, pp. 111–12. See J. Baxter, 'The Great Yorkshire Revival 1792–6: a study of mass revival among the Methodists', *A Sociological Yearbook of Religion in Britain*, 7, 1974, pp. 46–76; D. Luker, 'Revivalism in theory and practice: the case of Cornish Methodism', *Journal of Ecclesiastical History*, 37, no. 4, 1986, pp. 603–19; J. M. Turner, *Conflict and Reconciliation: Studies in Methodism and Ecumenism in England 1740–1982*, London, 1985; and Hempton, *Methodism and Politics*, pp. 92–8, 277–8.

38 Cited in D. G. Mathews, 'Evangelical America – the Methodist ideology', in R.

E. Richey, K. E. Rowe and J. M. Schmidt (eds), *Perspectives on American Methodism: Interpretive Essays*, Nashville, 1993, p. 19.

39 *Ibid.*, pp. 20–4.

40 D. H. Lobody, '"That language might be given me": women's experience in early Methodism', in Richey *et al.* (eds), *Perspectives*, p. 134; and *idem*, 'Lost in the ocean of love: the spiritual writings of Catherine Livingstone Garrettson', in Richey and Rowe (eds), *Rethinking Methodist History*, pp. 175–84. See also A. G. Schneider, *The Way of the Cross Leads Home: The Domestication of American Methodism*, Bloomington, 1993.

41 E. S. Gaustad, *Historical Atlas of Religion in America*, New York, 1976, p. 76.

42 W. H. Williams, *The Garden of American Methodism: The Delmarva Peninsula, 1769–1820*, Wilmington, Del., 1984; and *idem*, 'The attraction of Methodism: the Delmarva Peninsula as a case study, 1769–1820', in Richey *et al.* (eds), *Perspectives*, pp. 31–45.

43 R. E. Richey, 'The Southern accent of American Methodism', *Methodist History*, 27, 1988, pp. 3–24. I am grateful to Dr Richey for access to his unpublished paper entitled 'The Chesapeake coloration of American Methodism', Asbury, Ky., 1994.

44 Gaustad, *Historical Atlas*, pp. 43–82.

45 C. Sellers, *The Market Revolution: Jacksonian America, 1815–1846*, New York, 1991, pp. 157–61.

46 The most authoritative discussion of Wesley's views on the ownership and distribution of property is to be found in J. Walsh, 'John Wesley and the community of goods', in K. Robbins (ed.), *Protestant Evangelicalism: Britain, Ireland, Germany and America, c. 1750–c. 1950, Studies in Church History*, Subsidia 7, Oxford, 1990, pp. 25–50; and *idem*, 'Methodism and the common people', in R. Samuel (ed.), *People's History and Socialist Theory*, London, 1981, pp. 354–62.

47 W. Sutton, '"To extract poison from the blessing's of God's providence": Radical Methodist suspicions of the Methodist revolution', unpublished paper delivered at the conference on Methodism and the Shaping of American Culture, Asbury, Ky., 1994. For comparisons with popular politics in Britain, see Hempton, *Methodism and Politics*, pp. 208–16. See also, G. E. Milburn, 'Piety, profit and paternalism: Methodists in business in the North-East of England, c. 1760–1920', *Proceedings of the Wesley Historical Society*, 44, 1983, pp. 45–92; and D. Martin, 'Faith, flour and jam', *Times Literary Supplement*, 1 April 1983, pp. 329–30.

48 B. Gregory, *Side-Lights on the Conflicts of Methodism 1827–52*, London, 1898; J. H. S. Kent, *The Age of Disunity*, London, 1966; R. Currie, *Methodism Divided*, London, 1968; J. C. Bowmer, *Pastor and People*, London, 1975; D. A. Gowland, *Methodist Secessions: The Origins of Free Methodism in Three Lancashire Towns*, Manchester, 1979; and J. T. Wilkinson, 'The rise of other Methodist traditions', in Davies *et al.* (eds), *A History of the Methodist Church*, vol. 2, pp. 276–329. For interpretations located more distinctly in the social and political conditions of the period see Ward, *Religion and Society*, pp. 236–78; and Hempton, *Methodism and Politics*, pp. 197–208.

49 R. L. Moore, *Selling God: American Religion in the Marketplace of Culture*, New York, 1994, p. 64. I am grateful to Richard Carwardine for allowing me to see his forthcoming article '"Antinomians" and "Arminians": Methodists and the market revolution'.

50 Deming and Hamilton, 'Methodist revivalism', pp. 127–32.

51 R. Carwardine, *Trans-Atlantic Revivalism: Popular Evangelicalism in Britain and America, 1790–1865*, Westport, Conn., 1978, p. 10.

52 See P. Jenkins, *A History of Modern Wales 1536–1990*, London, 1992, ch. 10; I. G.

Jones, *Communities*, Dyed, 1987; and G. Williams, *Religion, Language and Nationality in Wales*, Cardiff, 1979.

53 N. O. Hatch, 'The puzzle of American Methodism', *Church History*, 63, no. 2, June 1994, pp. 175–89.

54 R. J. Carwardine, *Evangelicals and Politics in Antebellum America*, New Haven, 1993, pp. 113–32.

55 Hempton, *Methodism and Politics*, p. 230.

56 See the explanations offered by Hatch, 'The puzzle of American Methodism', p. 187.

57 W. R. Ward, 'The religion of the people and the problem of control, 1790–1830', *Studies in Church History*, 8, 1972, pp. 237–57; Hempton, *Methodism and Politics*, pp. 85–115.

58 J. H. S. Kent, 'The Wesleyan Methodists to 1849', in Davies *et al.* (eds), *A History of the Methodist Church*, London, 1978, vol. 2, pp. 213–75; and *idem*, *Age of Disunity*.

59 The best treatment of urban Methodism in the north of England remains Ward, *Religion and Society*. See also, D. C. Dews, 'Methodism in Leeds from 1791 to 1861', 2 vols, M.Phil. thesis, University of Bradford, 1984; Gowland, *Methodist Secessions*; and T. Koditschek, *Class Formation and Urban Industrial Society: Bradford 1750–1850*, Cambridge, 1990, ch. 10.

60 J. Walsh, C. Haydon and S. Taylor (eds), *The Church of England c. 1689–c. 1833: From Toleration to Tractarianism*, Cambridge, 1993; P. Virgin, *The Church in an Age of Negligence: Ecclesiastical Structure and Problems of Church Reform 1700–1840*, Cambridge, 1989; and D. Hempton, 'Religion in British society 1740–1790', in J. Black (ed.), *British Politics from Walpole to Pitt 1742–1789*, London, 1990, pp. 201–21.

61 M. Smith, *Religion in Industrial Society: Oldham and Saddleworth 1740–1865*, Oxford, 1994; D. Hempton, 'Bickersteth, Bishop of Ripon: the episcopate of a mid-Victorian evangelical', *Northern History*, 17, 1981, pp. 183–202. For more general treatments of urbanization and religion in Britain see S. Bruce (ed.), *Religion and Modernization: Sociologists and Historians Debate the Secularization Thesis*, Oxford, 1992; H. McLeod, *Religion and Irreligion in Victorian England*, Bangor, Gwynedd, 1993; and C. G. Brown, 'The mechanism of religious growth in urban societies: British cities since the eighteenth century', in H. McLeod (ed.), *European Religion in the Age of Great Cities*, London, 1995, pp. 239–62.

62 J. Wolffe, *God and Greater Britain: Religion and National Life in Britain and Ireland 1843–1945*, London, 1994; and K. Robbins, *Nineteenth-Century Britain: Integration and Diversity*, Oxford, 1988, pp. 63–96.

63 Carwardine, *Evangelicals and Politics*, pp. 130–1.

64 *Ibid.*, p. 1.

65 D. Hempton and M. Hill, *Evangelical Protestantism in Ulster Society 1740–1890*, London, 1992; D. Hempton, 'Methodism in Irish Society, 1770–1830', *Transactions of the Royal Historical Society*, 5th series, 36, 1986, pp. 117–42.

66 W. Arthur, *The Life of Gideon Ouseley*, London, 1876; W. G. Campbell, '*The Apostle of Kerry*', *The Life of the Rev. Charles Graham*, Dublin, 1868; F. J. Cole, *The Cavalry Preachers*, Belfast, 1945; C. H. Crookshank, *A Methodist Pioneer: The Life and Labours of John Smith*, London, 1881; and A. Stewart and G. Revington, *Memoir of the Life and Labours of the Rev. Adam Averell*, Dublin, 1848. An even more revealing picture emerges from the letters of early itinerants and missionaries which are unfortunately spread out between the Northern Ireland Public Record Office in Belfast, the School of Oriental and African Studies (Methodist missions) in London and the John Rylands Library in Manchester.

67 D. W. Miller, 'Presbyterianism and "modernization" in Ulster', *Past and Present*, no. 80, 1978, pp. 66–90.
68 Ward, 'The Evangelical Revival in eighteenth-century Britain', p. 268.
69 I am indebted to Dr J. C. Deming for allowing me to read his doctoral thesis entitled 'Protestantism and society in France: revivalism and the French Reformed Church in the Department of the Gard, 1815–1848', University of Notre Dame, Ind., 1989. See also J. L. Osen, 'The theological revival of the French Reformed Church, 1830–1852', *Church History*, 37, 1968, pp. 36–49.
70 Deming, 'Protestantism and society', p. 53.
71 Deming and Hamilton, 'Methodist revivalism', p. 139.
72 *Ibid.*, p. 147.
73 M. A. Noll, 'Revolution and the rise of evangelical social influence', in M. A. Noll, D. W. Bebbington and G. A. Rawlyk (eds), *Evangelicalism: Comparative Studies of Popular Protestantism in North America, the British Isles, and Beyond, 1700–1900*, New York and Oxford, 1994, pp. 113–36.
74 W. R. Ward, '"Reasonable Enthusiast"', *Proceedings of the Wesley Historical Society*, 47, pt 4, 1990, pp. 125–7.
75 Examples of good recent biographies of revival leaders include H. Rack, *Reasonable Enthusiast: John Wesley and the Rise of Methodism*, London, 1989; and H. S. Stout, *The Divine Dramatist: George Whitefield and the Rise of Modern Evangelicalism*, Grand Rapids, Mich., 1991, but little attention has been paid to the lower tiers of preachers in the period 1770–1830. For an indication of what can be done see K. D. Brown, *A Social History of the Nonconformist Ministry in England and Wales 1800–1930*, Oxford, 1988. The forthcoming *Dictionary of Evangelical Biography*, Oxford, 1995, edited by Donald Lewis, will offer some help, but more remains to be done.
76 The phrase is taken from an excellent chapter on popular evangelical enthusiasm by J. H. Wigger, 'Taking heaven by storm: Methodism and the popularization of American Christianity 1770–1820', Ph.D. thesis, University of Notre Dame, Ind., 1994.
77 Thompson, *Making*, p. 404.
78 I try to address this problem using the insights of early modern historians in '"Popular religion" 1800–1986", in T. Thomas (ed.), *The British: Their Religious Beliefs and Practices 1800–1986*, London, 1988, pp. 181–210.
79 Flora Thompson, *Lark Rise to Candleford*, London, 1973, ch. 14.
80 See W. R. Ward and R. P. Heitzenrater (eds), *The Works of John Wesley*, 18, *Journals and Diaries*, I (1735–1738), Nashville, 1988, pp. 1–79; and W. R. Ward, 'The renewed unity of the brethren: ancient church, new sect or interconfessional Movement?', in *idem*, *Faith and Faction*, p. 124.
81 See Chapter 7 for notes on sources.
82 Hatch, *Democratization of American Christianity*, p. 10.
83 G. A. Rawlyk, *Wrapped up in God: A Study of Several Canadian Revivals and Revivalists*, Burlington, Ontario, 1988; and *idem*, *Ravished by the Spirit*, Kingston, Ontario and Montreal, 1984.
84 Rawlyk, *Wrapped up in God*, p. 58.
85 Wigger, 'Taking heaven by storm', pp. 81–144; *idem*, 'Taking heaven by storm: enthusiasm and early American Methodism, 1770–1820', *Journal of the Early Republic*, 14, no. 2, summer 1994, pp. 167–94; K. L. Dvorak, 'Peter Cartwright and charisma', *Methodist History*, 26, no. 2, January 1988, pp. 113–26; and C. L. Lyerly, 'Francis Asbury and the opposition to early Methodism', *Methodist History*, 31, no. 4, July 1993, pp. 224–34.
86 W. R. Ward, 'The legacy of John Wesley; the Pastoral Office in Britain and America', in *idem*, *Faith and Faction*, p. 225–48.

87 C. D. Field, 'The social composition of English Methodism to 1830: a membership analysis', *Bulletin of the John Rylands University Library of Manchester*, 76, no. 1, spring 1994, pp. 153–69.

88 C. D. Field, 'The social structure of English Methodism: eighteenth–twentieth centuries', *British Journal of Sociology*, 28, no. 2, 1977, pp. 199–225; and J. Q. Smith, 'Occupational groups among the early Methodists of the Keighley circuit', *Church History*, 57, no. 2, 1988, pp. 187–96.

89 Such studies are valuable not only for explaining Methodist success in some areas, but also its failure in others. See, for example, J. N. Morris, 'The origins and growth of Primitive Methodism in East Surrey', *Proceedings of the Wesley Historical Society*, 48, pt 5, 1992, pp. 133–49. See also R. Currie, 'A micro-theory of Methodist growth', *Proceedings of the Wesley Historical Society*, 36, 1967–8, pp. 65–73. For a remarkably comprehensive and well-documented account of the various influences operating on the rise and development of Methodism in a particular setting see Dews, 'Methodism in Leeds'.

90 J. S. Werner, *The Primitive Methodist Connexion: Its Background and Early History*, Madison, 1984, p. 155.

91 *Ibid.*, p. 156.

92 See, for example, W. R. Ward (ed.), *Parson and Parish in Eighteenth-Century Surrey: Replies to Bishops' Visitations*, Surrey Record Society, XXXIV, Castle Arch, Guildford, 1994, vii–xxii.

93 Noll, 'Revolution and the rise of evangelical social influence', p. 130.

94 See, for example, R. O. Johnson, 'The development of the love feast in early American Methodism', *Methodist History*, 19, no. 2, January 1981, pp. 67–83; R. E. Richey, 'From quarterly to camp meeting: a reconsideration of early American Methodism', *Methodist History*, 23, no. 1, July 1985, pp. 199–213. Such evangelical enthusiasm, though characteristic of the Methodists, was not unique to them. See, for example, G. A. Rawlyk, *The Canada Fire: Radical Evangelicalism in British North America 1775–1812*, Montreal and Kingston, Ontario, 1994; L. E. Schmidt, *Holy Fairs: Scottish Communions and American Revivals in the Early Modern Period*, Princeton, 1989.

95 Wigger, 'Taking heaven by storm', pp. 300–45; H. D. Rack, 'The decline of the class-meeting and the problem of church membership in nineteenth-century Wesleyanism', *Proceedings of the Wesley Historical Society*, 39, 1973–4, pp. 12–21; and *idem*, 'Wesleyanism and "the World" in the later nineteenth century', *Proceedings of the Wesley Historical Society*, 42, 1979–80, pp. 34–54.

96 Compare, for example, the spread and content of the essays in Richey *et al.* (eds), *Perspectives on American Methodism* with the essays commissioned for the Davies *et al.* (eds), *A History of the Methodist Church in Great Britain* which was initiated by the Methodist Conference in 1953 and finally completed in 1988.

97 See, for example, the splendid bibliography in part two of Davies *et al.* (eds), *A History of the Methodist Church*, vol. 4, pp. 651–8.

98 N. Z. Davis, 'Some tasks and themes in the study of popular religion', in C. Trinkaus and H. A. Oberman (eds), *The Pursuit of Holiness in Late Medieval and Renaissance Religion*, Leiden, 1974, pp. 307–36; and *idem*, 'From "popular religion" to religious cultures', in S. Ozment (ed.), *Reformation Europe: A Guide to Research*, St Louis, 1982, pp. 321–41.

2 METHODISM IN IRISH SOCIETY, 1770–1830

1 J. Walker, *An Expostulatory Address to the Members of the Methodist Society in Ireland*, 3rd edn, Dublin, 1804, p. 9. Walker subsequently wrote seven letters on the same theme; they were published in Dublin between 1802 and 1804.

2   B. Semmel, *The Methodist Revolution*, London, 1974, pp. 48–55.

3   A. Knox, *Remarks on an Expostulatory Address to the Members of the Methodist Society*, Dublin, 1802, p. 29.

4   C. H. Crookshank, *History of Methodism in Ireland*, 3 vols, London, 1885–8. The Irish branch of the Wesley Historical Society in Belfast holds the largest collection of preachers' biographies and centenary histories.

5   W. R. Ward, 'The relations of enlightenment and religious revival in central Europe and in the English-speaking world', *Studies in Church History*, Subsidia 2, 1979, pp. 281–305; 'Power and piety: the origins of religious revival in the early eighteenth century', *Bulletin of John Rylands University Library of Manchester*, 63, 1980, pp. 231–52; and *The Protestant Evangelical Awakening*, Cambridge, 1992.

6   L. A. Clarkson, 'An anatomy of an Irish town: the economy of Armagh, 1770', *Irish Economic and Social History*, 5, 1978, pp. 27–45; W. H. Crawford, 'Landlord–tenant relations in Ulster 1609–1820', *Irish Economic and Social History*, 2, 1975, pp. 5–21; P. Gibbon, 'The origins of the Orange Order and the United Irishmen', *Economy and Society*, 1, 1972, pp. 134–63.

7   E. P. Thompson, *The Making of the English Working Class*, London, 1963; and W. R. Ward, *Religion and Society in England 1790–1850*, London, 1972.

8   A. Everitt, *The Pattern of Rural Dissent: The Nineteenth Century*, Leicester, 1972; E. P. Thompson, 'Anthropology and the discipline of historical context', *Midland History*, 1, 1972, pp. 41–55; J. Rule, 'Methodism, popular beliefs and village culture in Cornwall, 1800–50', in R. D. Storch (ed.), *Popular Culture and Custom in Nineteenth-Century England*, London, 1982.

9   C. D. Field, 'The social structure of English Methodism: eighteenth–twentieth centuries', *British Journal of Sociology*, 28, 1977, pp. 199–225; *idem*, 'The social composition of English Methodism to 1830: a membership analysis', *Bulletin of John Rylands University Library of Manchester*, 76, 1994, pp. 153–69; and D. Hempton, *Methodism and Politics in British Society 1750–1850*, London, 1984, pp. 74–7.

10 R. E. Davies, *Methodism*, London, 1963.

11 H. A. Snyder, *The Radical Wesley and Patterns for Church Renewal*, Downers Grove, Ill., 1980.

12 Cork Baptist Church Book, pp. 44–5. I am indebted to Kevin Herlihy for this reference.

13 W. Arthur, *The Life of Gideon Ouseley*, London, 1876; W. G. Campbell, 'The Apostle of Kerry', *The Life of the Rev. Charles Graham*, Dublin, 1868; F. J. Cole, *The Cavalry Preachers*, Belfast, 1945; *Sketch of the Life and Character of the late Rev. William Crook by His Son*, Dublin, 1863; C. H. Crookshank, *A Methodist Pioneer: The Life and Labours of John Smith*, London, 1881; R. H. Gallagher, *John Bredin*, Belfast, 1960; and *idem*, *Pioneer Preachers of Irish Methodism*, Belfast, 1965; A. Stewart and G. Revington, *Memoir of the Life and Labours of the Rev. Adam Averell*, Dublin, 1848.

14 Mrs R. Smith, *The Life of the Rev. Mr Henry Moore*, London, 1844, pp. 58–65.

15 Charles Graham told his son that 'we do more in spreading truth in one fair or market day, than we do in weeks or months in private places'. A copy of the original letter dated 22 October 1799 is in the uncatalogued Ouseley Collection in the Northern Ireland Public Record Office (hereafter NIPRO). The collection was gathered by J. O. Bonsall, Ouseley's nephew, in preparation for a biography which was never written. It contains transcripts of letters and journals no longer available elsewhere.

16 S. W. Christophers, *Class-Meetings in Relation to the Design and Success of Methodism*, London, 1873, p. 78. Also, G. Alley, *Our Class Meeting*, Dublin, 1868.

17 E. Smyth, *The Extraordinary Life and Christian Experience of Margaret Davidson*, Dublin, 1782.

18 R. L. Cole, *Love-Feasts: A History of the Christian Agape*, London, 1916, p. 279.

19 *Methodist Magazine*, xxv, 1802, pp. 37–40.

20 J. Baxter, 'The great Yorkshire revival 1792–6: a study of mass revival among the Methodists', in M. Hill (ed.), *A Sociological Yearbook of Religion in Britain*, 7, 1974, pp. 46–76; T. Shaw, *A History of Cornish Methodism*, Truro, 1967, p. 65.

21 C. H. Crookshank, *Memorable Women of Irish Methodism*, London, 1882; J. J. McGregor, *Memoir of Miss Alice Cambridge*, Dublin, 1832; Smyth, *Margaret Davidson*. See also D. M. Valenze, *Prophetic Sons and Daughters. Female Preaching and Popular Religion in Industrial England*, Princeton, 1985.

22 For the kind of business transacted in Methodist leaders' meetings see NIPRO, Methodist MSS, CR6/3, Minutes of the Dublin District Meetings 1826–48, the Belfast District Meeting 1826–43, and the Minute Book of the Dublin Leaders Meeting 1822–32.

23 Crookshank, *A Methodist Pioneer*. Smith was illiterate and passed on tales of special providences to his son.

24 L. Dow, *Works: Providential Experience of Lorenzo Dow in Europe and America*, 3rd edn, Dublin, 1806, p. 142. Also, NIPRO, Irish Wesley Historical Society Archives, L. Dow to G. Ouseley, 7 May 1819. For more on Dow see R. Carwardine, *Transatlantic Revivalism, Popular Evangelicalism in Britain and America, 1790–1865*, Westport, Conn., 1978; and J. Kent, *Holding the Fort: Studies in Victorian Revivalism*, London, 1978. On 'heavenly music' see F. Baker (ed.), *The Works of John Wesley*, vol. 26: *Letters II (1740–55)*, Oxford, 1982, pp. 526–8.

25 Smith, *Life of Moore*, p. 87.

26 Crookshank, *History of Methodism*, vol. 2, pp. 90–1.

27 Hempton, *Methodism and Politics*, pp. 151–8; and R. Gillespie, *'Wild as Colts Untamed'*, Lurgan, 1977, p. 30.

28 D. W. Miller, 'Presbyterianism and "modernization" in Ulster', *Past and Present*, no. 80, 1978, p. 73.

29 R. Currie, A. Gilbert and L. Horsley, *Churches and Churchgoers: Patterns of Church Growth in the British Isles since 1700*, Oxford, 1977, pp. 40–1, 139–46. A. D. Gilbert, *Religion and Society in Industrial England*, London, 1976, pp. 30–2.

30 W. H. Crawford, 'Economy and society in eighteenth century Ulster', Ph.D. thesis, Queen's University Belfast, 1982, p. 108; J. R. Binns, 'A history of Methodism in Ireland from Wesley's death in 1791, to the re-union of Primitives and Wesleyans in 1878', M.A. thesis, Queen's University Belfast, 1960, pp. 205–10.

31 Crookshank, *History of Methodism*, vol. 2, p. 130. See also Ordnance Survey of Ireland, 6 inch maps (1:10560): County Fermanagh, 1st edn, Dublin, 1835, and County Armagh, 1st edn, Dublin, 1836. They show that many Methodist chapels were located either on the margins of towns or in the surrounding countryside.

32 Stewart and Revington, *Life of Averell*, pp. 103–7, and Crookshank, *History of Methodism*, vol. 2, pp. 48, 82, 102–3.

33 R. L. Cole, *A History of Methodism in Dublin*, Dublin, 1932, p. 103.

34 Some eminent Methodist preachers were converts from Roman Catholicism, including Thomas Walsh, Matthias Joyce, John Bredin and James Lynch. Dr Coke was informed in 1802 that seventy-two out of 1,209 Methodists in the Clones Circuit were from Roman Catholic backgrounds: *Methodist Magazine*, 26, 1803, pp. 375–6. That was regarded as a high proportion.

35 Crookshank, *A Methodist Pioneer*.

36 Crawford, 'Economy and society', pp. 26, 71–2 and 168.

37 Campbell, 'The Apostle of Kerry', pp. 114–15.
38 T. Coke, Copies of Letters from the Missionaries who are Employed in Ireland, for the Instruction in their Own Language, and for the Conversion of the Native Irish, London, 1801. The output of letters by Irish Methodist missionaries in this period was prolific. Regrettably they are not yet catalogued, nor even collected in one place. The main collections are as follows: University of London School of Oriental and African Studies (hereafter SOAS), Methodist Missionary Society Mss, Irish folders; the John Rylands University Library of Manchester (hereafter Rylands), Methodist Church Archives, papers of Joseph Butterworth, Adam Clarke, Thomas Coke and Gideon Ouseley; NIPRO, Irish Wesley History Society Archives and the Ouseley Collection.
39 Methodist Magazine, 25, 1802, pp. 40–2.
40 NIPRO, Ouseley Coll., C. Graham and G. Ouseley to Dr Coke, 8 April 1800.
41 NIPRO, Ouseley Coll., J. O. Bonsall has left a transcription of Ouseley's Journal beginning in April 1803. See also Methodist Magazine, 25, 1802, pp. 225–6; 26, 1803, pp. 375–7, 420–4; 27, 1804, pp. 381–2; 28, 1805, p. 383; and 29, 1806, pp. 90–4.
42 NIPRO, Ouseley Coll., Journal, 10 October 1803.
43 NIPRO, Ouseley Coll., C. Graham and G. Ouseley to Dr Coke, 6 January 1800.
44 Moreover, the region itself became less prosperous in the early nineteenth century, especially after 1815. It was a latecomer to the linen industry and one of the earliest regions to contract. See W. A. McCutcheon, The Industrial Archaeology of Northern Ireland, Belfast, 1980, pp. 283–324.
45 W. R. Ward, 'The religion of the people and the problem of control, 1790–1830', Studies in Church History, 8, 1972, pp. 237–57; and idem, Religion and Society, pp. 75–85. Hempton, Methodism and Politics, pp. 92–6.
46 NIPRO, Wesley Hist. Soc. Mss, G. Ouseley to M. Tobias, 14 June 1820.
47 C. Gill, The Rise of the Irish Linen Industry, Oxford, 1925; L. M. Cullen, An Economic History of Ireland since 1660, London, 1972, pp. 77–133; Crawford, 'Economy and society', pp. 65–6, 82–103; and Clarkson, 'Anatomy of an Irish town', pp. 27–45.
48 M. Elliott, Partners in Revolution: The United Irishmen and France, New Haven, 1982, pp. 19–20.
49 W. J. Green, Methodism in Portadown, Belfast, 1960; R. H. Gallagher, Methodism in the Charlemont Circuit, Belfast, 1961; J. M. Lynn, A History of Wesleyan Methodism in the Armagh Circuit, 3rd edn, Belfast, 1887; and Gillespie, 'Wild as Colts Untamed'.
50 The Primitive Wesleyan Methodists split from the main connexion in 1816 in protest against the decision allowing Methodist preachers to administer the sacraments in Methodist societies. Binns, 'A history of Methodism', pp. 55–85.
51 Stewart and Revington, Life of Averell, pp. 115–17.
52 D. Savage, The Life and Labours of the Rev. Wm. McClure, Toronto, 1872; and Crookshank, History of Methodism, vol. 2, pp. 146–7. The term 'Jacobin Methodists' was used abusively against those who formed the Methodist New Connexion. They linked up with the Kilhamites in England.
53 J. Vickers, Thomas Coke: Apostle of Methodism, London, 1969, pp. 226–7; and D. N. Hempton, 'The Methodist crusade in Ireland 1795–1845', Irish Historical Studies, 22, no. 8, 1980, pp. 33–48.
54 Stewart and Revington, Life of Averell, pp. 165 and 194. See also A. F. Blackstock, 'The origin and development of the Irish yeomanry, 1796–c.1807', Ph.D. thesis, Queen's University Belfast, 1993.
55 Gillespie, 'Wild as Colts Untamed', pp. 27–8.
56 Irish Conference Minutes, Dublin, 1809. The financial statement shows that the

Dublin and Cork circuits contributed more money than all the other circuits in the linen triangle and Lough Erne rectangle added together.

57 Thompson, 'Anthropology and historical context', pp. 41–55.

58 Rule, 'Methodism', pp. 48–70. See also J. Rule, *The Experience of Labour in Eighteenth-Century Industry*, London, 1981, pp. 207–8.

59 Arthur, *Life of Ouseley*, pp. 165–70.

60 NIPRO, Wesley Hist. Soc. Mss, A. Clarke to G. Ouseley, 6 December 1806.

61 See D. Bowen, *The Protestant Crusade in Ireland 1800–1870*, Dublin, 1978; A. R. Acheson, 'The Evangelicals in the Church of Ireland 1784–1859', Ph.D. thesis, Queen's University Belfast, 1967; and J. Liechty, 'Irish Evangelicalism, Trinity College Dublin, and the mission of the Church of Ireland at the end of the eighteenth century', Ph.D. thesis, St Patrick's College, Maynooth, 1987.

62 NIPRO, Methodist Mss, CR6/3, Minutes of Conference, 1792–1813. Although the official minutes were published each year, this volume contains private minutes on sensitive subjects such as cases of spiritual discipline and relations with outside bodies.

63 S. J. Connolly, *Priests and People in Pre-Famine Ireland 1780–1845*, Dublin, 1982, pp. 74–134.

64 W. Gregory, 'Extracts of a Tour through the North of Ireland engaged under the Patronage of the Evangelical Society of Ulster, in the Summer of the year 1800', typescript, Linen Hall Library, Belfast. See also G. Hamilton, *The Great Necessity of Itinerant Preaching: a sermon delivered in Armagh at the formation of the Evangelical Society of Ulster*, Armagh, 1798; M. Lanktree, *Biographical Narrative*, Belfast, 1836, pp. 106–9; and *Report of a Deputation from the London Hibernian Society, respecting the Religious State of Ireland*, London, 1808, p.18.

65 Gregory, *Extracts*, pp. 12–13.

66 Miller, 'Presbyterianism', p. 73.

67 Crookshank, *History of Methodism*, vol. 2, pp. 399–400. S. Burdy, *The Life of Philip Skelton*, 2nd edn, Oxford, 1914, pp. 148, 171 and 236.

68 Crookshank, *History of Methodism*, vol. 2, pp. 75–6; J. Gamble, *Sketches of History, Politics and Manners in Dublin and the North of Ireland in 1810*, 2nd edn, London, 1826, pp. 173–7; and C. Forster, *The Life of John Jebb, with a Selection from his Letters*, London, 1836, pp. 2 and 70.

69 On the consequences of separation for the Church of Ireland see Binns, 'A history of Methodism', pp. 27 and 148–91.

70 P. Brooke, 'Controversies in Ulster Presbyterianism 1790–1836', Ph.D. thesis, University of Cambridge, 1980, pp. 65–9. A. J. Hayes and D. A. Gowland (eds), *Scottish Methodism in the Early Victorian Period, the Scottish Correspondence of the Rev. Jabez Bunting 1800–57*, Edinburgh, 1981, pp. 26 and 88.

71 *Records of the General Synod of Ulster*, 3, 1804, p. 279.

72 NIPRO, Methodist Mss, CR6/3, Minutes of Conference 1792–1813. See entry under Private Minutes for 1801.

73 *Fourth Report of the Commissioners of Irish Education Inquiry*, Belfast, 1825, pp. 148–9; A. T. Q. Stewart, 'The transformation of Presbyterian radicalism in the north of Ireland, 1792–1825', M.A. thesis, Queen's University Belfast, 1956, 177–93.

74 Miller, 'Presbyterianism', pp. 66–90; and Brooke, 'Controversies', pp. 26–35.

75 M. Hurley, SJ (ed.), *John Wesley's Letter to a Roman Catholic*, London, 1968. See also, D. Butler, *John Wesley and the Catholic Church in the Eighteenth Century*, London, 1995.

76 SOAS, Methodist Missionary Soc. Mss, Irish folders, C. Graham to Dr Coke, 11 September and 23 November 1802; Graham to J. Butterworth, 13 March 1805; Graham, J. Hamilton and W. Peacock to Dr Coke, 24 March 1806; W. Reilly to

J. Taylor, 15 December 1818; G. Ouseley to Taylor, 11 October 1819. Rylands, Methodist Archive and Research Centre, G. Ouseley to J. Butterworth, 29 May 1804, 3 August 1804 and 14 May 1813. NIPRO, Ouseley Coll., xxvii, 9–11.

77 NIPRO, Ouseley Coll., xxvii, G. Ouseley to Dr Bellew, 29 October and 2 December 1807.

78 NIPRO, Ouseley Coll., xxiii, Earl of Roden to G. Ouseley, 3 June 1837; xxvii, 11.

79 Hempton, 'Methodist crusade', pp. 33–48.

80 Binns, 'A history of Methodism', pp. 90–1 and 120–2.

81 N. W. Taggart, *The Irish in World Methodism 1760–1900*, London, 1986.

3 POPULAR RELIGION IN MODERN BRITAIN

1 D. M. Valenze, *Prophetic Sons and Daughters. Female Preaching and Popular Religion in Industrial England*, Princeton, 1985, p. 245.

2 R. C. Trexler, 'Reverence and profanity in the study of early modern religion', in K. von Greyerz (ed.), *Religion and Society in Early Modern Europe*, London, 1984, pp. 245–69.

3 S. Williams, 'Urban popular religion and the rites of passage', in H. McLeod (ed.), *European Religion in the Age of Great Cities 1830–1930*, London, 1995, pp. 216–36.

4 C. Brooke *et al.*, 'What is religious history?', *History Today*, 35, August 1985, pp. 43–52.

5 Trexler, 'Reverence and profanity', pp. 245–69.

6 N. Z. Davis, 'Some tasks and themes in the study of popular religion', in C. Trinkaus and H. A. Oberman (eds), *The Pursuit of Holiness in Late Medieval and Renaissance Religion*, Leiden, 1974, pp. 307–36; and N. Z. Davis, 'From "popular religion" to religious cultures', in S. Ozment (ed.), *Reformation Europe: A Guide to Research*, St Louis, 1982, pp. 321–41.

7 For church attendance figures in the British Isles since 1700 see R. Currie, A. Gilbert and L. Horsley, *Churches and Churchgoers: Patterns of Church Growth in the British Isles since 1700*, Oxford, 1977. See also, G. Davie, *Religion in Britain since 1945: Believing without Belonging*, London, 1994.

8 A. Briggs, 'The human aggregate', in H. J. Dyos and M. Wolff (eds), *The Victorian City: Images and Realities*, London, 1973, vol. 1, pp. 83–104.

9 Currie *et al.*, *Churches and Churchgoers*; R. Gill, *The Myth of the Empty Church*, London, 1993; and S. Bruce (ed.), *Religion and Modernization: Sociologists and Historians Debate the Secularization Thesis*, Oxford, 1992.

10 J. Cox, *The English Churches in a Secular Society: Lambeth, 1870–1930*, Oxford, 1982; D. N. Hempton, 'Bickersteth, Bishop of Ripon: the episcopate of a mid-Victorian Evangelical', *Northern History*, 17, 1981, pp. 183–202; K. S. Inglis, 'Patterns of religious worship in 1851', *Journal of Ecclesiastical History*, 11, 1960, pp. 74–86; and H. McLeod, *Class and Religion in the Late Victorian City*, London, 1974. For a different approach see C. G. Brown, 'The mechanisms of religious growth in urban societies: British cities since the eighteenth century', in McLeod (ed.), *European Religion*, pp. 239–62.

11 T. W. Laqueur, *Religion and Respectability: Sunday Schools and Working-Class Culture 1780–1850*, New Haven and London, 1976.

12 W. R. Ward, *Religion and Society in England 1790–1850*, London, 1972, p. 13.

13 For this and other controversies surrounding Sunday schools see D. Hempton, *Methodism and Politics in British Society 1750–1850*, London, 1984, pp. 86–92.

14 Currie *et al.*, *Churches and Churchgoers*, pp. 21–123.

15 A. Everitt, *The Pattern of Rural Dissent: The Nineteenth Century*, Leicester, 1972.
16 S. Connolly, *Religion and Society in Nineteenth-Century Ireland*, Dundalk, 1985; E. T. Davies, *A New History of Wales: Religion and Society in the Nineteenth Century*, Dyfed, 1981; A. D. Gilbert, *The Making of Post-Christian Britain*, London, 1980, pp. 75–6; R. F. G. Holmes, *Our Irish Presbyterian Heritage*, Belfast, 1985; R. Swift and S. Gilley (eds), *The Irish in the Victorian City*, London, 1985; R. Wallis, S. Bruce and D. Taylor, *'No Surrender!' Paisleyism and the Politics of Ethnic Identity in Northern Ireland*, Belfast, 1986; D. Hempton and M. Hill, *Evangelical Protestantism in Ulster Society 1740–1890*, London, 1992; and D. Hempton, *Religion and Political Culture in Britain and Ireland*, Cambridge, 1996.
17 Connolly, *Religion and Society*, pp. 58–9; H. McLeod, *Religion and the People of Western Europe 1789–1970*, Oxford, 1981; and *idem* (ed.), *European Religion*.
18 F. Thompson, *Lark Rise to Candleford*, London, 1973, ch. 14.
19 For suggestive comments on the complicated relationship between official and popular religion in nineteenth-century rural England see H. McLeod, 'Recent studies in Victorian religious history', *Victorian Studies*, 21, no. 2, 1978, pp. 245–55.
20 K. Thomas, *Religion and the Decline of Magic*, London, 1971.
21 J. Obelkevich, *Religion and Rural Society: South Lindsey 1825–1875*, Oxford, 1976; S. J. Connolly, *Priests and People in Pre-Famine Ireland 1780–1845*, Dublin, 1982.
22 Obelkevich, *Religion and Rural Society*, pp. 305–6.
23 G. Eliot, *Silas Marner*, Cambridge, 1995, ch. 1.
24 McLeod, 'Recent studies', p. 250.
25 *Silas Marner*, ch. 10.
26 N. Scotland, *Methodism and the Revolt of the Field*, Gloucester, 1981.
27 E. Gosse, *Father and Son*, London, 1989, ch. 6.
28 McLeod, 'Recent studies', n. 10.
29 See, for example, P. Horn, *The Rural World 1780–1850*, London, 1980, p. 156.
30 Obelkevich, *Religion and Rural Society*, pp. 149–50.
31 See A. Silver (ed.), *The Family Letters of Samuel Butler 1841–1886*, London, 1962; and S. Butler, *Ernest Pontifex or The Way of All Flesh*, London, 1964.
32 *The Way of All Flesh*, ch. 14.
33 *Ibid.*, ch. 15.
34 T. Hardy, *The Distracted Preacher*, in *Collected Short Stories*, London, 1988, ch. 6.
35 T. Hardy, *Under the Greenwood Tree*, London, 1985, pt 2, ch. 4.
36 *Lark Rise to Candleford*, ch. 14; and D. H. Lawrence, *Sons and Lovers*, Cambridge, 1992, ch. 2.
37 Obelkevich, *Religion and Rural Society*, pp. 149–50.
38 S. Budd, *Varieties of Unbelief*, London, 1977, pp. 105–6. For the impact of religious revivalism on Victorian society see R. Carwardine, *Trans-Atlantic Revivalism: Popular Evangelicalism in Britain and America, 1790–1865*, London, 1978; and J. Kent, *Holding the Fort: Studies in Victorian Revivalism*, London, 1978.
39 C. Moore, *Esther Waters*, London, 1962, ch. 4.
40 R. Moore, *Pit-Men, Preachers and Politics: The Effects of Methodism in a Durham Mining Community*, Cambridge, 1974; R. Colls, *The Collier's Rant: Song and Culture in the Industrial Village*, London, 1977; and Hempton, *Methodism and Politics*, pp. 214–16.
41 Coll, *The Collier's Rant*, p. 100.
42 E. T. Davies, *Religion in the Industrial Revolution in South Wales*, Cardiff, 1965; and *idem*, *A New History of Wales: Religion and Society in the Nineteenth Century*, Llandybie, Dyfed, 1981. See also, D. B. Rees, *Chapels in the Valley: A Study in the Sociology of Welsh Nonconformity*, Upton, Wirral, 1975.
43 Connolly, *Priests and People*, pp. 74–218; P. Corish, *The Irish Catholic Experience:*

A Historical Survey, Dublin, 1985, pp. 96–225; D. Keenan, *The Catholic Church in Nineteenth-Century Ireland: A Sociological Study,* Dublin, 1983; J. O'Shea, *Priest, Politics and Society in Post-Famine Ireland: A County Study of Tipperary, 1850–1891,* Dublin, 1983; D. Hempton, 'Irish religion', *Irish Economic and Social History,* 13, 1986, pp. 108–12; and D. W. Miller, 'Irish Catholicism and the historian', *Irish Economic and Social History,* 13, 1986, pp. 113–16.

44 Connolly, *Religion and Society,* p. 49.

45 Keenan, *Catholic Church,* p. 23.

46 Obelkevich, *Religion and Rural Society,* pp. 271–4.

47 E. Larkin, *The Historical Dimensions of Irish Catholicism,* New York, 1976; and *idem, The Making of the Roman Catholic Church in Ireland 1850–60,* Chapel Hill, NC, 1980.

48 Corish, *Irish Catholic Experience,* p. 167.

49 L. M. Cullen, *The Emergence of Modern Ireland 1600–1900,* London, 1981, pp. 135–9, 254–6.

50 W. Herberg, *Protestant–Catholic–Jew: An Essay in American Religious Sociology,* Garden City, NY, 1956; O. Handlin, *The Uprooted,* Boston, 1973; and K. A. Miller, *Emigrants and Exiles: Ireland and the Irish Exodus to North America,* New York, 1985.

51 Swift and Gilley (eds), *The Irish,* p. 10.

52 Ibid., see especially the articles by O'Tuathaigh, Aspinwall and McCaffrey, Connolly, Gilley and Samuel; S. Gilley, 'The Roman Catholic mission to the Irish in London', *Recusant History,* 10, 1969–70, pp. 123–41; *idem,* 'Protestant London, No-Popery and the Irish poor, 1830–60', pt 1, *Recusant History,* 10, 1969–70, pp. 210–30, and pt 2, *Recusant History,* 11, 1971–2, pp. 21–46; and H. McLeod, 'Building the "Catholic Ghetto": Catholic organisations 1870–1914', in W. J. Sheils and D. Wood (eds), *Voluntary Religion,* Oxford, 1986, pp. 411–44.

53 S. Gilley, 'Vulgar piety and the Brompton Oratory, 1850–1860', in Swift and Gilley (eds), *The Irish,* p. 263.

54 McLeod, *Class and Religion,* p. 72.

55 J. A. Banks, 'The contagion of numbers', and R. Samuel, 'Comers and goers', in Dyos and Wolff (eds), *The Victorian City,* pp. 105–60.

56 For the most recent contribution see Brown, 'The mechanism of religious growth', pp. 239–62.

57 J. Obelkevich, L. Roper and R. Samuel (eds), *Disciplines of Faith: Studies in Religion, Politics and Patriarchy,* London, 1987.

58 Valenze, *Prophetic Sons and Daughters;* G. Malmgreen, 'Economy and culture in an industrializing town: Macclesfield, Cheshire, 1750–1835', Ph.D. thesis, Indiana University, 1981; G. Malmgreen (ed.), *Religion in the Lives of English Women, 1760–1930,* London, 1986; and F. Prochaska, *Women and Philanthropy in Nineteenth-Century England,* Oxford, 1980.

59 J. F. C. Harrison, *The Second Coming: Popular Millenarianism 1780–1850,* London, 1979; E. P. Thompson, *The Making of the English Working Class,* London, 1963, pp. 116–20, 382–9 and 797–803; and C. Hill, *The World Turned Upside Down: Radical Ideas during the English Revolution,* London, 1972.

60 W. R. Ward, 'The religion of the people and the problem of control, 1790–1830', *Studies in Church History,* 8, 1972, pp. 237–57, and *Religion and Society,* pp. 75–85; J. Baxter, 'The great Yorkshire revival 1792–6; a study of mass revival among the Methodists', in M. Hill (ed.), *A Sociological Yearbook of Religion in Britain,* 7, 1974, pp. 46–76; D. Luker, 'Revivalism in theory and practice: the case of Cornish Methodism', *Journal of Ecclesiastical History,* 37, no. 4, 1986, pp. 603–19; Kent, *Holding the Fort;* and R. Carwardine, *Trans-Atlantic Revivalism.*

61 A. A. MacLaren, *Religion and Social Class: The Disruption Years in Aberdeen,*

London, 1974, pp. 1–49; A. L. Drummond and J. Bulloch, *The Scottish Church 1688–1843*, Edinburgh, 1973, pp. 114–41; and A. L. Drummond and J. Bulloch, *The Church in Late Victorian Scotland*, Edinburgh, 1978, pp. 126–214.

62 Cullen, *Emergence Of Modern Ireland*, chs 6 and 9; M. Elliott, *Partners in Revolution: The United Irishmen and France*, New Haven, 1982, pp. 19–20; P. Gibbon, 'The origins of the Orange Order and the United Irishmen', *Economy and Society*, 1, 1972, pp. 134–63; D. Hempton, 'Methodism in Irish society 1770–1830', *Transactions of the Royal Historical Society*, 5th series, 36, 1986, pp. 117–42; and Hempton and Hill, *Evangelical Protestantism*, pp. 20–44.

63 D. Hempton, 'Belfast: the unique city?', in McLeod (ed.), *European Religion*, pp. 145–64; Connolly, *Religion and Society*, pp. 31–41; and P. Gibbon, *The Origins of Ulster Unionism: The Formation of Popular Protestant Politics and Ideology in Nineteenth-Century Ireland*, Manchester, 1975.

64 This point is made with particular clarity by J. Rule, 'Methodism, popular beliefs and village culture in Cornwall 1800–50', in R. D. Storch (ed.), *Popular Culture and Custom in Nineteenth-Century England*, London, 1982, pp. 48–70. See also E. Yeo and S. Yeo (eds), *Popular Culture and Class Conflict 1590–1914*, Brighton, 1982.

65 H. McLeod, *Religion and the Working Class in Nineteenth-Century Britain*, London, 1984, pp. 57–66; H. McLeod, *Religion and Irreligion in Victorian England*, Bangor, Gwynedd, 1993; MacLaren, *Religion and Social Class*, pp. 121–43; C. G. Brown, 'Religion and the development of an urban society: Glasgow, 1780–1914', Ph.D. thesis, University of Glasgow, 1981; S. Yeo, *Religion and Voluntary Organisations in Crisis*, London, 1976, pp. 117–62; and E. R. Wickham, *Church and People in an Industrial City*, London, 1957.

66 S. Williams, 'Religious belief and popular culture: a study of the South London Borough of Southwark (c. 1880–1939)', D.Phil. thesis, University of Oxford, 1993; and Williams, 'Urban popular religion', pp. 216–36. See also, Cox, *The English Churches*; and J. Morris, *Religion and Urban Change: Croydon, 1840–1914*, London, 1992.

67 A notable exception is M. Smith, *Religion in Industrial Society: Oldham and Saddleworth 1740–1865*, Oxford, 1994.

68 J. Rule, *The Labouring Classes in Early Industrial England 1750–1850*, London, 1986, pp. 162–5; and S. Meacham, *A Life Apart*, London, 1977, pp. 199–200.

69 Although the dangers are only too obvious, both literary criticism and historical understanding have been advanced by sensitive books on this theme. See W. E. Houghton, *The Victorian Frame of Mind, 1830–1870*, New Haven, 1957; V. Cunningham, *Everywhere Spoken Against: Dissent in the Victorian Novel*, Oxford, 1975; E. Jay, *The Religion of the Heart: Anglican Evangelicalism and the Nineteenth-Century Novel*, Oxford, 1979; and D. Hempton, 'Popular religion and irreligion in Victorian fiction', in T. Dunne (ed.), *The Writer as Witness: Literature as Historical Evidence, Historical Studies*, 16, Cork, 1987.

70 M. Wolff, 'Victorian study: an interdisciplinary essay', *Victorian Studies*, 8, no. 1, 1964, pp. 59–70.

71 D. R. Schwarz, *Disraeli's Fiction*, London, 1979.

72 D. M. Thompson, 'The churches and society in nineteenth-century England: a rural perspective', *Studies in Church History*, 8, 1972, pp. 267–76; the articles by Rogers, Robson and Thompson in D. Baker (ed.), *The Church in Town and Countryside*, Oxford, 1979, pp. 335–59, 401–14 and 427–40; and Brown, 'The mechanism of religious growth', pp. 239–62.

73 These examples are taken from a range of so-called 'social problem' novels in the 1840s and 1850s including *Mary Barton* and *North and South* by Elizabeth Gaskell, *Alton Locke* and *Yeast* by Charles Kingsley, *Sybil* by Benjamin Disraeli,

and *Bleak House* and *Hard Times* by Charles Dickens. For a brief introduction to these themes see M. Wheeler, *English Fiction of the Victorian Period 1830–1890*, London, 1985, pp. 32–41.

74 William Hale White, *The Deliverance of Mark Rutherford*, London, 1893, ch. 6; and E. P. Thompson, 'Anthropology and the discipline of historical context', *Midland History*, 1, no. 3, 1972, pp. 41–55.

75 Moore, *Esther Waters*, ch. 3, where the heroine's father refers to the Brethren as 'your hymn-and-misery lot'; see B. Harrison, 'Religion and recreation in nineteenth-century England', *Past and Present*, no. 38, 1967, pp. 98–125; and J. Kent, 'Feelings and festivals', in Dyos and Wolff (eds), *The Victorian City*, pp. 855–72.

76 D. Vincent, *Bread, Knowledge and Freedom: A Study of Nineteenth-Century Working Class Autobiography*, London, 1981; Budd, *Varieties of Unbelief*; and J. A. Burdett, 'A study of the relationship between evangelical urban missionaries and the working-class poor in Birmingham, Norwich and Edinburgh, c. 1830–1860', M.Phil. thesis, University of Birmingham, 1994.

77 McLeod, *Class and Religion*, pp. 216–23.

78 Williams, 'Religious belief and popular culture', pp. iv and 43.

79 *Ibid.*, p. 296.

80 Hempton, *Methodism and Politics*, pp. 212–13; and H. McLeod, 'Religion in the British and German labour movements c. 1890–1914: a comparison', *Bulletin of the Society for the Study of Labour History*, 51, 1986, pp. 25–35.

81 P. Thompson, *The Edwardians: The Remaking of British Society*, London, 1975; P. Thompson, *The Voice of the Past: Oral History*, Oxford, 1978; E. Roberts, *A Woman's Place: An Oral History of Working-Class Women, 1890–1940*, Oxford, 1984; and H. McLeod, 'New perspectives on working-class religion: the oral evidence', *Oral History*, 14, no. 1, 1986, pp. 31-49. McLeod's references contain a much fuller bibliography of works on this subject than is possible here.

82 Kent, *Holding the Fort*, chs 5 and 9.

83 Obelkevich *et al.*, *Disciplines of Faith*, p. 555.

84 D. Clark, *Between Pulpit and Pew: Folk Religion in a North Yorkshire Fishing Village*, Cambridge, 1982, ch. 5.

85 H. G. Wells, *The New Machiavelli*, London, 1946, bk 1, ch. 3.

86 MacLaren, *Religion and Social Class*; Yeo, *Religion and Voluntary Organisations*; J. Foster, *Class Struggle and the Industrial Revolution: Early Industrial Capitalism in Three English Towns*, London, 1974, ch. 7; and P. Joyce, *Work, Society and Politics: The Culture of the Factory in Later Victorian England*, London, 1982, ch. 7.

87 Joyce, *Work, Society and Politics*, p. 261.

88 Cox, *The English Churches*, chs 4 and 8.

89 McLeod, *Class and Religion*, pp. 279–87.

90 Clark, *Between Pulpit and Pew*, pp. 65–6. For a helpful introduction to folk religion and its literature see D. Yoder, 'Toward a definition of folk religion', *Western Folklore*, 33, 1974, pp. 2–15.

91 A. D. Gilbert, *The Making of Post-Christian Britain: A History of the Secularization of Modern Society*, London, 1980; D. Martin, *A General Theory of Secularization*, Oxford, 1978; for a recent collection of articles and bibliography on the current state of play in this debate see Bruce (ed.), *Religion and Modernization*.

92 For good recent introductions to European religion in these periods see von Greyerz (ed.), *Religion and Society*; and J. van Engen, 'The Christian Middle Ages as an historiographical problem', *American Historical Review*, 91, no. 3, June 1986, pp. 519–52.

93 D. Lyon, *The Steeple's Shadow*, London, 1985, pp. 96–113.

94 D. Martin and P. Mullen (eds), *Strange Gifts? A Guide to Charismatic Renewal*, Oxford, 1984; E. Barker (ed.), *New Religious Movements: A Perspective for Understanding Society*, New York, 1982; and R. Wallis, *The Elementary Forms of the New Religious Life*, London, 1983.

95 P. Mullen, 'Confusion worse confounded', in Martin and Mullen (eds), *Strange Gifts?*, pp. 97–106. For a more sympathetic view see D. W. Bebbington, *Evangelicalism in Modern Britain: A History from the 1730s to the 1980s*, London, 1989, pp. 229–48.

96 Lambeth Palace Library Mss, Secker Papers, vol. 8 (Methodists). This includes the Lavington correspondence, parts of which are reproduced by O. A. Beckerlegge in *Proceedings of the Wesley Historical Society*, 42, 1980, pp. 101–11, 139–49 and 167–80. See also G. Lavington, *The Enthusiasm of Methodists and Papists Compar'd*, London, 1749–51; and E. Gibson, *Observations upon the Conduct and Behaviour of a Certain Sect usually distinguished by the Name of Methodists*, London, 1744.

97 Hempton, *Methodism and Politics*, pp. 164–6.

98 W. R. Ward, Review of H. McLeod, *Class and Religion in the Late Victorian City*, *Journal of Ecclesiastical History*, 26, 1975, pp. 424–5.

99 Obelkevich, *Religion and Rural Society*, p. 313.

100 W. R. Ward, 'The relations of enlightenment and religious revival in central Europe and in the English-speaking world', *Studies in Church History*, subsidia 2, 1979, pp. 281–305; *idem*, 'Power and piety: the origins of religious revival in the early eighteenth century', *Bulletin of the John Rylands University Library of Manchester*, 63, no. 1, 1980, pp. 213–52; *idem*, *The Protestant Evangelical Awakening*, Cambridge, 1992; H. McLeod, 'Building the "Catholic Ghetto"', pp. 411–44; McLeod, 'Religion in the British and German labour movements'; U. Gäbler and P. Schram (eds), *Erweckung am Beginn des 19. Jahrhunderts: Referate einer Tagung an der Freien Universität Amsterdam 26–29 März 1985*, Amsterdam, 1986; M. A. Noll, D. W. Bebbington and G. A. Rawlyk (eds), *Evangelicalism: Comparative Studies of Popular Protestantism in North America, the British Isles, and Beyond, 1700–1990*, New York and Oxford, 1994; and G. A. Rawlyk and M. A. Noll (eds), *Amazing Grace: Evangelicalism in Australia, Britain, Canada and the United States*, Montreal and Kingston, Ontario, 1994.

101 S. Mews (ed.), *Religion and National Identity*, Oxford, 1982; K. Robbins, *Nineteenth-Century Britain: Integration and Diversity*, Oxford, 1988; and Hempton, *Religion and Political Culture*.

102 Trexler, 'Reverence and profanity', pp. 245–69.

4 JOHN WESLEY AND ENGLAND'S *'ANCIEN RÉGIME'*

1 For a survey of some of this material see L. Colley, 'The politics of eighteenth-century British history', *Journal of British Studies*, 25, 1986, pp. 359–79. See also J. Black (ed.), *British Politics and Society from Walpole to Pitt 1742–1789*, London, 1990.

2 J. Innes, 'Review article: Jonathan Clark, social history and England's "Ancien Regime"', *Past and Present*, no. 115, 1987, pp. 165–200.

3 J. C. D. Clark, *English Society 1688–1832*, Cambridge, 1985, pp. 235–47.

4 *The Works of John Wesley*, XI, pp. 14–163.

5 B. Semmel, *The Methodist Revolution*, London, 1974, p. 66.

6 Clark, *English Society*, p. 242.

7 E. P. Thompson, *The Making of the English Working Class*, London, 1963, pp. 350–400.

8 M. Petersen, 'Thomas Jefferson: a brief life', in L. Weymouth (ed.), *Thomas Jefferson*, London, 1973, p. 14. See also, R. P. Heitzenrater, *The Elusive Mr Wesley*, 2 vols, Nashville, 1984, vol. 1, pp. 11–36.

9 H. D. Rack, *Reasonable Enthusiast: John Wesley and the Rise of Methodism*, London, 1989.

10 W. R. Ward, *The Protestant Evangelical Awakening*, Cambridge, 1992, pp. 327–8 and 332–5.

11 *Ibid.*, p. 300.

12 L. Colley, *In Defiance of Oligarchy*, Cambridge, 1982, pp. 112–15; and *idem*, 'Eighteenth-century English radicalism before Wilkes', *Transactions of the Royal Historical Society*, 5th series, 31, 1981, pp. 1–19.

13 Ward, *Protestant Evangelical Awakening*, p. 301. See also J. Wesley, *Concise History of England*, 4 vols, London, 1776, vol. 4, pp. 160–4.

14 I am grateful to John Walsh for talking through these ideas with me.

15 J. Wesley, *Thoughts Upon Liberty*, 1772, in *Works*, XI, p. 37.

16 *Ibid.*, p. 41.

17 J. Wesley, *Thoughts Upon Slavery*, 1774, in *Works*, XI, p. 71.

18 *Ibid.*, pp. 74–9.

19 *Ibid.*, p. 79.

20 J. Wesley, *Some Observations on Liberty Occasioned by a Late Tract*, 1776, in *Works*, XI, pp. 90–118.

21 *Ibid.*, p. 103.

22 J. Wesley, *A Calm Address to the Inhabitants of England*, 1777, in *Works*, XI, p. 13.

23 The phrase is taken from J. Wesley, *A Letter to the Printer of the 'Public Advertiser'*, London, 21 January 1780, in *Works*, X, pp. 159–61.

24 For a fuller discussion of these points see D. Hempton, *Methodism and Politics in British Society 1750–1850*, London, 1984, pp. 20–54.

25 Opinions expressed in an excellent unpublished typescript by L. O. Hynson, 'Human liberty as Divine Right: a study in the political maturation of John Wesley'. See also his 'Church and State in the thought and life of John Wesley', Ph.D. thesis, University of Iowa, 1971.

26 Hempton, *Methodism and Politics*, pp. 30–43.

27 Colley, *In Defiance*, and 'Eighteenth-century English radicalism'.

28 Heitzenrater, *Mr Wesley*, vol. 2, pp. 116–27.

29 The standard work on this subject is F. Baker, *John Wesley and the Church of England*, London, 1970.

30 Cited in Clark, *English Society*, p. 250.

31 *Ibid.*, pp. 247–76. See also, D. Hempton, 'Religion in British Society 1740–1790', in Black (ed.), *British Politics and Society*, pp. 201–21.

32 A. C. Outler (ed.), *The Works of John Wesley*, 2, *Sermons*, Nashville, 1985, pp. 462–3.

33 *The Works of John Wesley*, VII, p. 303.

34 *The Letters of John Wesley*, 4, p. 140.

35 M. Edwards, 'John Wesley', in R. Davies and G. Rupp (eds), *A History of the Methodist Church in Great Britain*, vol. 1, London, 1965, pp. 71–2.

36 F. Baker (ed.), *The Works of John Wesley*, 26, *Letters*, II, Oxford, 1982, p. 595.

37 Rack, *Reasonable Enthusiast*, p. 302.

38 Baker, *Wesley and the Church of England*, p. 135.

39 *Works*, 26, *Letters*, II, p. 189.

40 *Ibid.*, p. 135.

41 *Minutes of Some Late Conversations between the Rev. Mr Wesley and Others*, 27 June 1744, in *Works*, 8, pp. 280–1. See also F. Dreyer, 'A religious society under heaven: John Wesley and the identity of Methodism', *Journal of British Studies*,

25, 1986, pp. 62–83, in which he states that Wesley, both as an Anglican and a Methodist, 'thought of the church as a voluntary association that derived all the legitimacy it possessed from the agreement of its members', thereby rejecting notions of compulsory membership.

42 Baker, *Wesley and the Church of England*, p. 283.

43 The most recent and authoritative discussion of Wesley's views on property is to be found in J. Walsh, 'John Wesley and the community of goods', in K. Robbins (ed.), *Protestant Evangelicalism: Britain, Ireland, Germany and America, c. 1750–c. 1950, Studies in Church History*, Subsidia 7, Oxford, 1990.

44 R. Porter, *English Society in the Eighteenth Century*, London, 1982, p. 70.

45 N. McKendrick, 'The consumer revolution of eighteenth-century England', in N. McKendrick, J. Brewer and J. H. Plumb (eds), *The Birth of a Consumer Society: The Commercialization of Eighteenth-Century England*, London, 1983, pp. 9–33. See also, J. V. Beckett, *The Aristocracy in England 1660–1914*, Oxford, 1986.

46 Innes, 'Review article', pp. 165–200. See also P. Langford, *A Polite and Commercial People: England 1727–1783*, Oxford, 1989.

47 Thompson, *Making*, p. 355. Thompson's work has been particularly influential in this respect.

48 W. J. Warner, *The Wesleyan Movement in the Industrial Revolution*, London, 1930, pp. 136–247; J. Walsh, 'Methodism and the common people', in R. Samuel (ed.), *People's History and Socialist Theory*, London, 1981, pp. 354–62.

49 Cited in Warner, *The Wesleyan Movement*, p. 210.

50 Walsh, 'John Wesley', p. 30.

51 Outler (ed.), *Works*, vols 1–4, *Sermons*, Nashville, 1984–5. See especially Sermon on the Mount VIII and numbers 50, 87, 108 and 131.

52 J. Wesley, *Thoughts on the Present Scarcity of Provisions*, 1777, in *Works*, XI, p. 57.

53 Outler (ed.), *Works*, vol. 1, pp. 92–3.

54 *Works*, 26, *Letters*, II, pp. 544–5.

55 Warner, *The Wesleyan Movement*, p. 152; and Hempton, *Methodism and Politics*, pp. 231–4.

56 J. Brewer and J. Styles (eds), *An Ungovernable People: The English and their Law in the Seventeenth and Eighteenth Centuries*, London, 1980, p. 14. See also. J. Innes and J. Styles, 'The crime wave: recent writing on crime and criminal justice in eighteenth-century England', *Journal of British Studies*, 25, 1986, pp. 380–435.

57 See 2 Burr. 1041, Rex v. Moreley, 1760 and 4 Burr. 1991, Rex v. Justices and Clerk of the Peace for the County of Derby, 1766. For a more detailed discussion of the relationship between King's Bench and Quarter Sessions in this period see N. Landau, *The Justices of the Peace, 1679–1760*, London, 1984, pp. 345–53.

58 *Letters*, VIII, pp. 230–1.

59 Lambeth Palace Library Mss, Secker Papers, vol. 8, Methodists.

60 N. Curnock (ed.), *Journal*, 8 vols, London, 1909–16, vol. V, p. 184.

61 W. Blackstone, *Commentaries on the Laws of England*, vol. 1, London, 1830, pp. 6 and 143–4.

62 Hempton, *Methodism and Politics*, pp. 30–43. D. Butler, *Methodists and Papists: John Wesley and the Catholic Church in the Eighteenth Century*, London, 1995, pp. 47–59.

63 Semmel, *Methodist Revolution*, p. 44. Wesley thought that the doctrine of irresistible grace made man 'a mere machine'.

64 H. Abelove, 'The sexual politics of early Wesleyan Methodism', in J. Obelkevich, L. Roper and R. Samuel (eds), *Disciplines of Faith: Studies in Religion, Politics and Patriarchy*, London, 1987, pp. 86–99.

65 Rack, *Reasonable Enthusiast*, p. 237.

66 The evidence here is nevertheless a good deal more ambiguous, and the issues

more complex, than Clark allows. See W. R. Ward, *Religion and Society in England 1790–1850*, London, 1972, pp. 7–104; and Hempton, *Methodism and Politics*, pp. 55–115.

5 JABEZ BUNTING: THE FORMATIVE YEARS, 1794–1820

1 T. P. Bunting, *The Life of Jabez Bunting, D. D., with Notices of Contemporary Persons and Events*, London, 1887.

2 W. R. Ward, *The Early Correspondence of Jabez Bunting 1820–1829*, Camden Fourth Series, vol. 11, London, 1972; and *idem, Early Victorian Methodism: The Correspondence of Jabez Bunting 1830–1858*, London, 1976.

3 For a range of interpretations of Bunting's role in the connexional agitations between 1828 and 1851 see B. Gregory, *Side Lights on the Conflicts of Methodism 1827–1852*, London, 1898; J. H. Rigg, *Jabez Bunting, a Great Methodist Leader*, London, 1905; W. J. Townsend, H. B. Workman and G. Eayrs (eds), *A New History of Methodism*, London, 1909, vol. 1, pp. 381–433; J. Kent, *Jabez Bunting: The Last Wesleyan*, London, 1955; J. Kent, 'Historians and Jabez Bunting', in *idem, The Age of Disunity*, London, 1966, pp. 103–26; W. B. Maynard, 'The constitutional authority of Dr. Jabez Bunting over Wesleyan Methodism as seen through his correspondence', M.A. thesis, University of Durham, 1970; W. R. Ward, *Religion and Society in England 1790–1850*, London, 1972; R. Davies, A. R. George and G. Rupp (eds), *A History of the Methodist Church in Great Britain*, London, 1978, vol. 2; and D. Hempton, *Methodism and Politics in British Society 1750–1850*, London, 1984.

4 Much of what follows is based on the complete typescripts of Bunting's correspondence (hereafter referred to as Bunting Papers) prepared meticulously by W. R. Ward. I am grateful to Professor Ward for entrusting these materials to my care. Unless otherwise stated the originals are in the Methodist Archive and Research Centre in the John Rylands University Library of Manchester.

5 Bunting, *Life of Bunting*, p. 136.

6 Bunting to J. Whitaker, n.d., but probably 1801 or 1802.

7 Bunting to J. Wood, 14 October 1802.

8 Bunting to D. Alexander, 14 October 1802.

9 J. Barber to J. Bunting, 24 October 1799.

10 Bunting, *Life of Bunting*, pp. 44–9.

11 D. Alexander to J. Bunting, 28 February 1803.

12 Bunting, *Life of Bunting*, pp. 71–2.

13 *Ibid.*, p. 157.

14 Bunting to R. Reece, 15 July 1803.

15 Bunting to G. Marsden, 10 June 1803.

16 W. Jenkins to Bunting, 29 January 1806; J. Entwistle to Bunting, 26 March 1806; and J. T. Williams to Bunting, 28 April 1806.

17 Bunting to J. Gaulter, 24 February 1808.

18 Bunting to J. Wood, 15 March 1808. This letter has been inaccurately printed in Bunting, *Life of Bunting*. The original is in the United Methodist Church Archives, Lake Janaluska, USA.

19 Bunting, *Life of Bunting*, p. 182.

20 Bunting to T. Lessey sen., 30 May 1809.

21 *Ibid.* See also D. M. Valenze, *Prophetic Sons and Daughters. Female Preaching and Popular Religion in Industrial England*, Princeton, 1985.

22 J. Bunting, *A Great Work Described and Recommended in a Sermon before the*

Members of the Sunday School Union, London, 1805. See also Hempton, *Methodism and Politics*, pp. 86–92; and T. W. Laqueur, *Religion and Respectability: Sunday Schools and Working Class Culture, 1780–1850*, New Haven, 1976.

23 Bunting to R. Reece, 1 October 1808.

24 G. Marsden to Bunting, 3 November 1808; J. Entwistle to Bunting, 20 May 1809.

25 Bunting to T. Lessey sen., 30 May 1809.

26 W. Myles to J. Bunting, 26 September 1809; G. Newton to Bunting, 10 March 1810; J. Entwistle to Bunting, 28 March 1812.

27 J. Butterworth to Bunting, 9 November 1814.

28 Ward, *The Early Correspondence*, p. 228.

29 Z. Taft to Bunting, ? October 1812.

30 Bunting to Z. Taft, 11 November 1812.

31 Bunting, *Life of Bunting*, pp. 126–98.

32 *Ibid.*, pp. 127–8.

33 *Ibid.*, pp. 144–5.

34 See my 'The "Watchman" and religious politics in the 1830s', *Proceedings of the Wesley Historical Society,* 42, 1979, pp. 2–13.

35 Bunting to James Wood, 23 September 1803.

36 Bunting, *Life of Bunting*, p. 343.

37 *Ibid.*, p. 363.

38 Bunting to G. Marsden, 28 January 1813.

39 Hempton, *Methodism and Politics*, pp. 104–10.

40 Ward, *The Early Correspondence*, pp. 56–8.

41 *Ibid.*, p. 62.

42 *Ibid.*, p. 63.

43 *Ibid.*

44 S. Bamford, *Passages in the Life of a Radical*, Oxford, 1984, pp. 322–3.

45 E. P. Thompson, *The Making of the English Working Class*, Harmondsworth, 1968, pp. 385–440 and 916–39.

46 Ward, *Religion and Society,* p. 93.

47 *Ibid.*, p. 94.

48 Bunting, *Life of Bunting*, p. 210.

49 Bunting to J. Wood, 21 January 1805.

50 Bunting to G. Marsden, 24 June 1805.

51 I attempt to set out the reasons for this change of approach in *Methodism and Politics*, pp. 194–7.

52 T. Allan to Bunting, 28 July 1810.

53 Bunting, *Life of Bunting*, p. 410.

54 *Ibid.*, pp. 411–12.

55 B. Semmel, *The Methodist Revolution*, London, 1974, pp. 152–66. See also S. Piggin, 'Halevy revisited: the origins of the Wesleyan Methodist Missionary Society: an examination of Semmel's thesis', *Journal of Imperial and Commonwealth History,* 9, no. 1, 1980, pp. 19–20; R. H. Martin, 'Missionary competition between Evangelical Dissenters and Wesleyan Methodists in the early nineteenth century: a footnote to the founding of the Methodist Missionary Society', *Proceedings of the Wesley Historical Society,* 42, 1979, pp. 81–6; and *idem, Evangelicals United: Ecumenical Stirrings in Pre-Victorian Britain, 1795–1830,* London, 1983.

56 Semmel, *Methodist Revolution*, pp. 146–69.

57 Bunting to S. Taylor, 10 March 1814.

58 See D. Luker, 'Revivalism in theory and practice: the case of Cornish Methodism', *Journal of Ecclesiastical History,* 37, no. 4, 1986, pp. 603–19.

59 Bunting, *Life of Bunting*, p. 439.

60 *Ibid.*, p. 440.
61 M. Martindale to Bunting, 9 July 1816.
62 Bunting, *Life of Bunting*, p. 217.
63 Bunting to T. Lessey sen., 30 May 1809.
64 J. Butterworth to Bunting, 10 December 1808.
65 Bunting, *Life of Bunting*, p. 465.
66 The copy of a circular sent by Mr Isaac to the Superintendents of Circuits, relative to the foregoing publication and the Minute of the Conference concerning it. See also, D. Isaac to Bunting, 31 October 1816; and Bunting to Isaac, 16 November 1816, 23 December 1816.
67 See W. R. Ward, 'Pastoral Office and the general priesthood in the Great Awakening', and 'The legacy of John Wesley; the Pastoral Office in Britain and America', in *idem*, *Faith and Faction*, London, 1993, pp. 177–201 and 224–48.

6 THOMAS ALLAN AND METHODIST POLITICS, 1790–1840

1 I am grateful to Dr I. Green and Professor W. R. Ward for their comments on an earlier version of this chapter.
2 The John Rylands University Library of Manchester, Methodist Archives Research Centre, Thomas Allan manuscripts (hereafter MARC Allan Mss), T. Thompson to T. Allan, 31 August 1812.
3 W. R. Ward, *Religion and Society in England 1790–1850*, London, 1972, p. 57.
4 MARC Allan Mss. Some of Allan's correspondence is catalogued, but there are some twenty-two boxes of material arranged under broad subject headings.
5 MARC Mss Minutes of the Committee of Privileges 1803. See also S. Piggin, 'Halévy revisited: the origins of the Methodist Missionary Society: an examination of Semmel's thesis', *Journal of Imperial and Commonwealth History*, IX, no. 1, 1980, pp. 17–37.
6 MARC Allan Mss 7, Allan to J. Bunting, 28 July 1810.
7 Ward, *Religion and Society*, p. 53.
8 G. Pellew, *The Life and Correspondence of the Right Honourable Henry Addington, First Viscount Sidmouth*, 3 vols, London, 1847, vol. 3, p. 41.
9 See Piggin, 'Halévy revisited', for a comprehensive analysis of Sidmouth's negotiating tactics. Piggin is right to argue, as against Ward, that Clarke had already changed his mind before the meeting of the Committee of Privileges on 14 May. Allan and Butterworth convinced him on 11 May.
10 Hansard, 1st series, XIX, 1130.
11 MARC Allan Mss, J. Butterworth to T. Allan, 11 May 1811.
12 *Monthly Repository*, vi, 1811, pp. 303–5.
13 Pellew, *Life of Sidmouth*, vol. 3, p. 54.
14 MARC Allan Mss, T. Allan to T. Robinson, ? May 1811; Lord Erskine to T. Allan, 17 May 1811 (two letters).
15 MARC Allan Mss, J. Ward to R. Middleton (care of T. Allan), 20 May 1811.
16 Hansard, 1st series, XX, 247.
17 MARC Allan Mss, T. Allan to Marquis of Lansdowne, 23 May 1811; T. Allan to Lord Holland, 23 May 1811; and T. Allan to Lord Erskine, 23 May 1811.
18 MARC Allan Mss, private notes which have been reproduced by Ward, *Religion and Society*, pp. 60–1. Also, T. Allan to T. Robinson, 18 February 1812.
19 MARC Allan Mss, private notes.
20 MARC Allan Mss, T. Allan to S. Perceval, 15 February 1812.
21 MARC Allan Mss, private notes.

22 MARC Allan Mss, T. Allan to T. Robinson, 3 March 1812.

23 MARC Allan Mss, J. Ward to T. Allan, 29 February 1812.

24 MARC, printed copy, S. Perceval to J. Butterworth, 10 April 1812.

25 MARC, printed copy, T. Allan to S. Perceval, 9 May 1812.

26 MARC Allan Mss, T. Allan to Lord Liverpool, 11 June 1812, 18 June 1812, 27 June 1812, 2 July 1812, 11 July 1812, 29 July 1812. Also, T. Allan to T. Robinson, 7 July 1812; and T. Allan to W. Smith, 23 July 1812.

27 R. W. Davis, in *Dissent in Politics 1780–1830; the Political Life of William Smith M.P.*, London, 1971, states that, although the new Toleration Bill was drafted by the Methodists, the repeal of the Five Mile and Conventicle Acts was due entirely to the Dissenting Deputies, who urged this on Liverpool on 23 June. He overlooks the fact that Allan and Butterworth were convinced that these Acts had to go as early as 9 May. See MARC, printed letters of T. Allan to S. Perceval, 9 May 1812; and J. Butterworth to ?, 25 May 1812.

28 MARC, a circular letter from the Committee of Privileges to the circuit superintendents, 31 July 1812.

29 *Political Register*, xix, no. 42, 25 May 1811, p. 1283.

30 The manuscript Minutes of the Committee of Privileges, 1803–22 and 1835–45, which I discovered in the old Methodist Church Archives in City Road, London, are not known to have survived the move to Manchester. They may of course be located somewhere else.

31 MARC, address of the preachers to the Members of the Methodist Societies, Leeds, 27 July 1812.

32 Mss Committee of Privileges, 5 February 1817.

33 Mss Committee of Privileges, 9 January 1818.

34 Ward, *Religion and Society*, pp. 88–9.

35 R. Pilter to J. Bunting, 23 October 1819, in W. R. Ward, *The Early Correspondence of Jabez Bunting 1820–1829*, Camden 4th Series, vol. II, London, 1972, pp. 21–4.

36 MARC Allan Mss, draft resolutions of the Committee of Privileges, 22 October 1819.

37 MARC Allan Mss, T. Allan to J. Alan, 27 November 1819.

38 MARC, printed resolutions of the Committee of Privileges, 12 November 1819.

39 Mss Committee of Privileges, 12 November 1819.

40 Ward, *Religion and Society*, p. 93.

41 See, for example, E. P. Thompson, *The Making of the English Working Class*, Harmondsworth, 1968, pp. 385–440; H. Perkin, *The Origins of Modern English Society 1780–1880*, London, 1969, pp. 196–208; P. Stigant, 'Wesleyan Methodism and working-class radicalism in the north, 1792–1821', *Northern History*, vi, 1971, pp. 98–116; D. Hempton, *Methodism and Politics in British Society 1750–1850*, London, 1984, pp. 55–115; and A. D. Gilbert, 'Religion and political stability in early industrial England', in P. O'Brien and R. Quinault (eds), *The Industrial Revolution and British Society*, Cambridge, 1993, pp. 79–99.

42 H. T. Dickinson, *Liberty and Property; Political Ideology in Eighteenth-Century Britain*, London, 1977.

43 MARC resolutions of the Committee of Privileges, 12 November 1819.

44 See E. R. Taylor, *Methodism and Politics 1791–1851*, Cambridge, 1935.

45 J. Walsh, 'Methodism at the end of the eighteenth century', in R. Davies and E. G. Rupp (eds), *A History of the Methodist Church in Great Britain*, London, 1965, vol. 1, p. 306.

46 For the relationship between Methodism and party divisions after 1830 see my *Methodism and Politics*, pp. 179–223.

47 C. Butler, *An Address to the Protestants of Great Britain and Ireland*, London, February 1813. Allan's anonymous reply appeared in the *Papers of the Protestant*

Union, nos 4, 5, 6, 9 and 10. Butler later wrote that this was the ablest of all the replies to his pamphlet and that it was 'written with temper and moderation' (*Reminiscences of Charles Butler, Esq*, London, 1822, p. 250).

48 T. Allan, *Letters to a Protestant Dissenter Relative to the Claims of the Roman Catholics*, London, 1813, p. 17.
49 MARC Allan Mss, T. Allan to J. Butterworth, 3 December 1812.
50 MARC Mss, J. Barber to G. Marsden, 18 January 1813.
51 E. Halévy, *A History of the English People in the Nineteenth Century*, vol. 3, *The Triumph of Reform 1830–41*, London, 1950, p. 153.
52 J. Kent, 'M. Elie Halévy on Methodism', *Proceedings of the Wesley Historical Society*, 29, pt 4, 1953, and 34, pt 8, 1964. Also J. Kent, *The Age of Disunity*, London, 1966.
53 T. Jackson, *Recollections of My Own Life and Times*, London, 1873, p. 407.
54 MARC Mss, J. Mason to J. Bunting, 14 February 1829.
55 MARC Allan Mss, T. Allan to J. Eliot, 3 December 1819.
56 MARC Allan Mss, T. Allan to his son Thomas, 9 March 1829.
57 MARC Allan Mss, T. Allan to his son Thomas, 19 March 1829.
58 MARC Mss, journal of Joseph Entwistle. He inserted Mason's comments in his entry for 14 March 1829.
59 S. Dunn, *Recollections of Thomas Jackson and his Acts*, London, 1873, p. 5; Jackson, *Recollections*, pp. 215–22; and B. Gregory, *Side-Lights on the Conflicts of Methodism*, London, 1899, pp. 116–24.
60 J. Bunting to M. Tobias, in Ward, *Early Correspondence*, pp. 202–3.
61 Hansard, new series, XX, 1313.
62 Alnwick, 1795.
63 For more detail on this affair see my *Methodism and Politics*, pp. 67–73.
64 MARC Allan Mss, T. Allan to A. Kilham, 16 February 1796.
65 MARC Allan Mss, T. Allan to J. Benson, 15 August 1808.
66 MARC Allan Mss, J. Barber and ten preachers to T. Allan, 6 December 1811. Allan wrote several draft replies on the same day.
67 MARC Mss, T. Blanshard to T. Allan, 11 March 1814.
68 MARC Allan Mss, a series of draft replies dated 17 March 1814.
69 MARC Allan Mss, T. Allan to G. Morley, 9 August 1830.
70 MARC Allan Mss, T. Allan to J. Allan, 19 June 1834, 28 July 1834.
71 Hempton, *Methodism and Politics*, pp. 197–202.
72 R. Currie, A. Gilbert and L. Horsley, *Churches and Churchgoers: Patterns of Church Growth in the British Isles since 1700*, Oxford, 1977.
73 MARC Allan Mss, T. Allan to E. Grindrod, 9 March 1840.
74 For a useful discussion of the development of the pastoral office in Wesleyan Methodism see W. R. Ward, 'The legacy of John Wesley: the Pastoral Office in Britain and America', in A. Whiteman, J. S. Bromley and P. G. M. Dickson (eds), *Statesmen, Scholars and Merchants, Essays in Eighteenth-Century History presented to Dame Lucy Sutherland*, London, 1973; and J. C. Bowmer, *Pastor and People*, London, 1975.
75 Hansard, 3rd series, XLV, 280.
76 MARC Allan Mss, T. Allan to T. Jackson, 6 August 1838, 17 May 1839; and T. Jackson to T. Allan, 18 May 1839. See also W. Dealtry to T. Allan, 2 May 1839; and T. Allan to W. Dealtry, 27 May 1839.
77 T. Allan to J. Bunting, 11 June 1839, in W. R. Ward, *Early Victorian Methodism*, London, 1976, pp. 220–1.
78 *Ibid.*, p. 221.
79 J. Bunting to T. Binney, 5 April 1838, in Ward, *Early Victorian Methodism*, pp. 202–3.

80 Hansard, 3rd series, XLVII, 283.
81 E. Baines jun. to J. Bunting jun., 19 June 1839, in Ward, *Early Victorian Methodism*, p. 221.
82 MARC, printed resolutions, 3, pt 1, 12 June 1839.
83 I deal with this more fully in *Methodism and Politics*, pp. 149–78.
84 MARC Allan Mss, T. P. Platt to T. Allan, 11 April 1825, 29 April 1825. T. Allan to H. Drummond, 18 March 1825, 2 April 1825. Drummond to Allan, 29 March 1825. T. Allan to J. Scholefield, 3 August 1825 and reply 4 August 1825. R. Steven to T. Allan, 4 October 1825. W. Dealtry to T. Allan, 7 September 1825, 7 December 1825. T. Allan to the Secretaries of the British and Foreign Bible Society, 7 December 1825. J. Wardlaw to T. Allan, 4 May 1830 and reply 14 May 1830. A. Haldane to T. Allan, 28 May 1830.
85 D. Hempton, 'Evangelicalism and eschatology', *Journal of Ecclesiastical History,* 31, no. 2, 1980, pp. 179–94.

7 GIDEON OUSELEY: RURAL REVIVALIST, 1791–1839

1 Manchester, the John Rylands University Library, Methodist Archives Research Centre Mss, papers of Thomas Allan, Joseph Butterworth and Gideon Ouseley. Butterworth was MP for Coventry (1812–18) and for Dover (1820–6).
2 University of London School of Oriental and African Studies, Methodist Missionary Society Mss, boxes 1–3 and 74–5. Additional missionary correspondence is to be found in NIPRO, Irish Wesley Historical Society Mss under restricted consultation. See also T. Coke, *Copies of the Letters from the Missionaries who are employed in Ireland for the Instruction in their own Language, and for the Conversion of the Native Irish*, London, 1801.
3 Lack of space prevents a full list but the most important are: G. Ouseley, *The Substance of Two Letters to the Rev John Thayer, Once a Presbyterian Minister, but now a Roman Catholic Priest and Missionary. In Consequence of his Public Challenge to all Protestants*, Dublin, 1814; *Old Christianity Defended*, Dublin, 1820; *Letters to Dr Doyle on the Doctrines of his Church with an easy and effectual plan to obtain Immediate Emancipation*, Dublin, 1824; *Letters in Defence of the Roman Catholics of Ireland in which is opened the Real Source of their Many Injuries, and of Ireland's Sorrows, addressed to D. O'Connell*, London, 1829; *Letters on Topics of Vast Importance to all Roman Catholics and the State in reply to Dr Crolly's Letter to Lord Donegall*, Dublin, 1832; *An Easy Mode of Securing Ireland's Peace*, Dublin, 1833; and *A Dreadful Conspiracy against the Church of Christ Developed*, Dublin, 1837.
4 W. Arthur, *The Life of Gideon Ouseley*, London, 1876. See also C. H. Crookshank, *History of Methodism in Ireland*, 3 vols, London, 1885–8; and R. H. Gallagher, *Pioneer Preachers of Irish Methodism*, Belfast, 1965, pp. 144–7.
5 NIPRO mss, Ouseley Collection CR 6/3 ACC 13019, twenty-eight folders of paginated mss collected and transcribed by J. O. Bonsall and enlarged by John Hay in preparation for Arthur's biography.
6 Ouseley Coll., II fols 1–10; III fols 1–3; IV fols 1–7.
7 Ouseley Coll., XXVI fol. 4.
8 The importance of the military in the early dissemination of Irish Methodism is deserving of more attention. See Ouseley Coll., XXVI fol. 10. See also IX fol. 29; XII fols 3–5; XIII fol. 16.
9 *Ibid.*, V fols 1–24; VI fols 1–20; XXVIII fol. 3.
10 *Ibid.*, XXVIII fol. 4. See also NIPRO, Irish Wesley Historical Society Mss, G. Ouseley to M. Tobias, 14 June 1820.

11 For the flavour of Ouseley's labours see Bonsall's transcription of his journal in Ouseley Coll., IX, I5 July 1802 to 15 April 1803; and X, August 1804.

12 For a more complete background to this venture see my 'The Methodist crusade in Ireland 1795–1845', *Irish Historical Studies*, 22, 1980, pp. 33–48.

13 G. Taylor, *A History of the Rise, Progress and Suppression of the Rebellion in the County of Wexford in the year 1798*, Dublin, 1800.

14 Irish Conference Minutes, An Address from the Irish to the British Conference, Dublin, 13 July 1799.

15 Ouseley Coll., XI fol. 5; XII fol. 13; XV fol. 24; XXVIII fol. 43. See also L. Dow, *Works: Providential Experience of Lorenzo Dow in Europe and America*, 3rd edn, Dublin, 1805. For other American parallels see J. H. Wigger, 'Taking heaven by storm: Methodism and the popularization of American Christianity', Ph.D. thesis, University of Notre Dame, Ind. 1994.

16 D. M. Valenze, *Prophetic Sons and Daughters. Female Preaching and Popular Religion in Industrial England*, Princeton, 1985; and W. R. Ward, *Religion and Society in England 1790–1850*, London, 1972. Ouseley approved of English ranters and female preaching; see Ouseley Coll., XVII fols 9–10.

17 Arthur, *Life of Ouseley*, p. 278.

18 Ouseley Coll., XXVIII fols 7, 18–21, and 27–9.

19 *Ibid.*, XXI fol. 21; XXVIII fol. 13. G. Ouseley, *Calvinism–Arminianism. God's word and Attributes in Harmony, being an Affectionate Attempt to Promote Union among Christians*, Dublin, 1830.

20 Ouseley Coll., VIII fols 1 and 22–3; IX fol. 4; XVIII fols 9–14; XIX fol. 2.

21 *Ibid.*, XXVI fols 4–5.

22 *Ibid.*, VII fol. 10.

23 *Ibid.*, VII fol. 12.

24 *Ibid.*, XI fol. 23; XII fols 16–17; XX fol. 19.

25 *Ibid.*, XXVII fols 33–4. See also IX fol. 20.

26 D. W. Bebbington, *Evangelicalism in Modern Britain: A History from the 1730s to the 1980s*, London, 1989; and R. Anstey, *The Atlantic Slave Trade and British Abolition 1760–1810*, Atlantic Highlands, NJ, 1975, pp. 157–83.

27 For an enlightening discussion of Methodist attitudes towards the Irish language see Ouseley Coll., XI fols 18–22; and NIPRO, Irish Wesley Historical Society Mss, A. Clarke to G. Ouseley, 6 December 1806, in which Clarke stated that he was not 'willing that an ancient and dignified language should be lost'.

28 Arthur, *Life of Ouseley*, pp. 217–18.

29 Ouseley Coll., XXVIII fols 9–11.

30 *Ibid.*, XI fol. 2; and Arthur, *Life of Ouseley*, p. 175.

31 Ouseley Coll., XXVIII fol. 9.

32 Hempton, 'Methodist crusade', pp. 33–48.

33 Ouseley Coll., XII fols 30–5.

34 G. Ouseley, *The Substance of a Letter to the Rev Mr Fitzimmons, Roman Catholic Priest on some Chief Pillars or Principal Articles of his Faith*, Glasgow, 1815; *Five Letters in reply to the Rev Michael Branaghan PP*, Dublin, 1824; *Error Unmasked. Priest Walsh's Attack on Protestantism and its clergy defeated, his Professions proved vain, and his Faith deeply Erroneous*, Dublin, 1828; and *A Review of a Sermon preached by Dr Peter A. Baynes, Roman Catholic Bishop, at the opening of the R. Catholic Chapel in Bradford, Yorkshire*, Dublin, 1829.

35 Arthur, *Life of Ouseley*, p. 200.

36 The best accounts of this important decade of religious conflict, though different in emphasis, are D. Bowen, *The Protestant Crusade in Ireland 1800–1870*, Dublin, 1978; F. O'Ferrall, *Catholic Emancipation: Daniel O'Connell and the Birth of Irish Democracy 1820–30*, Dublin, 1985; I. M. Hehir, 'New lights and old

enemies: the Second Reformation and the Catholics of Ireland, 1800–1835', M.A. thesis, University of Wisconsin, 1983; and M. Hill, 'Evangelicalism and the churches in Ulster society, 1770–1850', Ph.D. thesis, Queen's University Belfast, 1987.

37 *Sligo Journal*, 21 May 1823.
38 Ouseley's views on this issue subsequently hardened as a result of the national education controversies and disillusionment with Maynooth College. In *A Dreadful Conspiracy*, Dublin, 1837, he stated 'what does the experience of more than forty years of Maynooth College teach? What gratitude to a Protestant Government that has hitherto been annually expending thousands of pounds in supporting it, has ever appeared?'
39 Ouseley Coll., XX fols 19–21; XXI fols 7–9.
40 *Ibid.*, XX fol. 20. Ouseley returned to England in 1836 and was much more impressed with the general public's knowledge of Irish affairs.
41 *Ibid.*, XXIII fols 14–15.
42 *Ibid.*, XII fol. 36. Ouseley was amazed to learn that over 3,000 people had supposedly been converted at an American camp meeting.
43 Arthur, *Life of Ouseley*, pp. 282–3.
44 N. Hatch, *The Democratization of American Christianity*, New Haven, 1989, pp. 36–40, 185–6.
45 Ouseley Coll., XVIII fol. 7; XX fols 3 and 8–9; XXIII fol. 20; XXVIII fol. 12.
46 *Ibid.*, XXII fols 14–17.
47 *Ibid.*, XXVI fol. 6.

8 METHODISM AND THE LAW IN ENGLISH SOCIETY, 1740–1820

1 I am grateful to Professor W. R. Ward, Dr John Walsh and Dr Martin Ingram for their comments on an earlier draft of this essay. The revision of the published article benefited also from the expert criticism of Dr Malcolm Gaskill. Remaining errors are entirely my own responsibility.
2 Lambeth Palace Library Mss, Secker Papers, 8 (Methodists), fos 4–5.
3 Much of this correspondence has been reproduced by O. A. Beckerlegg, 'The Lavington correspondence', *Proceedings of the Wesley Historical Society*, xlii, 1980, 101–11, 139–49 and 167–80.
4 P. Collinson, 'The English conventicle', in W. J. Sheils and D. Wood (eds), *Voluntary Religion, Studies in Church History*, 23, 1986, pp. 223–59.
5 22 Car. II, c. 1. Reproduced by J. P. Kenyon, *The Stuart Constitution*, Cambridge, 1966, pp. 383–6.
6 J. Wesley, *A Farther Appeal to Men of Reason and Religion*, London, 1745, in G. R. Cragg (ed.), *The Works of John Wesley*, 11, Oxford, 1975, pp. 178–83.
7 J. S. Simon, 'The Conventicle Act and its relation to the early Methodists', *Proceedings of the Wesley Historical Society*, xi, 1918, pp. 82–93.
8 Lambeth Palace Library Mss, Secker Papers, 8, fos 105–6.
9 1 Will. & Mary, c. 18: S.L. ix, 19. Reproduced by E. N. Williams, *The Eighteenth Century Constitution*, Cambridge, 1960, pp. 42–6.
10 N. Curnock (ed.), *The Journal of John Wesley*, London, 1909–16, ii, pp. 93–4. See also J. S. Simon, 'John Wesley and field preaching', *Proceedings of the Wesley Historical Society*, xi, 1918, pp. 54–63.
11 Published anonymously in London in 1744, but widely attributed to Gibson.
12 Cragg (ed.), *The Works of John Wesley*, 11, pp. 178–83.

13 F. Baker, *John Wesley and the Church of England*, London, 1970, p. 174. Also J. M. Turner, *Conflict and Reconciliation*, London, 1985, p. 15.

14 2 Burr. 1041, *Rex v. Moreley.*

15 4 Burr. 1991, *Rex v. Justices and Clerk of the Peace for the County of Derby.*

16 For the relationship between King's Bench and quarter sessions in this period see N. Landau, *The Justices of the Peace, 1679–1760*, London, 1984, pp. 345–53.

17 J. Walsh, 'Methodism and the mob in the eighteenth century', in G. J. Cuming and D. Baker (eds), *Popular Belief and Practice, Studies in Church History*, 8, 1972, pp. 213–27.

18 Cited in A. Warne, *Church and Society in Eighteenth-Century Devon*, Newton Abbot, 1969, p. 111.

19 See, for example, R. W. Malcolmson, '"A set of ungovernable people": the Kingswood colliers in the eighteenth century', in J. Brewer and J. Styles (eds), *An Ungovernable People: The English and their Law in the Seventeenth and Eighteenth Centuries*, London, 1980, pp. 85–127.

20 Walsh, 'Methodism and the mob', pp. 216–17.

21 F. Baker (ed.), *The Works of John Wesley*, 26, *Letters II, 1740–1755*, Oxford, 1982, p. 206.

22 Lambeth Palace Library Mss, Secker Papers, 8, fos 8–11, 22, 92–6.

23 Beckerlegge, 'The Lavington correspondence', pp. 103–11.

24 *Ibid.*, p. 145.

25 Lambeth Palace Library Mss, Secker Papers, 8, fos 8–10, 66 and 73–4. See also M. J. Naylor, *The Inantity* [sic] *and Mischief of Vulgar Superstitions. Four Sermons, Preached at All-Saints' Church, Huntingdon*, Cambridge, 1795.

26 Lambeth Palace Library Mss, Secker Papers, 8, fos 16–20.

27 F. Thompson, *Lark Rise to Candleford*, London, 1973, pp. 209–29.

28 See M. Hill, 'Evangelicalism and the churches in Ulster society, 1770–1850', Ph.D. thesis, Queen's University Belfast, 1987, pp. 400–12.

29 See Brewer and Styles (eds), *An Ungovernable People*, pp. 11–20; E. P. Thompson, 'The moral economy of the English crowd in the eighteenth century', *Past and Present*, no. 50, 1971, pp. 76–136; and J. Stevenson, *Popular Disturbances in England, 1700–1870*, London, 1979, pp. 301–23.

30 Baker (ed.), *The Works of John Wesley*, 26, pp. 324–7, 335–7, 340–1.

31 For a similar pattern elsewhere, see *ibid.*, pp. 474–5.

32 PRO, KB 122, Great Dogget of Trinity term in the 24th of George II, 240.

33 Baker (ed.), *The Works of John Wesley*, 26, p. 340. It is nevertheless possible that Wesley was not directly involved in the case brought by the Halifax Methodists against the rioters of Sowerby Bridge.

34 Curnock (ed.), *Journal of John Wesley*, vol. v, p. 184.

35 E. P. Thompson, *Customs in Common*, London, 1991, p. 350.

36 See, for example, W. B. Carnochan, 'Witch hunting and belief in 1751: the case of Thomas Colley and Ruth Osborne', *Journal of Social History*, 4, 1971, pp. 389–403.

37 T. D. Whitaker, *An History of the Original Parish of Whalley*, vol. 1, p. 206. I am grateful to Mike Snape for supplying this information.

38 C. H. Crookshank, *History of Methodism in Ireland*, 3 vols, London, 1885–8, vol. 1, pp. 43–72. See also Baker (ed.), *The Works of John Wesley*, 26, pp. 361–73, 427–9.

39 Lambeth Palace Library Mss, Secker Papers, 8, fos 73–4.

40 Baker (ed.), *The Works of John Wesley*, 26, p. 372.

41 D. Hempton, *Methodism and Politics in British Society 1750–1850*, London, 1984, pp. 34–42.

42 The Cork Baptist Church Book, 1653–1875, which is still in the possession of the Cork Baptist Church. I am grateful to Kevin Herlihy for this reference. See

K. Herlihy, 'The Irish Baptists, 1650–1780', Ph.D. thesis, Trinity College, Dublin, 1993.

43 Walsh, 'Methodism and the mob', p. 227.

44 Lambeth Palace Library Mss, Secker Papers, 8, fol. 75.

45 See J. Varley, 'Dissenters' certificates in the Lincoln diocesan records', *Lincolnshire Historian*, 4, 1949, 167–77; and E. Welch, 'The registration of meeting houses', *Journal of the Society of Archivists*, iii, 1965–9, pp. 116–20.

46 Borthwick Institute Mss, R Bp 5/34, Bishopthorne Papers, Bishopthorne to Rev. Robinson, 21 March 1770; and Mr Comber to Lord Bishop of York, 8 June 1770.

47 Baker (ed.), *The Works of John Wesley*, 26, p. 563.

48 Borthwick Institute Mss, D/C CP. 1755/2, 3; Trans. CP. 1756/1; the original presentment is preserved at York Minster Library, C3a, visitation papers, 1755. I am grateful to Dr W. J. Sheils for bringing this case to my attention.

49 Borthwick Institute Mss, Trans. CP. 1756/1, the fifth of eight articles brought before the dean and chapter of the cathedral.

50 Allegations that early Methodists were really Catholics in disguise were common, at least up to the 1760s. See Hempton, *Methodism and Politics*, pp. 31–4; Walsh, 'Methodism and the mob', pp. 226–7; C. Haydon, *Anti-Catholicism in Eighteenth-Century England: A Political and Social Study*, Manchester, 1993, pp. 63–6; and D. Butler, *Methodists and Papists: John Wesley and the Catholic Church in the Eighteenth Century*, London, 1995.

51 A. C. H. Seymour, *The Life and Times of Selina, Countess of Huntingdon*, 2 vols, London, 1840, pp. 307–14; and E. Welch (ed.), *Two Calvinistic Methodist Chapels, 1743–1811*, London Record Society, 1975, pp. xvi–xvii.

52 Turner, *Conflict and Reconciliation*, p. 17.

53 T. Townsend, curate of Pirbright and Worplesdon to Brownlow North, Bishop of Winchester, 29 March 1788, in W. R. Ward (ed.), *Parson and Parish in Eighteenth-Century Surrey: Replies to Bishops' Visitations*, Guildford, 1994, pp. 127–9.

54 Staffordshire Record Office Mss, D240/E/F/8/30, Rev. Johnson to Lord Talbot, 18 May 1789.

55 *Gentleman's Magazine*, 70, 1800, pp. 241, 1077.

56 For figures covering the country as a whole see B. L. Manning, *The Protestant Dissenting Deputies*, Cambridge, 1952, pp. 130–1. They too show a remarkable rise in meeting-house registrations in the period 1790–1810.

57 W. R. Ward, *Religion and Society in England, 1790–1850*, London, 1972, p. 72.

58 D. W. Lovegrove, *Established Church, Sectarian People: Itinerancy and the Transformation of English Dissent, 1780–1830*, Cambridge, 1988.

59 *Returns of the Archbishops and Bishops of the Number of Churches and Chapels of the Church of England, in every Parish of 1000 Persons and upwards: also of the Number of other Places of Worship not of the Establishment*, London, House of Lords, 5 April 1811.

60 See 14 East 286, *Rex v. Justices of Denbighshire*; 15 East 577, *Rex v. Justices of Gloucestershire*; and 15 East 591, *Rex v. Justices of Suffolk*.

61 15 East 577, *Rex v. Justices of Gloucestershire*, 6 May 1812.

62 See W. R. Ward, 'The religion of the people and the problem of control, 1790–1830', in G. J. Cuming and D. Baker (eds), *Popular Belief and Practice, Studies in Church History*, 8, 1972, pp. 237–57.

63 For a fuller discussion of the Kilhamite secession, see Hempton, *Methodism and Politics*, pp. 65–73.

64 A. Kilham, *The Progress of Liberty amongst the People called Methodists. To which is added Out-Lines of a Constitution*, Alnwick, 1795, p. 17.

65 Paul and Silas (Kilham), *An Earnest Address to the Preachers Assembled in*

Conference, Manchester, 1795; A. Kilham, *A Candid Examination of the London Methodistical Bull*, Alnwick, 1796.

66 A. Kilham, *An Account of the Trial of Alexander Kilham, Methodist Preacher, before the General Conference in London*, Nottingham, 1796; J. Brewer, 'The Wilkites and the law, 1763–74: a study of radical notions of governance', in Brewer and Styles (eds), *An Ungovernable People*, pp. 128–71. See also A. Mather, J. Pawson and J. Benson, *A Defence of the Conduct of the Conference in the Expulsion of Alexander Kilham. Addressed to the Methodist Societies*, n.p., n.d.

67 Hempton, *Methodism and Politics*, pp. 197–202.

68 The John Rylands University Library of Manchester, Methodist Archives Research Centre Mss, J. Pawson to C. Atmore, 15 July 1795.

69 Stevenson, *Popular Disturbances*, pp. 301–23.

9 POPULAR EVANGELICALISM, REFORM AND POLITICAL STABILITY IN ENGLAND, C. 1780–1850

1 W. R. Ward, *Religion and Society in England 1790–1850*, London, 1972, p. 1.

2 See, for example, M. A. Noll, *A History of Christianity in the United States and Canada*, Grand Rapids, Mich., 1992; R. Currie, A. Gilbert and L. Horsley, *Churches and Churchgoers: Patterns of Church Growth in the British Isles since 1700*, Oxford, 1977; and the essays in M. A. Noll, D. W. Bebbington and G. Rawlyk (eds), *Evangelicalism: Comparative Studies of Popular Protestantism in North America, the British Isles, and Beyond, 1700–1900*, Oxford, 1994.

3 E. P. Thompson, *The Making of the English Working Class*, Harmondsworth, 1968; and G. W. Olsen (ed.), *Religion and Revolution in Early Industrial England: The Halévy Thesis and its Critics*, Lanham, Md., 1990.

4 A. D. Gilbert, *Religion and Society in Industrial England: Church, Chapel and Social Change 1740–1914*, London, 1976.

5 S. Drescher, 'Public opinion and the destruction of British colonial slavery', in J. Walvin (ed.), *Slavery and British Society 1776–1846*, London, 1982, pp. 22–48.

6 D. A. Hamer, *The Politics of Electoral Pressure: A Study in the History of Victorian Reform Agitations*, Hassocks, W. Sussex, 1977; D. W. Bebbington, *The Nonconformist Conscience*, London, 1982.

7 T. Clarkson, *The History of the Rise, Progress and Accomplishment of the Abolition of the African Slave Trade by the British Parliament*, 2 vols, London, 1808.

8 The various historiographical traditions are well set out by S. Drescher, *Capitalism and Anti-slavery: British Mobilization in Comparative Perspective*, Oxford, 1987, pp. 1–24.

9 R. Anstey, *The Atlantic Slave Trade and British Abolition 1760–1810*, Atlantic Highlands, NJ, 1975.

10 E. F. Hurwitz, *Politics and the Public Conscience: Slave Emancipation and the Abolitionist Movement in Britain*, London, 1973, p. 15.

11 W. R. Ward, *Early Victorian Methodism: The Correspondence of Jabez Bunting, 1830–58*, London, 1976, p. 29.

12 Drescher, *Capitalism and Anti-Slavery*.

13 Quoted by R. Anstey, in 'Religion and British slave emancipation', in D. Eltis and J. Walvin (eds), *The Abolition of the Atlantic Slave Trade*, Madison, 1981, p. 47. For a wider interpretation of Methodism and anti-slavery see my *Methodism and Politics in British Society 1750–1850*, London, 1984, pp. 208–16.

14 See E. Halévy, *The Birth of Methodism in England*, trans. B. Semmel, Chicago, 1971 and *England in 1815*, vol. 1 of his *A History of the English People in the Nineteenth Century*, London, 1961.

15 Hempton, *Methodism and Politics*, ch. 2.
16 D. W. Bebbington, *Evangelicalism in Modern Britain*, London, 1989.
17 R. Wearmouth, *Methodism and the Working-Class Movements of England 1800–1850*, London, 1947, p. 11.
18 *Ibid.*, p.174.
19 *Ibid.*, p. 176.
20 *Ibid.*, p. 224.
21 V. Kiernan, 'Evangelicalism and the French Revolution', *Past and Present*, no. 1, 1952, pp. 44–56.
22 E. P. Thompson, *Witness Against the Beast: William Blake and the Moral Law*, Cambridge, 1993. Much of the discussion of Edward Thompson and the Methodists is borrowed from a forthcoming article written in collaboration with John Walsh. The most insightful ideas are his, the rest are mine.
23 *Ibid.*, pp. 44 and 72.
24 Thompson, *Making*, p. 429.
25 *Ibid.*, p. 409.
26 W. R. Ward, *The Protestant Evangelical Awakening*, Cambridge, 1992.
27 W. R. Ward, 'Church and society in the first half of the nineteenth century', in R. Davies, A. R. George and G. Rupp (eds), *A History of the Methodist Church in Great Britain*, London, 1978, vol 2, pp. 11–96. See also Ward, *Faith and Faction*, London, 1993, pp. 264–98.
28 Ward, *Religion and Society*, p. 53.
29 D. A. Gowland, *Methodist Secessions: The Origins of Free Methodism in Three Lancashire Towns: Manchester, Rochdale, Liverpool*, Manchester, 1979; D. C. Dews, 'Methodism in Leeds from 1791 to 1861', 2 vols, M.Phil. thesis, University of Bradford, 1984; T. Koditschek, *Class Formation and Urban Industrial Society: Bradford 1750–1850*, Cambridge, 1990, pp. 252–92; and M. Smith, *Religion in Industrial Society: Oldham and Saddleworth 1740–1865*, Oxford, 1994.
30 Ward, *Religion and Society*, pp. 279–92.
31 Smith, *Religion in Industrial Society*, pp. 168–242.
32 Ward, *Religion and Society*, p. 6.
33 Hempton, *Methodism and Politics*.
34 A. Gilbert, 'Religion and political stability in early industrial England', in P. O'Brien and R. Quinault (eds), *The Industrial Revolution and British Society*, Cambridge, 1993, pp. 79–99. See also Gilbert, 'Methodism, Dissent and political stability in early industrial England', *Journal of Religious History*, 10, no. 4, 1979, pp. 381–99.
35 *Ibid.*, p. 98.
36 *Ibid.*, p. 88.
37 J. Obelkevich, *Religion and Rural Society: South Lindsey 1825–1875*, Oxford, 1976; and Hempton, *Methodism and Politics*, pp. 55–84.
38 Gilbert, 'Religion and political stability', p. 94. See also *idem*, *Religion and Society*.
39 Gilbert, 'Religion and political stability', p. 93.
40 See, for example, A. M. Urdank, *Religion and Society in a Cotswold Vale: Nailsworth, Gloucestershire 1780–1865*, Berkeley, 1990.
41 *Ibid.*, pp. 307–11.
42 Smith, *Religion in Industrial Society*, p. 256.
43 M. Winstanley, 'Oldham radicalism and the origins of popular liberalism, 1830–52', *Historical Journal*, 36, no. 3, 1993, pp. 619–43. See also J. Foster, *Class Struggle and the Industrial Revolution: Early Industrial Capitalism in Three English Towns*, London, 1974; and J. Vincent, *The Formation of the British Liberal Party*, Hassocks, W. Sussex, 1976.
44 E. J. Hobsbawm, *Primitive Rebels*, Manchester, 1959.

45 See, for example, many of the essays in Olsen (ed.), *Religion and Revolution*.
46 W. R. Ward, 'The Evangelical Revival in eighteenth-century Britain', in S. Gilley and W. J. Sheils (eds), *A History of Religion in Britain*, Oxford, 1994, pp. 252–72.

10 WOMEN AND EVANGELICAL RELIGION IN IRELAND, 1750–1900

1 L. Kerber, 'Separate spheres, female worlds, woman's place: the rhetoric of women's history', *Journal of American History*, 75, no. 1, 1988, pp. 9–39.
2 A. Vickery, 'Historiographical review: golden age to separate spheres? A review of the categories and chronology of English women's history', *Historical Journal*, 36, no. 2, 1993, p. 412.
3 *Ibid.*, p. 413.
4 L. Davidoff and C. Hall, *Family Fortunes: Men and Women of the English Middle Class 1780–1850*, London, 1987, pt 1.
5 D. W. Bebbington, *Evangelicalism in Modern Britain: A History from the 1730s to the 1980s*, London, 1989; D. Hempton and M. Hill, *Evangelical Protestantism in Ulster Society 1740–1890*, London, 1992; and M. Noll, D. Bebbington and G. Rawlyk (eds), *Evangelicalism: Comparative Studies of Popular Protestantism in North America, the British Isles, and Beyond, 1700–1990*, Oxford, 1994.
6 A. C. H. Seymour, *The Life and Times of Selina, Countess of Huntingdon*, 2 vols, London, 1884; C. H. Crookshank, *Memorable Women of Irish Methodism in the Last Century*, London, 1882, pp. 151–60.
7 J. W. James (ed.), *Women in American Religion*, Philadelphia, 1980; G. Malmgreen (ed.), *Religion in the Lives of English Women, 1760–1930*, London, 1986, pp. 9–10; E. K. Brown, 'Women in church history: stereotypes, archetypes and operational modalities', *Methodist History*, 18, 1980, pp. 109–32.
8 C. D. Field, 'The social composition of English Methodism to 1830: a membership analysis', *Bulletin of the John Rylands University Library of Manchester*, 76, no. 1, 1994, pp. 153–69.
9 G. Malmgreen, 'Domestic discords: women and the family in East Cheshire Methodism, 1750–1850', in J. Obelkevich, L. Roper and R. Samuel (eds), *Disciplines of Faith: Studies in Religion, Politics and Patriarchy*, London, 1987, p. 60.
10 Field, 'Social composition', p. 158.
11 A. M. Urdank, *Religion and Society in a Cotswold Vale: Nailsworth, Gloucestershire 1780–1865*, Berkeley, 1990, pp. 138–52.
12 In a paper on 'The history women' at the Irish Conference of Historians in Belfast in 1993, Joan Thirsk stated that at the opening of all new enterprises women were able to play an important part before the structures were later cemented by men.
13 M. Weber, *Sociology of Religion*, London, 1966.
14 K. Thomas, 'Women and the Civil War sects', *Past and Present*, no. 13, 1958, pp. 42–62; H. McLeod, *Religion and the People of Western Europe 1789–1970*, Oxford, 1981, p. 28–35. See also C. Cross, 'He-goats before the flocks', *Studies in Church History*, 8, 1972, pp. 195–202. For a wider study of this aspect see G. F. Moran, '"Sisters" in Christ: women and the church in seventeenth-century New England', in James (ed.), *Women in American Religion*, pp. 47–65; J. Rendall, *The Origins of Modern Feminism in Britain, France and the United States 1780–1860*, London, 1985.
15 C. H. Crookshank, *History of Methodism in Ireland*, 3 vols, London, 1885–8, vol. 1, pp. 25, 58, 180, 203, 362. See also R. Haire, *Wesley's One-and-Twenty Visits to Ireland*, London, 1947, pp. 87, 117. For American comparisons, see G. Schneider,

The Way of the Cross Leads Home: The Domestication of American Methodism, Bloomington, 1993; H. F. Thomas and R. S. Keller, *Women in New Worlds*, Nashville, 1981.

16 Crookshank, *History of Methodism*, vol. 1, p. 229.

17 W. H. Williams, 'The attraction of Methodism: the Delmarva Peninsula as a case study, 1769–1820', in R. E. Richey, K. E. Rowe and J. M. Schmidt (eds), *Perspectives on American Methodism: Interpretive Essays*, Nashville, 1993, p. 42.

18 Cited in D. C. Dews, 'Ann Carr and the female revivalists of Leeds', in G. Malmgreen (ed.), *Religion in the Lives of English Women 1760–1830*, London, 1986, pp. 68–87.

19 Cited in Crookshank, *History of Methodism*, vol. 2, p. 31.

20 Crookshank, *Memorable Women*, p. 67; E. Smyth, *The Extraordinary Life and Christian Experience of Margaret Davidson*, Dublin, 1782.

21 Crookshank, *Memorable Women*, pp. 191–202; J. J. McGregor, *Memoir of Miss Alice Cambridge*, Dublin, 1832.

22 *Minutes of the Methodist Conference in Ireland*, vol. 1, 1744–1819, p. 152.

23 D. M. Valenze, *Prophetic Sons and Daughters. Female Preaching and Popular Religion in Industrial England*, Princeton, 1985; E. D. Graham, 'Chosen by God: the female itinerants of early Primitive Methodism', Ph.D. thesis, University of Birmingham, 1986; W. F. Swift, 'The women itinerant preachers of early Methodism', *Proceedings of the Wesley Historical Society*, 28, 1951–2, pp. 89–94; and 29, 1953–4, pp. 76–83.

24 J. Holmes, 'Religious revivalism and popular evangelicalism in Britain and Ireland, 1859–1905', Ph.D. thesis, Queen's University Belfast, 1995, pp. 161–214.

25 NIPRO, Ouseley Collection, CR6/3, Z. Taft to G. Ouseley, 15 February 1823.

26 E. Thomas, *Irish Methodist Reminiscences: Memorials of the Life and Labour of the Late Reverend S. Nicholson*, London, 1889, p. 10.

27 H. Bingham, *The Life Story of Ann Preston*, Toronto, 1907, p. 33.

28 Crookshank, *History of Methodism*, vol. 2, p. 31.

29 *Ibid.*, p. 405.

30 NIPRO, Ouseley Collection, Ouseley, 22 September 1802.

31 Valenze, *Prophetic Sons and Daughters*; C. Brekus, 'Female evangelism in the early Methodist movement, 1784–1845', Ph.D. thesis, Yale University, 1994.

32 D. H. Lobody, '"That language might be given me": Women's experience in early Methodism', in Richey *et al.*, *Perspectives*, pp. 141–2.

33 E. P. Thompson, 'Anthropology and the discipline of historical context', *Midland History*, 1, no. 3, 1972, pp. 41–55; *idem*, 'Patrician society, plebeian culture', *Journal of Social History*, 7, no. 4, 1974, pp. 382–405; J. Rule, 'Methodism, popular beliefs and village culture in Cornwall, 1800–50', in R. D. Storch (ed.), *Popular Culture and Custom in Nineteenth-Century England*, London, 1982.

34 Anon., *An Address to the Clergy of the United Church in Ireland on the Present Crisis, by an aged Minister of the Gospel*, Dublin, 1800.

35 Crookshank, *History of Methodism*, vol. 1, pp. 218–19.

36 NIPRO, Methodist Mss, CR6/3, Private minutes of the Methodist Conference in Ireland. I am grateful to the Methodist Church for permission to read this source.

37 C. H. Crookshank, *A Methodist Pioneer: The Life and Labours of John Smith*, London, 1881.

38 *Minutes of the Methodist Conference in Ireland*, vol. 1, 1744–1819, p. 152.

39 The literature on the Ulster Revival of 1859 is prolific and is conveniently summarized by Hempton and Hill, *Evangelical Protestantism*, pp. 145–60. For the role played by women, see M. Hill, 'Ulster awakened: the '59 revival reconsidered', *Journal of Ecclesiastical History*, 41, no. 3, 1990, pp. 443–62; J. E.

NOTES

Holmes, 'Lifting the curtain on popular religion: women, laity and language in the Ulster revival of 1859', M.A. thesis, Queen's University, Kingston, Ontario, 1991, pp. 63–97; and *ibid.*, 'The "world turned upside down": women in the Ulster revival of 1859', in J. Holmes and D. Urquhart (eds), *Coming into the Light: The Work, Politics and Religion of Women in Ulster 1840–1940*, Belfast, 1994, pp. 126–53.

40 Anon., *Hints for Conducting Sunday Schools, Useful also for Day Schools and Families*, 2nd edn, Dublin, 1819.
41 *Report of the Hibernian Bible Society*, Dublin, 1822.
42 *Religious Tract and Bible Society, 16th Report*, Dublin, 1830.
43 *24th Annual Report of the London Hibernian Society*, Dublin, 1830. See also the *Annual Reports of the Irish Society for Promoting the Education of the Native Irish through the Medium of their own Language*, especially 1834 and 1836.
44 F. E. Bland, *How the Church Missionary Society came to Ireland*, Dublin, 1935. See also Representative Church Body Library, Dublin, Hibernian Church Missionary Society papers, auxiliary letter book, Report of the Deputation to the North, 26 September 1820.
45 W. D. Killen, *Memoir of John Edgar*, Belfast, 1867, p. 249.
46 M. Luddy, *Women and Philanthropy in Nineteenth-Century Ireland*, Cambridge, 1995, pp. 4–5.
47 F. Prochaska, *Women and Philanthropy in Nineteenth-Century England*, Oxford, 1980, p. 230.
48 A. E. Brożyna, 'Creating the ideal Christian woman: female piety in Ulster, 1850–1914', Ph.D. thesis, Queen's University, Kingston, Ontario, 1995, pp. 327–8. See also, *idem.*, '"The cursed cup hath cast her down": constructions of female piety in Ulster evangelical temperance literature, 1863–1914', in Holmes and Urquhart (eds), *Coming into the Light*, pp. 154–78.
49 Brożyna, 'Creating the ideal Christian woman', pp. 365–74.
50 The printed reports of the Female Association for Promoting Christianity among the Women of the East are held in Presbyterian Church House, Belfast.
51 *Report of the Female Association*, Belfast, 1876.
52 *Report of the Female Association*, Belfast, 1875.
53 *Report of the Female Association*, Belfast, 1876.
54 Brożyna, 'Creating the ideal Christian woman', pp. 393–406.
55 *Report of the Debates which took place at the Two Meetings of the Ladies Auxiliary to the London Hibernian Society, held at Cork, 8th and 9th September, 1824*, Dublin, 1824.
56 *Belfast People's Magazine*, 1 (1847).
57 *Report of the Debates at Cork*.
58 Brożyna, 'Creating the ideal Christian woman', p. 120.
59 Luddy, *Women and Philanthropy*, pp. 214–18.
60 M. Hill and V. Pollock, *Image and Experience: Photographs of Irishwomen c. 1880–1920*, Belfast, 1993.

INDEX

Page numbers in bold denote a chapter devoted to subject